What people are saying about …

The Fresh Life Series

"I'm touched and blessed by Lenya's heart for His kingdom."

—**Kay Arthur**, Bible teacher and author of many bestselling Bible studies

"What a great way for women to learn to study the Bible: interesting stories, thought-provoking questions, and a life-changing approach to applying Scripture. Lenya provides a great method so women can succeed and grow spiritually in a short period of time. Kudos!"

—**Franklin Graham**, president and CEO of Billy Graham
Evangelistic Association and Samaritan's Purse

"Skip and Lenya Heitzig have been friends of my wife, Cathe, and I for more than twenty years. Lenya loves to study God's Word and teach it to women in a way that is both exciting and accessible. I trust her latest book will be a blessing to you."

—**Greg Laurie**, pastor and evangelist of Harvest Ministries

"Lenya's love for the Lord and knowledge of His Word uniquely equips her to help other women discover the pathway to God through these in-depth Bible studies."

—**Kay Smith**, wife of Chuck Smith (Calvary Chapel)

"The Fresh Life Series is an insightful and in-depth look at God's Word. Through these Bible studies, Lenya Heitzig leads women to deeper intimacy with God."

—**K. P. Yohannan**, president of Gospel for Asia

"Lenya has created another wonderful Bible study series that invites participants to spend time in God's Word and then see the Word come to fruition in their lives. What a blessing! These studies are perfect for small groups or personal daily devotions."

—**Robin Lee Hatcher**, women's event speaker and award-winning author

Live Brilliantly

The Fresh Life Series

Live Brilliantly

A Study in the Book of 1 John

Lenya Heitzig

David C Cook

transforming lives together

LIVE BRILLIANTLY
Published by David C Cook
4050 Lee Vance Drive
Colorado Springs, CO 80918 U.S.A.

David C Cook U.K., Kingsway Communications
Eastbourne, East Sussex BN23 6NT, England

The graphic circle C logo is a registered trademark of David C Cook.

LCCN 2017949594
ISBN 978-1-4347-1248-6
eISBN 978-0-8307-7256-8

© 2018 Lenya Heitzig

Published in association with William K. Jensen Literary Agency, 119 Bampton Ct., Eugene, OR 97404.

The Team: Alice Crider, Amy Konyndyk, Rachael Stevenson, Heather Gemmen Wilson, Susan Murdock
Cover Design: Nick Lee and Ashley Ward
Cover Photo: Getty Images

Contributors: Christy Willis, Laura Sowers, Maria Guy, Misty Foster, Trisha Petero, Vicki Perrigo
Printed in the United States of America

First Edition 2018

1 2 3 4 5 6 7 8 9 10

102717

Contents

Introduction

Why do we crave authenticity? Corporate supermarkets get nudged out of the neighborhood by local co-op stores and farmers markets that offer real food (i.e., organic). Starbucks skyrocketed in the 1980s, but "indie" coffee shops force the mermaid-laden brand into megastores like Target and Albertsons. Back-to-school shopping used to include a new pair of Levi's. But today's jeans come with rips, tears, and fraying, bearing the label "vintage" as if they were fine wines. Remember when kids from big families dreaded hand-me-downs? Today trendy stores are popping up in Soho and Rodeo Drive to offer customers "upcycled" (aka secondhand) merchandise with exorbitant price tags. All of this strategic remarketing is designed to make people feel more authentic.

So, what is the deal with being real? Sociologists suggest that with the emergence of blogs, tweets, and Facebook we have created virtual identities for ourselves online. As a result, we now need a host of social networking coaches to help us become authentic—some delicate balance between embarrassing ourselves by airing our dirty laundry and being unapproachable by sharing our successes. Even e-dating services encourage their clients to present their most authentic selves because you don't want to shock your date when you show up ten years older and ten pounds heavier than in the college photo you posted. Finally, high-profile actors, politicians, and sports celebrities have so overused the word it has lost its original meaning. Just like "awesome" isn't so awesome anymore, authentic is some inauthentic fabrication of one's identity for public consumption.

Author: John, a disciple of Jesus and the author of the gospel of John

Audience: "Little Children," which includes Christians from the New Testament era until today

Theme: Christian assurance. *"These things I have written to you who believe in the name of the Son of God, that you may know that you have eternal life, and that you may continue to believe in the name of the Son of God"* (1 John 5:13).

Date: AD 90–95

Setting: Unlike most of the other epistles, 1 John offers no formal greeting. Although it includes no personal addressees, 1 John is one of the most intimate documents included in Scripture.

Jesus is, truly, the real deal. First John begins with the apostle's personal testimony to this fact. Not only was John an eyewitness to Jesus, but his rough fisherman hands touched the Savior's body. Jesus and John shared meals together, walked Israel's dusty roads side by side, and enjoyed conversations around a bonfire. Just like Coca-Cola's campaign boasted of being the "real thing," since it was the first cola on the market, John informs us that Jesus is the real deal because He's the original light source for the world. He is the light, and in Him is no darkness at all. He is *the* authentic light of life.

Three key phrases found in John's writings—the gospel of John and his three epistles—repeat the theme of Christ's authenticity: manifest, eternal life, and bear witness.

Manifest

Manifest appears seven times in 1 John. It is often translated as "light," to appear outwardly, to make more visible, or to shine.

The first time John used this term was in the opening of his gospel as he proclaimed that the life of Jesus was "the light of men" and that this "light shines in the darkness" (see John 1:1–5). In this text, the word *light* means "manifest." Thus, the incarnation of Jesus Christ made the shining light of God visible to the whole world, to all of humanity.

First John gives three reasons why the light of Jesus was made manifest to the world:

1. To stop sin: *"You know that He was manifested to take away our sins"* (1 John 3:5).

2. To destroy the Devil: *"For this purpose the Son of God was manifested, that He might destroy the works of the devil"* (1 John 3:8).

3. To extend eternal life: *"The love of God was manifested toward us, that God has sent His only begotten Son into the world, that we might live through Him"* (1 John 4:9).

In this epistle, he assured the reader that Christ's manifestation was not merely universal but also personal. John exclaimed that the light of the world was also his own light.

What about you? Has Jesus been manifest personally in your life? Has His light illuminated your world? Can you describe a time when Jesus was elevated from a good man to the God man, from the speaker of fine words to the Savior of your soul, from a radical religionist to the righteous Redeemer? Let His light shine!

Eternal Life

Eternal life appears most often in the gospel of John at a total of nine times. However, it is used six times in 1 John. In John 20:31, the apostle explains why he wrote his gospel: so that "you may believe that Jesus is the Christ, the Son of God, and that believing you may have life in His name." In other words, he hopes that reading his account of the life of Jesus will lead you to eternal life. He hopes to instill confidence. He wants those who have already received eternal life to know, without a doubt, that they are saved—a complete assurance of salvation.

Eternal life has been greatly misrepresented. The idea is not quantity of life but quality. Literally it is interpreted as "age abiding or abundant life."[1] Eternal life is not what you know, like the secret to eternal youth, but who you know. *"And this is eternal life, that they may know You, the only true God, and Jesus Christ whom You have sent"* (John 17:3).

First John gives three expressions of eternal life:

1. It's a personal promise from God: *"This is the promise that He has promised us—eternal life"* (1 John 2:25).

2. It's a "just give me Jesus" attitude: *"God has given us eternal life, and this life is in His Son"* (1 John 5:11).

3. It's an ongoing belief in God's Son: *"These things I have written to you who believe in the name of the Son of God, that you may know that you have eternal life, and that you may continue to believe in the name of the Son of God"* (1 John 5:13).

Those who have experienced eternal life embrace the idea of being "born again." This describes our spiritual birth into a spiritual family. Just like physical birth passes on genetic identifying markers such as eye or hair color, spiritual regeneration includes certain behavior "birth marks." If you emulate the following family characteristics of your Heavenly Father, you are an authentic part of Christ's family:

- Cessation of Sin: *"Whoever has been born of God does not sin"* (1 John 3:9).
- Really Righteous: *"If you know that He is righteous, you know that every-one who practices righteousness is born of Him"* (1 John 2:29).
- Safely Separated: *"We know that whoever is* born of God *does not sin; but he who has been born of God keeps himself, and the wicked one does not touch him"* (1 John 5:18).

Bear Witness

Bearing witness literally means to testify, often in a legal court setting where there is consider-able concern for the truth of the testimony. Witnesses not only tell others what they have personally experienced; they must also express how the experience impacted them. This term is repeated seven times in 1 John and reveals the ever-widening span of those who bear witness to Jesus' authenticity—from God, to the disciples, to all Christians.

- God's Witness: *"If we receive the witness of men, the witness of God is greater; for this is the witness of God which He has testified of His Son"* (1 John 5:9).
- John's Witness: *"And we have seen and testify that the Father has sent the Son as Savior of the world"* (1 John 4:14).
- Our Witness: *"He who believes in the Son of God has the witness in him-self; he who does not believe God has made Him a liar, because he has not believed the testimony that God has given of His Son"* (1 John 5:10).

First John asks whether you have personally heard the gospel and let the light of Christ illuminate your life. Do you live brilliantly, shining the light of salvation to the world around you? Can you testify of His light and grace to change an outlook, a marriage, or a hopeless situation?

Remember that a testimony goes beyond words; both your lips and your life can sparkle. A witness is twofold. It is something you do and something you are. One must follow the other. The words can *testify*, the life must *magnify*, for God to be *glorified*. Join us in living brilliantly so that the whole world sees the light.

How to Get the Most out of This Study

Has your life lost its luster? Perhaps the abundance of things has tarnished the abundant life God offers. The best way to polish your life is through the cleansing power of God's Word. That's why doing a Bible study like this is so vital—because God's Word has the power to do God's work in our lives. It's the catalyst that refreshes your heart, renews your mind, and restores your soul—His Word makes life worth living!

In this study, we're going to explore the short yet powerful book of 1 John. While in today's world we see darkness and despair with no sign of true love and light, we can find assurance in God's Word and in the One who created real love.

Each week of the study is divided into five days for your personal time with God. Each day's lesson has five elements. They are designed to help you fully "live" as you apply the truths you learn to your life.

1. Lift Up … Here we ask you to "Lift Up" prayers to God, asking Him to give you spiritual insight for the day.

2. Look At … This portion of the study asks you to "Look At" the Scripture text using inductive questions. These questions help you discover *What are the facts?* You'll learn the basic who-what-when-where-how aspects of the passage as well as some of the important background material.

3. Learn About … The "Learn About" sidebars correlate to specific questions in order to help you understand *What does this text mean?*

These sidebar elements offer cultural insight, linguistic definitions, and biblical commentary.

4. Live Out … These questions and exercises are designed to help you investigate *How should this change my life?* Here you're challenged to personally apply the lessons you have learned as you "Live Out" God's principles in a practical way. I encourage you to write out all of the answers to the questions in this study. You may want to write the answers to the personal application questions in a journal to ensure privacy. By writing your insights from God day by day, you'll have a record of your relationship with Him that you can look back on when you need a faith boost.

5. Listen To … We finish with inspiring quotes from authors, speakers, and writers. You'll be able to "Listen To" the wisdom they've gleaned in their lives and relate it to your own.

Live Brilliantly: A Study in the Book of 1 John is ideal for discussion in a small group setting as well as for individual study. The following suggestions will help you and your group get the most out of your study time.

Personal Checklist

*   Be determined. Examine your daily schedule, then set aside a consistent time for this study.
*   Be prepared. Gather the materials you'll need: a Bible, this workbook, a journal in which to write your thoughts, and a pen.
*   Be inspired. Begin each day with prayer, asking the Holy Spirit to be your teacher and to illuminate your mind.
*   Be complete. Read the suggested Bible passage and finish the homework each day.

- Be persistent. Answer each question as fully as possible. If you're unable to answer a question, move forward to the next question or read the explanation in the "Learn To ..." question and allow the Lord to search your heart and transform your life. Take time to reflect honestly about your feelings, experiences, sins, goals, and responses to God.
- Be blessed. Enjoy your daily study time as God speaks to you through His Word.

Small-Group Checklist

- Be prayerful. Pray before you begin your time together.
- Be biblical. Keep all answers in line with God's Word; avoid personal opinion.
- Be confidential. Keep all sharing within your small group confidential.
- Be respectful. Listen without interrupting. Keep comments on track and to the point so that all can share.
- Be discreet. In some cases, you need not share more than absolutely necessary. Some things are between you and God.
- Be kind. Reply to the comments of others lovingly and courteously.
- Be mindful. Remember your group members in prayer throughout the week.

Small-Group Leader Checklist

- Be prayerful. Pray that the Holy Spirit will "guide you into truth" so that your leadership will guide others.
- Be faithful. Prepare by reading the Bible passage and studying the lesson ahead of time, highlighting truths and applying them personally.
- Be prompt. Begin and end the study on time.

- Be thorough. For optimum benefit, allot one hour for small-group discussion. This should allow plenty of time to cover all of the questions and exercises for each lesson.

- Be selective. If you have less than an hour, you should carefully choose which questions you will address and summarize the edited information for your group. In this way, you can focus on the more thought-provoking questions. Be sure to grant enough time to address pertinent "Live Out …" exercises, as this is where you and the women will clearly see God at work in your lives.

- Be sensitive. Some of the "Live Out …" exercises are very personal and may not be appropriate to discuss in a small group. If you sense that this is the case, feel free to move to another question.

- Be flexible. If the questions in the study seem unclear, reword them for your group. Feel free to add your own questions to bring out the meaning of the verse.

- Be inclusive. Encourage each member to participate in the discussion. You may have to draw some out or tone some down so that all have the opportunity to participate.

- Be honest. Don't be afraid to admit that you don't have all the answers! When in doubt, encourage the women in your small group to take difficult questions to their church leadership for clarification.

- Be focused. Keep the discussion on tempo and on target. Learn to pace your small group so that you complete a lesson on time. When participants get sidetracked, redirect the discussion to the passage at hand.

- Be patient. Realize that not all people are at the same place spiritually or socially. Wait for the members of your group to answer the questions rather than jumping in and answering them yourself.

Partners in Faith

1 John 1:1–2:2

Attending a symphony is a joyous and inspiring occasion. Many schoolchildren are introduced to this musical experience through annual excursions to hear the likes of *Peter and the Wolf* or *Pinocchio*. The diversity of eighty or ninety instruments creates a reverberating effect. While there are occasional solos in a symphony, the true purpose is to hear the instruments resound in harmony. In fact, the word *symphony* comes from a Greek word that means the agreement or accord of sound.

Harmony is a beautiful thing in music, but it is also wonderfully expressed among people who have a common love for the Lord. In the book of Acts, Luke chronicled about the new fellowship of the Jews and Gentiles under the banner of Jesus Christ. The infant church was a noisy and disruptive group, and despite relatively small numbers, its members set the world at large on its ear. Out of the cacophony of voices, the Holy Spirit formed a bond of fellowship, or *koinonia*.

This was a unique period of time within the ancient church. Their bond laid the foundation for the growing body of Christ. In Acts 2, we read about the day of Pentecost—the precise dawn of the church age. We are still living in the church age and will continue to do so until the Lord gathers His followers at the rapture of the church.

As we delve into 1 John, we are brought into fellowship with those early believers and, more importantly, with the Lord Jesus. Their love for each other and for God was composed of a chorus of elements: love, obedience, and truth. Be encouraged, Christian, and add your unique voice to this divine symphony.

Day 1: 1 John 1:1–4   **Partakers of Joy**

Day 2: 1 John 1:5–6   **Practicing Truth**

Day 3: 1 John 1:7–8   **Partners in Light**

Day 4: 1 John 1:9–10   **Professing Iniquity**

Day 5: 1 John 2:1–2   **Propitiation for Sin**

DAY 1

—

Partakers of Joy

Lift Up ...

Thank You, Father, for the joy that comes from knowing the heart of the early church and living with the expectation of eternal life through faith in Jesus Christ. In the meantime, I pray that the joy of knowing You today will resonate in fellowship with other believers and will draw nonbelievers to You. In Jesus' name. Amen.

Look At ...

When John wrote this book, the Gnostics, a particularly prideful group of people, insisted they were superior believers who had received special knowledge above and beyond the teachings of the apostles. They attacked the claims of Jesus on the most fundamental and destructive level: they asserted that He could not be both man and God simultaneously. Because they claimed to have a greater knowledge, they created an atmosphere of doubt among many Christians. They implied that something important had been withheld from them, not unlike Satan's assertion to Eve that God had withheld the fruit of the tree of knowledge of good and evil.

In these first verses of 1 John, the aged apostle John set about to refute these lies and reaffirm both the eternal and earthly life of the Son of God.

Read 1 John 1–4.

That which was from the beginning, which we have heard, which we have seen with our eyes, which we have looked upon, and our hands have handled, concerning the Word of life—the life was manifested, and we have seen, and bear witness, and declare to you that eternal life which was with the Father and was manifested to us—that which we have seen and heard we declare to you, that

1 Genesis of Life

In his gospel, John uses the phrase "In the beginning" (John 1:1), which means eternity past. However, "That which was from the beginning" does not refer to eternity past but to the *beginning* of Jesus' ministry and the preaching of the gospel message.

3 Word of Life

God's Word is His powerful self-expression in creation, wisdom, revelation, and salvation as revealed through the person of Jesus Christ. The phrase *Word of Life* refers to the person of Jesus and the proclamation of *the message about life,*[1] the gospel. "In Him was life, and the life was the light of men" (John 1:4).

5 Declaration of Life

John saw, testified, and declared that the eternal life of God was manifested or appeared to him through the incarnation, the coming of God's Son into the world as a human being.[2] A genuine experience with Jesus leads to honest testimony and an uninhibited declaration of His reality and the gospel message.

you also may have fellowship with us; and truly our fellowship is with the Father and with His Son Jesus Christ. And these things we write to you that your joy may be full. 1 John 1:1–4

1. What phrase does John use to introduce the subject of his letter? To whom do you think he refers with the pronoun *we*?

2. Describe the ways John and others physically encountered Jesus. How did this affirm the humanity of Jesus Christ?

3. After John relates his personal encounter with Christ, what phrase does he use to describe Jesus?

4. What happened to the Word of Life?

5. What did John and the apostles declare?

6. Explain why John shared what he had seen and heard with his readers.

7. John says that being in fellowship with the apostles unites his readers with each other and with whom?

Live Out ...

8. Explain why John wrote his letter.

9. We learned that John actually heard, saw, and touched Jesus. These experiences convinced him that Jesus was truly the Messiah, God made flesh. Based on the gospel accounts of Christ's life, name some things

John heard, saw, or touched and how they led him to believe Jesus was the Christ (e.g., he saw Jesus in glory on the Mount of Transfiguration).

10. John was an eyewitness to the Word of life, but it wasn't his physical nearness to Jesus that gave him eternal life; it was spiritual nearness. John trusted Jesus as his Savior and the gospel as the truth.

a. Have you trusted Christ as your Savior and accepted the gift of eternal life?

b. If so, write in your journal about your experience of salvation. How did Jesus draw you to Himself?

c. If you haven't accepted the gift of eternal life through Jesus Christ, this is the perfect time to do so. Say a prayer and repent of your sin—that's the first step. Then receive Jesus into your heart as your Lord and Savior. Write in your journal about this life-changing decision.

d. Now that you've memorialized this occasion in writing, share the good news of your decision with another person. This is a great day in your life. Welcome to the family of God!

11. Today we learned that a genuine experience with Jesus leads to a testimony, which leads us to declare the truth. In what practical ways do you testify to the reality of Jesus in your life?

❑ Loving the unlovable

❑ Practicing patience

❑ Selflessly serving others

❑ Praise and worship

❑ Praying for those who persecute you

❑ Other: _____

7 Security of Life

The apostles' firsthand experience with the incarnate Christ united them for eternity with the Father and His Son. John wanted his readers to be secure in their fellowship with him and the apostles regarding their salvation and eternal life—through Jesus Christ.

8 Certainty of Life

Certainty of salvation and eternal life with the Father and Son produces confident joy and calm delight in the believer's life. "Though now you do not see Him, yet believing, you rejoice with joy inexpressible and full of glory, receiving the end of your faith—the salvation of your souls" (1 Pet. 1:8–9).

10 Prayer of Life

Whether you are a new believer or one who is seasoned in the faith, it's reassuring to know the Holy Spirit both guides us and prays for us as we go through life. "Likewise the Spirit also helps in our weaknesses. For we do not know what we should pray for as we ought, but the Spirit Himself makes intercession for us with groanings which cannot be uttered" (Rom. 8:26).

In your journal give an example of one of the boxes you checked above.

12. Describe the joy you experience as a result of secure fellowship with God.

———————————

We are a country that is serious about our happiness. In fact, we affirmed our inalienable right to pursue happiness in the Declaration of Independence. While we are not *guaranteed* happiness, our right to pursue it cannot be revoked or given away. In 1776 when the Declaration of Independence was drafted, there may have been a different understanding of the word *happiness,* a more down-to-earth meaning of the right to meet the physical needs of food and shelter and of the right to enjoy religious freedoms without fear of persecution.

When we talk about *joy,* there is a distinction between the happy state that comes from pleasant circumstances and the deeper sense of secure rejoicing. The certainty of eternal fellowship with the Father and His Son produces this joy in a believer's life. God wanted our joy to be solid, so He manifested it in His Son and verified His life through reliable witnesses. John's epistle was written so our joy would be enhanced with truth and certainty and, therefore, made full.

Listen To ...

Human fellowship can go to great lengths, but not all the way.
Fellowship with God can go to all lengths.
—*Oswald Chambers*

DAY 2

Practicing Truth

Learning to do anything well requires practice. Whether it is something complicated like playing the piano or learning a new language or a simple task like brushing your teeth, consistency and practice bring success. Even natural talent requires a studied repetition before mastery is achieved.

Telling the truth is a lifelong practice and pursuit. Yet the plumb line for truth is only as reliable as its source. As believers, our truth is founded on the person of Jesus Christ and the authority of the Bible.

When Jesus stood in Pontius Pilate's court, He was asked, "Are You the King of the Jews?" (John 18:33), and Jesus affirmed that He was. He further stated, "Everyone who is of the truth hears My voice" (v. 37), to which Pilate responded, "What is truth?" (v. 38).

Pilate's comment was ambiguous. Was he genuinely curious, perpetually cynical, or hopelessly indifferent? We don't know. But this is certain: when we know Jesus and who He is, we know that He is Truth.

Lift Up ...

Thank You, Lord, for guiding me along life's path by way of Your truth and light. Help me to always walk according to Your divine character and Your divine truth. In doing so, I pray that I will be a light that glorifies You and leads others to know You. In Jesus' name. Amen.

Look At ...

John began his letter with the clear goal of affirming the reality of the life of Jesus, the truth of the gospel, and the joy that comes from eternal fellowship with God. Yesterday we looked at

3 Direct Revelation

The message John and the apostles heard was a truth they had learned directly from the Lord Jesus. John was passing this truth on to his readers, who would in turn carry the message on to future generations.

4 Divine Illumination

The word *light* means to shine or to illuminate.[3] God's character and divine nature are pure light. As a flashlight illuminates the path through darkness, so God's light, as revealed through Jesus and the Word, illuminates the righteous path Christians are to walk in this world.

the way he validated his personal qualifications as an eyewitness, an ear-witness, and a touch-witness of the Lord. He declared his intent to bring believers into an eternal fellowship with each other and with the Father and His Son.

Today we find that John's next goal was to address the fundamental principles of the behaviors that signify true fellowship with God. He gave us a reliable message that enabled us to recognize the true Son of God and the veracity of our relationship with Him. John made it simple to recognize: it's as clear as light and dark.

Read 1 John 1:5–6.

This is the message which we have heard from Him and declare to you, that God is light and in Him is no darkness at all. If we say that we have fellowship with Him, and walk in darkness, we lie and do not practice the truth. 1 John 1:5–6

1. What had John heard?

2. Considering what you learned yesterday, from whom do you think John heard the message?

3. To whom did John declare this message?

4. In your own words, explain the content of the message.

5. Undoubtedly John was drawing on the rich Old Testament imagery of God as light. Read the following Scriptures and record how God's Word offers moral guidance and direction for living according to His will.

Scripture	God's Word as Light
Job 29:3	
Psalm 119:105	
Psalm 119:130	

6. What do people become when they claim fellowship with God but walk in darkness?

7. What do they fail to practice?

8. Scripture has much to say about light and darkness. Read the following verses and record how God views these two opposing realities.

Scripture	Light	Darkness
John 1:4–5		
John 3:19–20		
John 8:12		
John 12:35		

Live Out ...

9. John heard Jesus' message and then passed it on to the next generation of believers. To whom are we responsible to pass on the truth about God?

10. Today we learned that God's character and nature are pure light and that light has nothing in common with darkness. Draw a large circle around the words God/Light and another around the words World/Darkness. Do not allow the circles to intersect or touch in any way. Within each circle write the attributes that characterize the words they surround. (Hint: purity, love—sin, hatred.)

7 Distinct Behaviors

What do light and dark have in common? Absolutely nothing. A person cannot serve God, who is light, and walk (live or dwell) in the realm of sin and darkness. To do so is to live a lie. When we have genuine fellowship with God, we practice truth by living in conformity with God's character and doing His will.

9 Definite Commission

When we think of "the Great Commission," we are inclined to think on a massive, missionary scale. But we are to teach first within our own four walls. "You shall teach them diligently to your children, and shall talk of them when you sit in your house, when you walk by the way, when you lie down, and when you rise up" (Deut. 6:7).

God / Light   World / Darkness

Write in your journal about how you endeavor to practice the truth and live according to the light and character of God.

_____

10 Dynamic Difference

Sin and shame drive us into darkness and deceit and away from the bright light of examination and exposure. But as we live by the Word, our lives manifest clarity and transparency.

Every day we make decisions that have consequences. At a fundamental level, we decide if we will walk in the light of God's Word or in the darkness of sin and depravity. More often than not, the initial decisions are small ones: What TV program or movie will I watch? What book or magazine will I read? What sites will I visit on the Internet? These can be small portals that can lead to big problems.

Satan is cunning and can turn us just slightly off course day by day until we find we are veering further and further away from a truthful and light-filled life. The danger is in both overestimating and underestimating the power of darkness. When Jesus addressed the chief priest and captains of the temple as they came to seize Him at Gethsemane, He said, "When I was with you daily in the temple, you did not try to seize Me. But this is your hour, and the power of darkness" (Luke 22:53).

Beware of being oblivious to the presence of sin and the power of darkness. We make a choice to walk in the light of God's Word and in the presence of God. It's a choice made minute by minute, hour by hour, day by day.

Listen To ...

Where I found truth, there found I my God, who is the truth itself.

—*Augustine*

Partners in Light

We all know who invented the light bulb: Thomas Alva Edison, right? Well, that's partly right. At the same time Edison was pursuing this invention, other inventors were hot on the same idea leading to incandescent lights. Yet Edison's efforts stood apart.

The early light bulbs were flawed by short periods of illumination, extremely expensive production, and high draws on the electrical current. These problems made the light bulb inaccessible to the public at large. Edison turned his efforts toward finding the proper metal filaments, and eventually he arrived at the carbon filament. The first successful testing of this bulb was in 1879, and it glowed for an astonishing 13.5 hours. He applied for and was granted a patent. After further refinement of the filament, Edison's team discovered a way to enable the light to last over 1,200 hours.

The other not-so-famous inventors were partners in the pursuit of light, but it was Edison who made the light bulb affordable to the masses. Flying high on his success, he said, "We will make electricity so cheap that only the rich will burn candles."[4]

While Edison grabbed the glory, he clearly benefitted from the efforts and discoveries of other inventors. In our physical lives as in our spiritual lives, we have the advantage of people whose knowledge and maturity help us progress in our own journeys. We stand on the shoulders of those who came before us and help us in our own pursuit of the light.

Lift Up ...

Lord Jesus, I am so grateful for my relationship with You and the light You bring to my life. Much of my appreciation comes from the fact that I was once in darkness. Lost. Afraid. Your truth brings me great joy and hope for the future. In Jesus' name. Amen.

1 Walk in the Light

On our own, we human beings cannot achieve the sinless perfection of God. "There is none righteous, no, not one" (Rom. 3:10), but we can persist in walking in the light where Holy God dwells. A genuine believer's life is characterized by living the truth according to God's will.

2 Live in the Light

When we truly live in the light, mutual fellowship among God, ourselves, and other believers is possible. In the life shared with other believers, we are like sparks combined to create a blaze that glorifies God.

3 Receive the Light

God's holiness spotlights the impurities in our hearts, convicts us of our sins, and convinces us of our need for cleansing. We can be confident that Jesus' blood purifies us from all our sins so that we may continue in fellowship with God. Acceptance of Jesus' death on our behalf is an ongoing part of our walk in the light.

Look At ...

Yesterday we saw that the message John declared was this: people who have genuine fellowship with God are shaped both by His character and by their individual commitment to Him. Regardless of what we say, our behaviors and proclivities tell the truth of our beliefs. God's character and nature are that of light. There is nothing dark or shadowy about Him.

Today we find that John revealed that the results of genuine commitment to God are communion with Him, continual conviction, confession, and cleansing from sin. We are works in process, and we know we will occasionally sin. If we say differently, the sin of that statement will stunt our growth and ruin our witness to others. Our light-guided walk brings others into fellowship with us and strengthens our relationships.

Read 1 John 1:7–8.

But if we walk in the light as He is in the light, we have fellowship with one another, and the blood of Jesus Christ His Son cleanses us from all sin. If we say that we have no sin, we deceive ourselves, and the truth is not in us. 1 John 1:7–8

1. Rather than walking in darkness, where are believers to walk? Who is there with us?

2. What is the result of walking in the light?

3. How are we cleansed from our sin?

4. If we claim to be sinless, what disservice do we do ourselves?

5. Read 1 John 1:8–10 and answer the following questions.

    a. What does honest fellowship with God mean (v. 8)?

    b. How is fellowship with God achieved (v. 9)?

    c. What happens when we lie to God, others, and ourselves (v. 10)?

Live Out ...

6. What is *not* at work in us when we deceive ourselves?

7. Today we learned that a genuine commitment to God produces a consistent walk in the light. A consistent walk in the light results in communion with our King.

Write in your journal about how you have experienced communion with the Lord as a result of a determined walk in His truth and holiness.

8. God's holiness and Word spotlight what is false and impure in our hearts. Use your Bible concordance to find a verse that speaks of the condition of our hearts before we are washed clean from our sins. Research words like *heart, deceitful, wicked*. Write your verse below and share it with your small group.

9. As believers, we are confident that the blood of Jesus continually purifies us from all our sins, restoring us into fellowship with Him. Read Hebrews 4:14–16 and answer the following questions.

    a. Who is our great High Priest?

    b. What understanding does He have of us? Why?

    c. Because of Jesus' sinless sacrifice, where are we free to go? In what manner can we go there?

    d. What will we find when we get there?

6 Lies in the Light

Deception means to cause to roam from safety, truth, or virtue. When people believe they are sinless, they leave the safety of God's truth and are deceived by the greatest lie of all, "You will be like God" (Gen. 3:5), told by the greatest liar of all—Satan. "When he speaks a lie, he speaks from his own resources, for he is a liar and the father of it" (John 8:44).

7 Abide in the Light

Jesus gave us a wonderful definition of what it is to *abide*: "Abide in Me, and I in you. As the branch cannot bear fruit of itself, unless it abides in the vine, neither can you, unless you abide in Me" (John 15:4). The fruit does not have to *try* to bear fruit—it's the natural result of life on the vine.

Jesus' death would have been pointless if people were sinless. A sinless person has no need for a Savior. Surprisingly, there are times when being an outwardly *good* person actually interferes with the insight and self-reflection necessary to be aware of our basic inclination to sin.

When Jesus walked to Samaria on His way to Galilee, He entered a city that was avoided and hated by the Jews. Jesus didn't avoid it, though; He went directly into Samaria because He wanted to have a conversation with someone there. That person was a sinful woman. She knew she was sinful and had the tough shell that defends a tough life. So when Jesus asked a favor of her (a drink of water), she was curious and interested. He did not play games but told her immediately that at that very moment, she had the opportunity to receive the gift of God in the form of belief in His beloved Son—the man right in front of her.

It was in the heat of the day when respectable women were in the cool comfort of their homes. But this woman ventured out into the hot, bright spotlight of the reality of her sins. There, she received her gift of forgiveness and the promise of eternal life.

She may have lived on the margins of society, but when Jesus exposed the truth of her life, she knew she was in the presence of a prophet. She left her waterpot and went into the city proclaiming this event. "Could this be the Christ?" she asked. Indeed.

Listen To ...

There are two ways of spreading the light: to be the candle or the mirror that reflects it.
—*Edith Wharton*

Professing Iniquity

It was a photograph that captured the imagination of the world.

Since the early 1930s there had been musings about the existence of a prehistoric-type monster living in the lake of Ness in the Scottish Highlands. The Loch Ness Monster was apparently very clever and managed to elude capture by both fishermen and photographers until 1934. At that time, a man by the name of Dr. Robert Kenneth Wilson offered a picture to the *Daily Mail* newspaper. It revealed a long-necked creature with a small head and humped back in a swirl of water. Dr. Wilson told the newspaper he saw something in the lake, stopped his car, and took five pictures—two of which produced images clear enough to make out. For decades they were considered the best evidence for the existence of the Loch Ness Monster.

Sixty years later, in 1994, at the age of 93, another man, Christian Spurling, made a deathbed confession. The photographs taken by Dr. Wilson were a fake and a hoax. When the tale finally unraveled, it turned out that Wilson, Spurling, and a third man had conspired in this elaborate scheme to mislead the public and the authorities.[5]

Deception by any name is a lie. It doesn't matter whether we call it a hoax, a joke, a prank, or outright fraud. Spurling's deathbed confession revealed a man whose sin haunted him. He may have spent countless days smiling through fear or sleepless nights worrying about being discovered.

As believers we have the incredible gift and assurance that God welcomes our confession of sin. He does not reject us; He delights to forgive us.

Lift Up ...

I praise You, Lord, for Your faithfulness to convict me of my sin, draw me to repentance, and forgive me when I confess. Lord, You are faithful and true. In Jesus' name. Amen.

1 Confession

To *confess* means to acknowledge God's perspective of our sin or say the same thing about our sin that God does. When we resist acknowledging our offense, fellowship with God and with others is broken. A Christian is characterized by consistent confession of sin.

Look At ...

Yesterday we looked at the black-and-white contrast between living in the dark or living in the light. Fellowship flourishes in the light of truth and a genuine commitment to God. Our fellowship with other believers hinges on our mutual standing in the light of God's Word. We can enjoy intimate fellowship and a cleansing from sin by the blood of Jesus Christ.

Today we will learn about the way God wants us to regard sin. He tells us just how we are to deal with it when we inevitably sin. Our human part of the process is the easiest: we recognize the sin for what it is and confess it. The balance of the process rests on God's divine character, His love, and His forgiveness. God gave us a concise protocol to deal with sin and maintain fellowship with Him.

Read 1 John 1:9–10.

If we confess our sins, He is faithful and just to forgive us our sins and to cleanse us from all unrighteousness. If we say that we have not sinned, we make Him a liar, and His word is not in us. 1 John 1:9–10

1. What is our responsibility when God spotlights our sin?

2. What attributes does God display when we confess our sins?

3. Read 2 Timothy 2:13. Why does God remain faithful to us even when we are unfaithful to Him?

4. Read Deuteronomy 32:4. What does this verse say about God's character?

5. According to 1 John 1:9, God is faithful and just to do what two things?

    1.

    2.

6. What are people saying about God when they claim to be sinless?

Live Out ...

7. Although Christians are cleansed from sin and eternal death by the blood of Christ, we still walk in the world, get dirty, and need a daily spiritual bath. Confessing our sins means we agree with God and see ourselves from His perspective. Take an honest look at yourself. In what ways do you sin?

    ❏ Judge others   ❏ Gossip   ❏ Foul language

    ❏ Pride   ❏ Fear   ❏ Hypocrisy

    ❏ Other: _____

8. What do people prove when they claim to be sinless?

9. Stop for a moment, close your eyes, and ask God to reveal any other sin harbored or hidden in your heart. Write the confession of your sin below.

    Lord, I confess ...

4 Profession

God's nature is *faithful* (dependable, loyal, and stable). He is faithful to His children because He is first faithful to Himself. God is also just (righteous). His actions and decisions are true and right. Confession is possible and profitable in the atmosphere of God's love.

5 Admission

God *forgives* (the act of excusing or pardoning another in spite of one's errors) and washes us clean from our unrighteousness when we recognize and acknowledge our need for forgiveness. God sees us as righteous because of our faith in His Son, Jesus Christ.

8 Accusation

To deny sin in the face of God's testimony that "all have sinned and fall short of the glory of God" (Rom. 3:23) is to level a serious accusation—that God is a liar. Those who claim to be sinless prove that God's Word (truth and light) is not in them.

11 Condemnation

Jesus made it clear that judging or blaming others comes with intense consequences: "Judge not, and you shall not be judged. Condemn not, and you shall not be condemned. Forgive, and you will be forgiven" (Luke 6:37). Judgment and condemnation are reserved for the Lord. He alone is the perfect judge.

10. We can be assured of the forgiveness that is promised us because we serve a loving, faithful, righteous God.

In your journal write a prayer based on Jeremiah 24:6–7.

For I will set My eyes on them for good, and I will bring them back to this land; I will build them and not pull them down, and I will plant them and not pluck them up. Then I will give them a heart to know Me, that I am the LORD; and they shall be My people, and I will be their God, for they shall return to Me with their whole heart. (Jer. 24:6–7)

Father, forgive me for … Humble yourself before God, seek His face, and ask Him to forgive your specific sins. Thank Him for His faithfulness to heal you.

11. Why is it important for us to forgive others when they sin against us?

12. When people claim to be without sin, they call God a liar. Read the following Scriptures and record God's indictment of fallen humanity.

Scripture	God's Indictment of Humanity
Romans 3:10–11	
Romans 3:12–13	
Romans 3:14–15	
Romans 3:16–17	
Romans 3:18–19	

———————

Confessing our sins isn't easy. Our tendency is to try to make ourselves look better than we are, not worse. Jesus is repelled by overt pride and self-righteousness—so much so that He told a parable to illustrate this truth. The Pharisee was a religious legalist who prided himself in being knowledgeable and righteous on his own merit. The publican was probably a tax collector who had undoubtedly sinned by extorting taxes above and beyond the ones demanded by Rome.

The parable takes place in the temple. The Pharisee made a production of his superiority by praying loudly, saying, "God, I thank You that I am not like other men—extortioners, unjust, adulterers, or even as this tax collector" (Luke 18:11). At the same time, the tax collector stood back from the limelight and demeaned himself, saying, "God, be merciful to me a sinner!" (v. 13). The first man needed a Savior, but he didn't know it, and the second man needed a Savior, and he knew it.

We are sinners who need to confess our sins to the Lord. God hates our sins, but He loves us. He sent His Son, our Savior, to save us from our sins. Confession hurts in the short term and heals in the long term.

Listen To ...

I believe that I have received Jesus Christ into my heart. I
believe that He has covered all of my sins.
—*Billy Graham*

DAY 5

Propitiation for Sin

In 1741 Jonathan Edwards preached a powerful sermon on the subject of sin to his church in Northampton, Massachusetts. At a later date, he preached the same message to a congregation in Connecticut. His teaching dramatically illustrated the fact that sin is an offense that arouses the wrath of God.

The name of the sermon was "Sinners in the Hands of an Angry God." Edwards' message was unvarnished: he described the danger of sin, the horrors of hell, and the eternal terror of being lost. He urged his listeners to receive the gift of the propitiation for sins provided through the death of Jesus Christ, a death we all deserve.

During the course of his sermon, he was interrupted several times by people pleading, "What shall I do to be saved?" This discourse and similar teachings by other preachers were credited as factors leading to the "Great Awakening," a time of massive religious revival.[6]

Each one of us has a reckoning with the Lord. Edwards used the illustration of the sinner hanging from a slender thread poised over a pit of everlasting separation from God. While we love thoughts of heaven, thoughts of hell repel us.

Is now the time for your personal Great Awakening? Wake up to the realities of sin, wrath, and hell, and grab hold of the hand of salvation reaching out to you from our propitiation, Jesus Christ.

Lift Up ...

Lord, although I sin, I can rest in the knowledge that I am not condemned because You mediate on my behalf. Your death on the cross paid the penalty I deserved. Thank You for loving me, praying for me, and paying my debt. In Jesus' name. Amen.

Look At ...

Yesterday we read that when we are confronted by God's Word about our sins, we should be prompted to confess our sins and trust our faithful, righteous God to forgive us. As believers, we carry on God's reputation in our every action. If we fail to recognize our sin, we are essentially making God a liar.

2 Children

The word *children* is translated from the Greek word *teknia*, which means little born ones.[7] As a pastor, John had a fatherly concern for his flock of fledgling believers. He wrote to encourage them to walk righteously in the world.

Today John affirmed God's grace and mercy to cover our sins by the all-sufficient sacrifice of Jesus on the cross. We *will* sin. And John stated that we have no power to redeem ourselves. But we have a covering, a propitiation, an act of appeasement before God the Father. The payment for our sins has been made and is ours to receive. And not just for us, but for all who believe.

5 Defender

Jesus Christ, the righteous (just, holy), is our defense attorney in heaven. Eternal life is not in question here, as faith in Jesus has already ensured our salvation. But the consequences of a believer's sin, restoration, and future usefulness are urgent matters that Jesus takes up with God when we sin.

Read 1 John 2:1–2.

My little children, these things I write to you, so that you may not sin. And if anyone sins, we have an Advocate with the Father, Jesus Christ the righteous. And He Himself is the propitiation for our sins, and not for ours only but also for the whole world. 1 John 2:1–2

1. With what endearing phrase does John address his readers?

2. Why did John exhort his readers with the previous truths?

3. How do you know John recognizes that his readers are not perfect?

4. Of what does he assure all sinners?

6 Appeaser

Propitiation means to appease or satisfy. Jesus died on the cross to pay the price for sin or satisfy God's demand for payment of sin. Although Jesus was sinless, He took our sins upon Himself and delivered us from the penalty of death that our sins demanded. "For Christ also suffered once for sins, the just for the unjust, that He might bring us to God" (1 Pet. 3:18).

7 Remover

The cross of Christ appeased God and has met His righteous demands so that His grace and mercy are abundantly available to everyone.[8] "For the Lamb who is in the midst of the throne will shepherd them and lead them to living fountains of waters. And God will wipe away every tear from their eyes" (Rev. 7:17). Each of us needs a Savior.

9 Advocate

The word *advocate* is translated from *parakletos* (par-ak'-lay-tos) and means an intercessor.[9] It conveys the idea of a defense attorney who defends a client before a judge and jury. Regardless of our guilt, we stand with our great Advocate who loves and defends us.

5. Who is this? What title does John give Him?

6. What is Jesus on our behalf?

7. Who else does He do this for?

Live Out ...

8. John wrote to his "little born ones" to encourage them to walk righteously in the world. Think of a missionary you know and complete the following in your journal:

   a. Write his or her name.

   b. Write a prayer for the Lord to encourage this person in his or her walk with Him. Include a Scripture that speaks of the joy that comes from *koinonia* with God.

9. Imagine standing in the heavenly courtroom of Judge God Almighty. Satan, the prosecuting attorney, stands up and reads a seemingly endless list of crimes you have committed against God and your fellow human beings. There you sit, guilty as sin, without a glimmer of hope that anything you've ever done can cancel out your inevitable life sentence.

Immediately, your Attorney, Jesus Christ, rushes to your defense. Based upon what you've learned in this lesson about walking in the light, practicing the truth, confessing our sin, forgiveness of sin, and propitiation for sin, finish this story. What do you say? What does Jesus say? How does God respond? And what is the verdict?

_____

There's a popular bumper sticker that reads, "God bless the whole world, no exceptions." This sentiment sounds loving, but it is flawed. First, God *did* bless the whole world when He configured it at creation to meet our every human need. Adam and Eve were the only ones to experience the world in perfection, and they were the first ones to spoil that perfect gift with sin.

God's justice and love prevent Him from pouring His favor on the rebellious and continuously sinful person. But He loved us so much that He provided a means for us to be fit for His presence through the death of His Son, Jesus.

Our Advocate is Jesus, who not only speaks on our behalf but paid the penalty at a great cost. Because of His death on the cross, freedom and blessings are ours for the taking. God *has* blessed the whole world through His Son, Jesus. Yet we must humbly receive Him and His gift. There is no other way to eternal blessings. No exceptions.

Listen To ...

We trample the blood of the Son of God if we think we are forgiven because we are sorry for our sins. The only explanation for the forgiveness of God and for the unfathomable depth of His forgetting is the death of Jesus Christ.

—*Oswald Chambers*

The Genuine Article

1 John 2:3–11

Dietrich Bonhoeffer was a Lutheran pastor and Nazi opponent who was hanged in a Nazi concentration camp in 1945. Bonhoeffer wrote *The Cost of Discipleship,* which is considered a modern classic. He coined the term "cheap grace," which refers to a doctrine that offers the forgiveness of Jesus Christ but makes obedience optional.[1] In contrast to "cheap grace," this week's text demonstrates genuine faith that is evidenced by obedience and love.

To determine whether we are genuine believers, we are prompted to answer several questions: Do I really know Jesus Christ? Does my life demonstrate that knowledge? What do unbelievers see when they look at my life? How can I live to please Him more?

John's love for believers led him to draw attention to our chief aim, which is to "know Him." In other words, we seek an intimate relationship with Jesus characterized by heartfelt obedience. John knew that our sin nature is inclined to sabotage this kind of relationship, so he addressed an area of struggle common to us all: loving our brothers and sisters. We see him draw a picture comparing the perfected love of God in and through us as we walk in the light, as opposed to the dark, aimless wanderings of those unwilling to love those around them.

Day 1: 1 John 2:3   **Showing That We Know**

Day 2: 1 John 2:4–5   **Living What We Say**

Day 3: 1 John 2:6   **Walking as He Walked**

Day 4: 1 John 2:7–8   **Loving as He Loved**

Day 5: 1 John 2:9–11   **Abiding in the Light**

Showing That We Know

Lift Up ...

Dear Lord, as I grow in the knowledge of You through this Bible study, transform my character. Let my decisions and behaviors demonstrate that I truly know You. May I glorify You in every passing and lasting relationship. In Jesus' name. Amen.

Look At ...

Last week we discovered what it means to walk in the light and deal honestly with our sin. Upon experiencing God's amazing grace and forgiveness, we should respond with dedicated hearts, desiring to grow in the knowledge of God.

This week's lesson reveals that obedience is required in our relationship with God. When we understand His love and devotion to us, we are able to obey with grace and gratitude. Our obedience manifests in a way that honors and glorifies Him. In the process, believers and nonbelievers alike will be able to recognize that we know our God.

Read 1 John 2:3.

Now by this we know that we know Him, if we keep His commandments. 1 John 2:3

1. Last week's lesson ended with the good news that we have an "Advocate" with God the Father. Who is He? In today's text, "Him" refers to this same person.

2. What should we know about Him?

3. According to John, what evidence validates that we know Him?

4. According to John 12:49–50, where did Jesus' teachings originate?

5. Read Matthew 22:36–40 concerning Jesus' view of the commandments.

   a. What does Jesus say are the two greatest commandments?

   b. Why do you think they are the greatest of the commandments?

6. Read John 14:15. What should motivate us to keep His commandments?

Live Out ...

7. Simply *knowing* the Bible does not mean we know God; however, our *response* to God's Word validates whether we know *Him*. Look up Psalm 119:1–2, 44–47 to discover how someone who knows God responds to His Word. Fill in the blanks with the missing words.

   Psalm 119:1–2: "Blessed are the undefiled in the way, who _walk_ in the law of the LORD! Blessed are those who _Keep_ His testimonies, who _Seek_ Him with the whole heart!"

   Psalm 119:44–47: "So shall I _Keep_ Your law continually, forever and ever. And I will walk

3 Watchful Obedience

Keep conveys the idea of watchful, observant obedience motivated by love rather than external pressure.[2] Under the law, obedience was an obligation, but under grace, it is a demonstration of love and devotion.

4 Perfect Obedience

When Jesus came into this world to redeem us from our sin and reconcile us to the Father, He acted in obedience and was under a commission from God. Jesus' every word was backed by God's authority. Jesus was the ultimate example of perfect obedience.

6 Loving Obedience

Jesus reduced the law to two commandments, both rooted in love. C. S. Lewis said, "We might think that God wanted simply obedience to a set of rules; whereas He really wants people of a particular sort."[3]

at liberty, for I _seek_____ Your precepts. I will _speak_____ of Your testimonies also before kings, and will not be ashamed. And I will _delight_____ myself in Your commandments, which I _love_____."

9 Sacrificial Obedience

Psalm 119 is a treasure trove of thoughts, desires, prayers, and observations about God's commands. It was originally divided into twenty-two parts, one for each letter in the Hebrew alphabet. This made it easy to learn and teach to the young.

10 Greatest Obedience

There are many ways to demonstrate love, but none greater than by sacrifice. Jesus said, "Greater love has no one than this, than to lay down one's life for his friends" (John 15:13). Amazingly, Jesus saw beyond our sin, beyond His own death, and into a time when we would be friends.

8. Think about your current circumstances. In your journal write about the last time you heard and obeyed God's command. If you are struggling with obedience, also write a prayer for strength. Now, go and obey.

9. The psalmist prefers God's Word over other objects of delight. Match the Scripture references below with the objects of delight.

Psalm 119:72   Food

Psalm 119:103   Riches

Psalm 119:147–148   Sleep

10. Just as we demonstrate our love for God by obedience, God demonstrates His love for us in specific ways. Look up Romans 5:6–8. Copy it onto an index card or slip of paper, then post it in a conspicuous place. Throughout the week, reread it and be reminded of His love for you.

————————————

Life is full of tests, and they start early on in life. When a child first enters school, he or she takes a placement test to evaluate which classes to take. By middle school, tests are a regular part of life. In high school, students take the rite-of-passage driver's test to earn a license and then the all-important college entrance exams.

Other specialized tests can follow. For instance, before a person can practice law, he or she must take a test. Pretests weed out those who are unqualified to pursue a particular course of study. Progression tests evaluate interim learning. Posttests determine whether the standards of knowledge have been met.

Jesus took the pretest that allowed us to have a relationship with God. The test John wrote about is something like a posttest. As we walk through life, we are undoubtedly met with progress tests to strengthen our faith. The ultimate test is one that determines if we know God at all: Are we obediently seeking to keep His commands?

There is no better credential than obedience—it's how you and everyone else know that your relationship with God is the genuine article. Obedience demonstrates our devotion to Him and makes our relationship real and intimate.

Listen To ...

The Bible recognizes no faith that does not lead to obedience, nor does it recognize any obedience that does not spring from faith. The two are opposite sides of the same coin.

—A. W. Tozer

Living What We Say

At a masquerade ball, guests are encouraged to dress in costumes and wear elaborate masks to conceal their identities. Others try to guess who's behind each mask. Part of the fun is being anonymous while assuming a false persona. But if we were being entirely serious, we could say that it's a purposeful attempt to deceive.

At a ball, of course, this is part of the fun; but too often deception can creep into real life, and we wear masks to hide the conditions of our lives. Maybe we are concealing trouble at home or betraying someone in a business dealing with a fake reassuring smile. At church, believers have been known to wear masks that gives the impression that they're walking from one blessing to the next when in reality they are struggling—or worse, lost.

Why would anyone do such a thing? Because it's easier to pretend to be who we should be than to be honest about who we really are. Masks do a good job of diverting attention from reality, but the situation is made worse because our relationship with God suffers from the ruse.

Deception reaps a crop of troubles, both in daily life and in our pursuit of a genuine relationship with God. When we refuse to face our true selves and obey the Lord, we waste our lives hiding behind a disguise.

Lift Up ...

Dear Lord, I want to live an authentic life. Help me to be honest with You, others, and myself about my sin. What a privilege it is to say I know You. Let my life reflect Your truth and character more each day. In Jesus' name. Amen.

Look At ...

Yesterday we learned that obedience to God is evidence of knowing Him and that obedience in all facets of life—including our love for Jesus Christ—is the mark of a believer. Yet no matter how diligently we strive for obedience, the perfectly obedient and sacrificial death of Jesus Christ humbles us.

Today we see the contrast between living a lie as opposed to living an authentic life in Christ. Once again, we acknowledge that there are no acts or righteous-sounding words that can replicate a genuine walk with the Lord. When we know Him through His Word, we are permeated with the love of God. Others recognize Him through us. The simple truth is that there can be no love without obedience to God's commands.

Read 1 John 2:4–5.

He who says, "I know Him," and does not keep His commandments, is a liar, and the truth is not in him. But whoever keeps His word, truly the love of God is perfected in him. By this we know that we are in Him.
1 John 2:4–5

1. How does John describe the person who claims to know Jesus Christ but disregards His commandments?

2. Read the words of Jesus in Matthew 7:15–20. Do you think John is being unfair by calling those who don't obey God's commands "liars"? Why or why not?

3. Continue reading Matthew 7:21–23.

1 Works of Denial

A *liar* is someone who is insincere before God and others and lives a life that is not genuine. This person's behavior contradicts his or her claim to know Jesus Christ. "They profess to know God, but in works they deny Him, being abominable, disobedient, and disqualified for every good work" (Titus 1:16).

3 Words of Deceit

Jesus' response can be interpreted as "I never came to observe you as having experienced Me."[4] These people looked good on the outside but *practiced* disobedience, whereas a true believer experiences Jesus on the inside and *practices* obedience.

4 Lives of Love

The Greek word for love in
this verse (*agape*) refers to
God's unconditional love.
Perfected implies comple-
tion and fulfillment. When
we submit our thoughts,
choices, and actions to
God, His plan for our lives
is accomplished and His
perfect love flows through
us to others.

7 Proof of Knowledge

Just as a passport validates
our citizenship, an obedient lifestyle proves we
know Jesus Christ. John
MacArthur said, "The
faith that says but does
not do is really unbelief....
True faith will not fail to
produce the fruit of good
works."[5]

8 Reach of Faith

Sanctification is the process
of being separated from
sin and set apart for
God's service, and it will
continue until we awake
in His likeness (see Ps.
17:15). We are encouraged
to "press on ... forgetting
those things which are
behind and reaching
forward to those things
which are ahead" (Phil.
3:12–13).

a. What will happen to those who "say" versus those who "do" (v. 21)?

b. How do these verses warn that things are not always as they appear (v. 22)?

c. What two tests did these fraudulent believers fail (v. 23)?

4. What does John say about the person who "keeps His word"?

5. What can we "know" when we keep His Word?

6. Look up the following scriptures to discover the blessings that belong to those who are "in Him."

Scripture	Blessings of Being "in Him"
2 Corinthians 5:21	
Ephesians 1:7	
Ephesians 1:11	
Colossians 2:9–10	

Live Out ...

7. Today we learned that having a relationship with Jesus Christ means following His commandments. Good works are the natural result of this relationship. According to Ephesians 2:8–10, how do grace, faith, and works go together?

8. In which of the following areas do you find it difficult to walk what you talk—to make choices and behave in ways that keep God's Word?

❑ Marriage   ❑ Workplace   ☑ Entertainment choices
❑ Public places   ❑ Parenting   ☒ Family
☑ Financial matters   ❑ Other: _____

Write in your journal about how your actions have failed to match your words.

    a.

    b.

Write a prayer of rededication to God. Ask Him to make those attitudes and actions as distasteful to you as they are to Him.

9. Recall a time when you surrendered an area of disobedience to God. Be bold and share the story with another believer. Your experience might encourage someone else to obey.

    a. What blessings did you experience as a result of your decision?

    b. How did your obedience affect others?

Most children are not naturally obedient; obedience has to be learned, experienced, and incorporated into everyday life. It is natural to resist someone else's agenda when you can't see how it benefits you. Young children don't understand that cleaning up their toys is the beginning of developing a work ethic. They don't see that turning in homework is the start of developing a habit of meeting commitments. They don't realize that letting Mom and Dad know where they will be when they go out with friends is developing transparency, a trait that will benefit future relationships. But as time goes on, they begin to see the correlation between hard work and rewards. They find that meeting commitments gives them a sense of pride and accomplishment. Trustworthiness is a trait that leads to successful friendships, successful business advancements, and a successful marriage.

The love of God that John spoke about is a mature love that is perfected in us as we consistently obey God and come to truly know Him. Obedience to God has to start somewhere, usually with a small step like stopping a bad habit, developing daily prayer, and consistently reading His Word. The journey is well worth taking because the ultimate benefit is in knowing the Almighty God. One day He will welcome us home—like a longtime friend.

Listen To ...

It does not require great learning to be a Christian and be convinced of the truth of the Bible. It requires only an honest heart and a willingness to obey God.

—*Albert Barnes*

Walking as He Walked

During the Middle Ages, master craftsmen took on apprentices between the ages of ten and fifteen who would usually train under them for seven years in order to learn a trade. The master craftsman would take the apprentice into his own home and care for the child, who, in turn, provided labor and learned the trade. When the apprentice completed his training, he earned the title of "journeyman."[6]

An apprentice started his tenure with none of the needed skills, and the master craftsman knew that. The apprentice would learn methodically, step by step. Over the seven-year period, there would be an emphasis on technique and quality, with the goal of producing another master of the trade.

New Christians also need to learn how to "be" Christians in a patient and methodical way. The greatest example was the Master Himself, Jesus Christ. He demonstrated the behaviors that exemplify forgiveness, love, mercy, prayer, and obedience—the marks of a genuine believer. Apprentice Christians also have the benefit of being surrounded by journeyman Christians, who can provide an example of walking the Christian walk.

Lift Up ...

Thank You, Lord, for the gift of the Holy Spirit. Without Your Spirit I can never hope to walk as You walked. Help me to empty myself daily of my arrogance and pride so that I may be filled with the power to do Your will. In Jesus' name. Amen.

Look At ...

Yesterday, we pondered the differences between living a lie and living an authentic life of knowing and following Jesus. No mask can substitute for the genuine life of the daily, purposeful

2 Willing Spirit

The word *ought* conveys a dutiful obligation to walk or live as Jesus did. Although it sounds like an impossible standard, since "the spirit indeed is willing, but the flesh is weak" (Matt. 26:41–42), Jesus did not leave us helpless.

3 Identical Essence

"Another Helper" indicates a person of equal quality. The Holy Spirit has the same essence of deity and oneness with the Father as does Jesus Christ.[7] "His divine power has given to us all things that pertain to life and godliness, through the knowledge of Him who called us" (2 Pet. 1:3).

4 Gradual Transformation

The primary work of the Holy Spirit in the life of a believer is to transform us into the image of Christ. Transformations are gradual and take time. It is how we "keep in step with the Spirit" (Gal. 5:25 NIV) and walk as Jesus walked.

walk of obedience. Humble obedience is the sign of a true believer. When we obey, His love is perfected in us.

Today we focus on how to live an obedient life in Christ. Who could possibly walk as Jesus walked? He is perfect, and we are but dust. But there is a way to walk so that He is glorified and we are blessed. We must understand that transformation is a lifelong pursuit. Thankfully, God made the way known to us. Today we find that the key to a faithful walk is an abiding life.

Read 1 John 2:6.

He who says he abides in Him ought himself also to walk just as He walked. 1 John 2:6

1. John describes the person who makes what claim?

2. To what standard does he hold such a person?

3. Read John 14:16–17. What kind of help did Jesus promise His disciples?

4. Review 2 Corinthians 3:18 and answer the following questions.
   a. Who works in us?
   b. For what purpose does He work?

5. The phrases on the left describe some of the ways Jesus walked. Look up the Scriptures on the right and match them to the appropriate phrase.

a. Reached out to religious outcasts   _d_ Matthew 14:23

b. Lived to do God's will   _c_ Mark 1:40–41

c. Showed compassion for social outcasts   _a_ Luke 5:30–31

d. Spent time with God in prayer   _b_ John 4:34

e. Demonstrated humility   _e_ John 13:13–15

6. To walk as Jesus walked, we must walk in the Spirit. Fill in the chart below to discover how to walk His way.

Scripture	Walk His Way
2 Corinthians 5:7	
Galatians 5:24–25	
Ephesians 4:1–2	
Ephesians 5:15–16	

7 Complete Dependence

To abide in Christ means to depend completely on Him for all that we need in order to live for Him and serve Him. It is a living relationship.[8] Our Christian walk can't survive without drawing upon His strength.

Live Out ...

7. Read Jesus' description in John 15:4–5 of what it means to "abide in Him."

a. Summarize this relationship in your own words.

b. Compare and contrast situations in your own life where (1) you have struggled to produce fruit (good deeds, godly attitudes, pure thoughts) on your own, and (2) God has produced the fruit of His Spirit (love, joy, peace, patience, kindness, goodness, faithfulness, gentleness, and self-control) in you.

9 Mutual Reliance

God intended the body of Christ to be interdependent. We need one another, especially when we are limping spiritually. Yet this is often the time we isolate ourselves and hide our struggle from other believers. Be available either to minister or to be ministered to by others.

8. Look at your answers to question 5.

In your journal, write about some practical ways that you will walk more like Jesus walked.

❏ Be a friend to _____ even though:

❏ Seek God's will in:

❏ Show compassion to:

❏ Sacrifice the following to spend more time in prayer and Bible study:

❏ Demonstrate a servant's heart by:

9. Compare your spiritual walk with the verses in question 6.

a. How often do you "walk in the Spirit"? More or less often than last year? Last month?

b. What helps you to walk this way?

c. What hinders you?

10. The Bible reminds us to "consider one another in order to stir up love and good works, not forsaking the assembling of ourselves together, as is the manner of some, but exhorting one another, and so much the more as you see the Day approaching" (Heb. 10:24–25).

a. How have you grown in your walk with God as a result of being in a small group?

b. Name someone in your life who is struggling to walk with God.

c. How will you encourage that person and spur him or her on to love and good deeds?

❏ Pray   ❏ Listen   ❏ Offer practical help

❏ Share Scripture   ❏ Other: _____

_____

Although cooking shows have been around for decades, they have recently exploded in popularity. What is it that we find so interesting about watching someone cook? Perhaps it's the ease with which these chefs are able to produce amazing dishes, or maybe we believe that by watching them, kitchen mastery is within our reach.

Anyone who has attempted to duplicate a recipe from television has probably been confronted with the reality that it's a lot harder than it looks. TV cooks have all the right ingredients at hand (premeasured with exact precision), all the necessary equipment, and a pristine kitchen. No wonder they get it done in minutes! At-home cooks who have tried and succeeded know that it is indeed possible to produce great meals in their own kitchens. Even a small success can fuel encouragement to try again and again.

The Christian walk is not much different. We see other Christians who seem to walk through their spiritual lives with ease, but even for mature Christians, following in the footsteps of Jesus is a continual learning process. Successes such as when we exhibit the fruit of the Holy Spirit, have an answered prayer, and understand God's Word are ways that God encourages us to keep abiding. The satisfaction of walking in the Master's footsteps can bring more fulfillment than the finest gourmet meal.

Listen To ...

> *To be in Christ is the source of the Christian's life; to be like Christ is the sum of His excellence; to be with Christ is the fullness of His joy.*
> —*Charles Hodge*

Loving as He Loved

Just the thought of moving to another country brings up many considerations. Yet despite the obvious differences from our current homes, many aspects of our lives would remain the same. For instance, a different climate might necessitate either a heavier or lighter wardrobe, but one way or another, we would still wear clothing. A new country's cuisine might be more concentrated on vegetables, fish, or spicier foods, but eating every day would still be part of our routines. And then there's the culture itself. It might be more formal, requiring a study of new protocols, or it could be a friendly come-as-you-are type of social interaction.

For a new believer, the Christian life can seem a bit like moving to a foreign country. Yet when it comes to interacting with others, much remains the same. We are closer to some than others, but the Christian life enables us to treat everyone with sincere respect and selfless love. Essentially we have taken up residence in a new and eternal country. The cultural standards have been set high by none other than Jesus, because He loves us with unsurpassed sacrificial love. No matter how we try, we will never out-love Him.

Lift Up ...

Lord, You lavish love upon me even when I am unlovable. The only love I can muster on my own is conditional and dependent on circumstances and emotions. Purify my heart and give me insight into Your love for others. In Jesus' name. Amen.

Look At ...

Yesterday we found that abiding in Christ is a lifelong process that involves an eager determination, patient expectation, and clear understanding that we depend on the encouragement of others along the way. Ultimately, we learned that we are dependent on God. We explored the ways believers grow and develop in ways that coincide with the challenges of consciously seeking to follow Jesus' example.

Today we see that those who truly know Jesus abide in Him and are being transformed constantly by His power. It's easier to follow a list of Old Testament commandments than to love as Jesus loved. Love, we will see, is at once given, commanded, required, extended, and a natural result of abiding in Christ.

Read 1 John 2:7–8.

Brethren, I write no new commandment to you, but an old commandment which you have had from the beginning. The old commandment is the word which you heard from the beginning. Again, a new commandment I write to you, which thing is true in Him and in you, because the darkness is passing away, and the true light is already shining. 1 John 2:7–8

1. What type of commandment does John describe?

2. When did the recipients of this letter originally receive the commandment?

3. With what phrase does John identify the old commandment?

4. What seemingly contradictory statement does John make at the beginning of verse 8?

5. Who embodied the truth of this *new* brand of love according to John?

6. Who else demonstrated this love?

3 Commanded Love

"From the beginning" refers to the time when the recipients of John's letter embraced the teachings of Jesus. As we will see from the context of this verse, John is talking about the commandment to love. *"The word which you heard"* is the gospel message, the purest example of love.

4 Extended Love

The commandment is new in that it raised love to an entirely new emphasis and level by Jesus' teaching and example.[9] The love He spoke about extended to sinners and Gentiles. This was new to the orthodox Jew.

7 Highest Love

New refers to a quality of freshness rather than age. *The darkness* describes the old way of doing things prior to the dawning of the "true light" of the gospel message. While Jesus upheld the Old Testament commands to love God and others, He took love to its highest level.

8 Selfless Love

Jesus' life demonstrated a new kind of love, one that was sacrificial and selfless. This is the same "love of God [that] has been poured out in our hearts by the Holy Spirit who was given to us" (Rom. 5:5).

10 Abiding Love

Jesus never commanded us to like everyone, but He *does* command us to love them. John 15:10 says, "If you keep My commandments, you will abide in My love, just as I have kept My Father's commandments and abide in His love." To love others is to abide in God's love.

7. How does John contrast darkness and light?

Live Out ...

8. Read these verses and explain how Jesus shed "new" light on the "old" commandment to love.

    a. Matthew 5:43–48:

    b. John 13:34–35:

9. Loving others does not always mean pleasing them. Sometimes acting in love—which is acting in the person's best interest—is difficult. Is God asking you to love someone in any of these ways?

❑ Be truthful with them (Eph. 4:15)

❑ Confront them about habitual sin (Gal. 6:1)

❑ Withdraw fellowship (2 Thess. 3:6)

❑ Stop carrying a load they need to carry themselves (Gal. 6:5)

10. Think of someone you know who is difficult to love. Find a verse that encourages you to demonstrate love to him or her. Find a way to show His love to that person this week.

Anyone who has planted a garden knows the joy and anticipation of waiting until something breaks through the soil. Seeds are fascinating, and the fact that everything required for a full-grown plant is present in something as tiny as a pebble speaks of God's creative power. Once the seed is planted, there isn't anything you can do but watch, water, and wait. Growth is a natural process that follows its own course and timing. When the plant has grown, it is critical that the leaves or branches stay connected to the main stalk so the plant can receive nourishment and produce fruit.

This basic concept also applies to spiritual growth. Jesus instructed us to abide in Him, which means we need to stay connected to Him just like a branch on a plant. When we do, we receive the nourishment to bear His chosen fruit. Invariably, that will include love for both the loveable and unlovable.

If that seems like a tall order, remember that the seeds of love were planted when you accepted Jesus as Savior. Let them take their course and stay connected to the nourishment of prayer and Bible study, and God will bear His fruit of love supernaturally in you.

Listen To ...

> *Do not waste time bothering whether you "love" your neighbor; act as if you did. As soon as we do this we find one of the great secrets. When you are behaving as if you loved someone you will presently come to love him.*
>
> —C. S. Lewis

Abiding in the Light

Have you ever ridden in a car with a driver who is lost, and you both know it? That's bad enough, but it's even worse when the driver refuses to admit to being lost. Denial multiplies the strain of the moment and delays a solution.

There are some common indicators that signal when you're lost: You know you are lost when you're concentrating so hard to read the street signs, you have to turn off the radio. You know you're lost when someone gives you a series of directions ending with "You can't miss it," and you still miss it. Even a GPS device is no guarantee that you won't get lost. Then add the stress of being in a moving vehicle, making quick decisions, obeying traffic laws, and avoiding collisions with other cars. Stress upon stress.

Now, translate this scenario into our spiritual life. When we hate our brothers or sisters, we are behaving much like a driver in denial of being lost. We are wasting time insisting we know where we're going, while in reality we have lost our way. John pictured this as stumbling through darkness as opposed to confidently walking in the light.

Lift Up ...

Lord, You have chosen me and called me for Your special purposes. I know how easily I can get lost. All it takes is a hateful attitude toward others or shifting my focus from You. I want to remain in the certainty of Your marvelous light. In Jesus' name. Amen.

Look At ...

We've seen how Jesus embodied pure love and learned that His love flows through us by the power of the Holy Spirit. Achieving a standard of love is possible only through the light of the Spirit's power, although we must determine to walk in that light. Light and love come through abiding in Christ Jesus.

John brought this new concept of love to a practical level by comparing our words and actions. Today is a study of contrasts: light and dark, blessings and curses, blindness and sight, stumbling and walking, and hatred and love. John missed no opportunity to communicate the power of love and the darkness of hatred. There are no gray shadows when it comes to love.

Read 1 John 2: 9–11.

He who says he is in the light, and hates his brother, is in darkness until now. He who loves his brother abides in the light, and there is no cause for stumbling in him. But he who hates his brother is in darkness and walks in darkness, and does not know where he is going, because the darkness has blinded his eyes. 1 John 2:9–11

1. John describes the contradictory lifestyle of someone who claims to be where?

2. In reality, this person is where? Why?

3. Describe two characteristics of someone who "loves his brother."

4. Someone who "hates his brother" is doing what two things in relation to darkness?

5. Describe what happened to this person's sense of direction. Why?

6. Scripture is clear that anger must be handled appropriately "lest any root of bitterness springing up cause trouble, and by this many

2 Sinful Hatred

In Scripture, hatred is used to describe God's reaction to sin (see Heb. 1:9) or different levels of love (see Luke 14:26 and Rom. 9:13). In this context, hatred describes conduct or words characterized by ill will and a persecuting spirit.[10] A life consumed by hatred, therefore, cannot coexist with light.

3 Blessings for Curses

John used the word *brother* to emphasize the special obligation we have to love other believers. But we are also required to love our enemies and unbelievers. "Love your enemies, do good to those who hate you, bless those who curse you, and pray for those who spitefully use you" (Luke 6:27–28).

5 Spiritual Vision

Hatred blinds us to God's light, making us lose our way. As we abide in the light, God's love attracts others to Christ. But when we allow hatred to reign, we compromise our spiritual eyesight and our walk with God.

become defiled" (Heb. 12:15). Summarize the instruction given by the following verses.

    a. Romans 12:17–19

    b. Ephesians 4:26–27, 31

Live Out ...

7 Clear Direction

When Christians "walk in the light," they know where they are going. They are having fellowship with God and other Christians; they are not causing others to stumble, and they are growing spiritually. These are all deliberate choices facilitated by clear eyesight.

7. Just as walking in the Spirit is an active process, our choices determine whether we walk in light or darkness. Summarize the choices described in the verses below.

    a. Luke 9:23

    b. Romans 13:12–14

    c. 2 Corinthians 6:14–15

    d. Ephesians 5:8–11

8 Solid Footing

A "cause for stumbling" describes trapping someone and causing his or her demise or downfall." Unloving people are themselves stumbling because they walk in darkness and are causing others to stumble as well.

8. Has your sin ever caused someone to stumble by affecting that person's relationship with God or causing that person to sin? Confess this to God now. Then go to that individual and express your remorse.

9. Is there a root of bitterness in your heart? Has it developed into hatred? Work through the following steps in your journal so that you might experience the freedom of forgiveness.

Step 1. Honestly express your feelings about this person to God.

Step 2. Confess the bitterness and hatred as sin. Ask for God's forgiveness.

Step 3. Ask God to remove the bitterness and hatred from your heart.

Step 4. Replace your negative thoughts about this person with loving thoughts. Write down some things you admire about him or her.

While walking down a dark street one night, a man saw a faltering pinpoint of light coming toward him. He thought perhaps the person carrying the light was ill or drunk, but as he drew nearer, he could see a man with a flashlight walking with a white cane.

Why would a blind man be carrying a light? the man wondered. When he came close to the blind man, he decided to ask.

The blind man smiled and said, "I carry my light, not so I can see, but so that others can see me. I cannot help being blind, but I can help being a stumbling block to someone else."[12]

The man had probably experienced a few unfortunate collisions leading him to establish this precaution when walking at night. What a considerate man. He could do nothing about his blindness, so he protected both himself and others as best he could.

Fortunately, people who are spiritually blind have better options. They can turn to God to remove the hatred in their hearts. Spiritual sight can be restored. Most Christians don't want to be a stumbling block and would be horrified to know they had caused another to stumble. Why risk it? Learn to abide in God so His love can flow through you, and His light will illuminate your way. You'll save yourself and others the anguish of a fall.

Listen To ...

> *Darkness cannot drive out darkness; only light can do that.*
> *Hate cannot drive out hate; only love can do that.*
> —*Martin Luther King Jr.*

What in the World?

1 John 2:12–17

In the book *Where the Red Fern Grows*, the main character, ten-year-old Billy, longed to buy a couple of raccoon-hunting dogs. Living in the poverty-stricken Ozarks, the boy earned the money himself and bought two puppies. In order to train the dogs to recognize the scent of a raccoon, he needed to capture one. Together, Billy and his grandfather constructed a trap and placed a shiny object in it as a lure. These pesky and often destructive critters are curious and drawn to shiny things. Once the animal gets hold of the object and tries to pull it out, his clenched fist becomes caught in the trap. Ironically, if the raccoon would simply let go of the object, he could go free—but he won't let go. He doesn't realize that grasping the treasure will lead to his capture. We tend to shake our heads at this, but Christians can sometimes get trapped in a similar way. In this world, Satan uses many shiny things to distract us and capture our attention. Before we know it, just like the raccoon, we're trapped because we won't let go of the shiny distraction.

Jon Courson compared Satan to a football team with only three strategies: "From the beginning of time, Satan has had only three plays: the lust of the eyes, the lust of the flesh, and the pride of life. To this day, every temptation, every attack from the enemy, and every worldly seduction falls into one of these three categories because Satan has no other plays."[1]

Paul warned us not to fall into the snare of the things of this world but to overcome the temptation. By remaining in God's Word, we remain in His will.

Are you holding onto something shiny? Drop the baubles of this world and hold tightly to Christ.

Day 1: 1 John 2:12–14   **Knowing the Father**

Day 2: 1 John 2:13–14   **Overcoming the Enemy**

Day 3: 1 John 2:15   **Receiving a Warning**

Day 4: 1 John 2:16   **Avoiding the World**

Day 5: 1 John 2:17   **Remaining in God's Will**

DAY 1

Knowing the Father

Lift Up ...

Thank You, Lord, for forgiving my sins and for making Yourself known to me. I know I will not experience any temptation that is unknown to You or to humanity. Yet I also know I am vulnerable to being diverted and fooled. I want to know You so well that I cannot be led astray. In Jesus' name. Amen.

Look At ...

Last week we learned that God tells us we know that we know Him by being obedient to His commandments and by abiding in Him. We put this into action by walking in the light of Christ and loving those around us. In order to love God, we have to move away from the things of this world; otherwise, we will drift away from God's love and our love for others.

This week John sternly warns us of the things that can trip us up in today's world. God made it clear in His Word that either we are marked by love and obedience to God or we are in rebellion against Him. For a believer, there is no middle ground. Just as Joshua told the Israelites, "Choose for yourselves this day whom you will serve" (Josh. 24:15), John made it clear that we must do the same today.

Read 1 John 2:12–14.

I write to you, little children, Because your sins are forgiven you for His name's sake. I write to you, fathers, Because you have known Him who is from the beginning.... I write to you, little children, Because you have known the Father. I have written to you, fathers, Because you have known Him who is from the beginning. 1 John 2:12–13a, 13c, 14a

1 Children

We learned in Lesson One that *little children* means little born ones. All believers, regardless of age, have been born from above and belong to the family of God. Jesus said, "You must be born again" (John 3:7). When you are born again, you're one of God's little children.

3 Christ

The name *Jesus* means Savior. The name *Christ* means Anointed One.[2] God forgives our sins on account of our Savior, the Anointed One of God, and His selfless sacrifice on the cross. "Therefore God also has highly exalted Him and given Him the name which is above every name" (Phil. 2:9).

7 Infant

"Little children" comes from the Greek word *paidion* (pahee-dee'-on), which means an infant or half-grown child.[3] Rather than addressing all born-again believers, John addresses newborns in the faith. "Truly I tell you, unless you change and become like little children, you will never enter the kingdom of heaven" (Matt. 18:3 NIV).

1. Last week John directed his attention to those who walk in darkness. Who does he turn his attention to today?

2. Of what truth does John assure them?

3. What makes forgiveness possible?

4. Who does John speak to next?

5. When John said, "from the beginning," to whom does he refer?

6. John addresses them again as little children but changes the next part. What does he say?

7. What phrase is repeated here? Why do you think John does this?

Live Out ...

8. Read Romans 8:15–17 and answer the following questions.
   a. By what other name can we cry out to our Father?
   b. To what does the Spirit of God bear witness?
   c. What privileged status do we receive as God's children, and with whom do we share this?

9. Today we learned that because of the name of Jesus Christ, all believers are forgiven and born into the family of God. Read John 3:3–7 and answer the following questions.
   a. What has to happen in order for a person to see the kingdom of God?

b. In addition to a natural birth, how must a person be born in order to enter the kingdom of God?

10. John wrote to the church elders to encourage them in their walk with God.

a. Name someone you know who is a spiritually mature believer.

b. What godly characteristics does this person exhibit that confirms he or she has experienced genuine fellowship with God?

c. Contact this person by phone, through email, or in person and encourage him or her to continue to "pursue righteousness, godliness, faith, love, patience, gentleness" and to continue to "fight the good fight of the faith" (1 Tim. 6:11–12).

11. Earthly inheritance is based on the wealth our parents accumulated over a lifetime. Spiritual inheritance is based on the glorious riches of our heavenly Father through Jesus Christ. Read the following verses to discover some of the riches of our spiritual inheritance.

Scripture	Riches of Our Spiritual Inheritance
Psalm 73:25–26	
Matthew 25:34	
Titus 3:7	
Hebrews 1:2	

In your journal write a prayer thanking God for the abundant spiritual inheritance He has provided for you. Thank Him for the honor of being a co-heir with Christ. Thank Him for the people He has placed in your life to hold you accountable and encourage you.

8 Co-Heirs

The word *Abba* means Daddy or Papa. It connotes tenderness, dependence, and a relationship free of fear or anxiety. What a powerful privilege to be able to call the Creator our Daddy! We are co-heirs with Jesus Christ for every good work God has done and will do.

9 Cleansed

Water figuratively refers to renewal or spiritual cleansing. Spiritual washing is accomplished by the Holy Spirit through the Word of God (see Eph. 5:26). When we trust in the name of the Savior, Jesus Christ, we are cleansed of our sins and experience new spiritual birth into God's family.

———————

Studies of animals have discovered a phase of sensitive learning known as "filial imprinting," which occurs when a young animal observes and acquires several behavioral characteristics from its parent. It is most obvious in birds that leave the nest shortly after hatching. These birds "imprint" on their parents and follow them around, copying their behavior and actions. From turkeys to geese, birds will imprint on the first suitable source in the critical period of thirteen to sixteen hours after hatching. They have even been known to imprint on inanimate objects.[4] In 1993 using this technique, Bill Lishman of Ontario, Canada, flying in an ultralight aircraft, led a flock of Canadian geese to North Carolina.[5]

It's believed that unborn babies hear their parents' voices and then recognize them after birth. Just as babies and birds imprint on their parents, God wants us to imprint our minds and hearts on Him. By knowing God, reading His Word, and copying His behavior, we are able to follow Him and grow to be likeminded. What better example could we emulate than our Heavenly Father?

Listen To ...

Forgiveness is the remission of sins. For it is by this that what has been lost, and was found, is saved from being lost again.

—*Augustine*

Overcoming the Enemy

Recently, in Baytown, Texas, Dorothy Baker-Flugence left the CVS Pharmacy with her children, ages two and five. She got in her vehicle and drove off, when a man wielding a knife popped up from the back of her van. She wrestled with him over the knife, and after he bit her hand, she punched him in the face and tried to veer her car off the road into a telephone poll to disorient him. When she stopped her vehicle, he jumped out, and in the process, she ran him over.

When asked why she took such drastic measures, Baker-Flugence said, "I thought, 'If you swerve and hit the pole, he's not wearing a seatbelt, [so] he'll go through the windshield or at least hit his head, and you can stop him. You can do something to make sure that he doesn't hurt your kids.' That's all I was thinking of really, was just to get him away from my kids."

A Baytown resident cheered Baker-Flugence's actions, saying, "She's trying to protect herself and her kids. I'd do the same thing."[6]

In this world of danger and crime, there are times when we must take drastic measures to protect and preserve our lives. The same is true when we come up against the attacks of Satan. At such times, we should recognize we are in a battle and must protect ourselves by whatever means necessary. What drastic measures will you take to overcome the enemy?

Lift Up ...

Lord, thank You for overcoming evil by Your death on the cross. Knowing You and Your Word prepares me for dealing with the enemy and becoming strong and sure. Help me in my desire to abide in You daily. In Jesus' name. Amen.

2 Victory

Overcome means to conquer, prevail over, or be victorious. John isn't saying believers *will* overcome or that they *can* overcome but that we *have* overcome through the name of Jesus Christ. "Yet in all these things we are more than conquerors through Him who loved us" (Rom. 8:37).

3 Enemy

Satan, aka the wicked one and the Devil, is God's enemy and ours. Satan's influence in worldly affairs is clearly revealed throughout Scripture. Believers have assurance that "the God of peace will crush Satan under your feet" (Rom. 16:20). But such personal victory depends on our will to resist Satan's temptations.

4 Mighty

Strong means mighty and powerful. Strength for a Christian's victory over Satan is provided through the power of Jesus Christ's death and resurrection. "Finally, my brethren, be strong in the Lord and in the power of His might" (Eph. 6:10).

Look At ...

In yesterday's lesson, John addressed two groups of believers: children and fathers. He spoke to some who were new to the faith. Although they were still learning what it means to follow Christ, they were forgiven and clean. He was speaking to those who had walked longer with God and knew Him in a deeper way. He wanted all of them to be assured that they were saved and had intimate access to God.

Today we meet another group of solid believers: the young men. James Montgomery Boice notes these believers were "those who are bearing the brunt of the church's spiritual warfare."[7] Distinct from the children and fathers, these believers were fighting the good fight and overcoming Satan with their strong knowledge of the Word.

Read 1 John 2:13–14.

I write to you, young men, Because you have overcome the wicked one.... I have written to you, young men, Because you are strong, and the word of God abides in you, And you have overcome the wicked one. 1 John 2:13b, 14b

1. Who does John write to next?

2. What accomplishment does he credit to them?

3. Who have they overcome?

4. What characteristic does John commend the "young men" for exhibiting?

5. What abides in this set of believers that would help them overcome the enemy?

6. Read the Scriptures below. What do they say about resisting the Devil?

    a. James 4:7

    b. 1 Peter 5:8–10

8 Maturity

God calls believers to grow in their spiritual walks, not to stay spiritual babies. "You therefore, beloved, since you know this beforehand, beware lest you also fall from your own steadfastness, being led away with the error of the wicked; but grow in the grace and knowledge of our Lord and Savior Jesus Christ" (2 Pet. 3:17–18).

Live Out ...

7. Read the Scriptures below. How is Satan referred to in each, and what do they say about him?

    a. John 12:31

    b. 2 Corinthians 4:4

    c. Ephesians 2:2

8. Today we met the third group in a church's congregation—young believers. As believers mature in their faith and the Word of God abides in them, they grow strong against Satan and sin. Read the following verses and record what God's Word helps you to overcome and why or how it helps you to conquer.

Scripture	God's Word Helps Me to Overcome	Why or How
Deuteronomy 31:6		
Job 33:14–18		
Colossians 3:8–10		

In your journal paraphrase Ephesians 6:11–12 as a prayer, asking God to equip you to deal with Satan in your daily life.

9 Diversity

Each of us is at a different level in our walk with God. Paul admitted that even he had not arrived. "Not that I have already attained, or am already perfected; but I press on, that I may lay hold of that for which Christ Jesus has also laid hold of me" (Phil. 3:12).

Put on the whole armor of God, that you may be able to stand against the wiles of the devil. For we do not wrestle against flesh and blood, but against principalities, against powers, against the rulers of the darkness of this age, against spiritual hosts of wickedness in the heavenly places.

9. Circle the stage of spiritual development that you are in now.

New Believer   **Young Believer**   **Mature Believer**

- If you are a new believer, write in your journal about how you will make an effort daily to receive God's Word and continue to grow in the knowledge of the Lord.
- If you are a young believer, write in your journal about how you will continue to stay strong and cultivate God's Word to overcome sin and Satan.
- If you are a mature believer, write in your journal about how you will allow God's Word in you to glorify Him and teach others about Him.

10. What keeps God's Word from continuing to abide in you? What choices do you make that cause you to compromise the Word of God in your life?

❑ Consulting your horoscope   ☑ Worrying about the world

❑ Adopting pop psychology   ❑ Watching certain television shows

❑ Listening to or engaging in gossip   ❑ Socializing exclusively with unbelievers

❑ Other: _____

———————

Spiritual warfare is nothing new. Saints who have gone before us have battled against the same spiritual forces of evil that we do today. Thankfully, believers know the ultimate outcome of the war: victory! Because Jesus conquered death on the cross, we fight *from* a place of victory, not *for* it.

Revelation 12:7–9 says, "And war broke out in heaven: Michael and his angels fought with the dragon; and the dragon and his angels fought, but they did not prevail, nor was a place found for them in heaven any longer. So the great dragon was cast out, that serpent of old, called the Devil and Satan, who deceives the whole world; he was cast to the earth, and his angels were cast out with him."

Satan will be cast down and conquered once and for all, but until then, we must equip ourselves for the daily battles we face. Ephesians 6 details the armor we should be putting on each day, in order to "stand against the wiles of the devil.... Therefore take up the whole armor of God, that you may be able to withstand in the evil day, and having done all, to stand" (vv. 11, 13).

So today, be sure you are equipped with the truth, the breastplate of righteousness, the preparation of the gospel of peace, the shield of faith, the helmet of salvation, and the sword of the Spirit, which is the Word of God. Spend time every day praying in the Spirit and then prepare to battle.

Listen To ...

Enemy-occupied territory—that is what this world is. Christianity is the story of how the rightful king has landed, you might say landed in disguise, and is calling us all to take part in a great campaign of sabotage.

—C. S. Lewis

Receiving a Warning

Even with the advanced technology of early warning systems, each year sixty people die in tornadoes. One article posed the question of "why people neglect to acknowledge tornado warnings."[8] According to the article, people don't heed these warnings for reasons varying from just not taking the warning seriously to believing the warning is wrong because they live in an area where tornadoes are uncommon.

Expert senior meteorologist for AccuWeather.com, Henry Margusity, believes people have become desensitized because too many false alarms are issued. It is referred to as the "cry wolf syndrome." People won't believe the accuracy of a weather warning unless they actually see the tornado. Those living on flat lands might decide they will wait until they see the tornado before taking action, but sadly, ignoring these warnings results in destruction of property, injury, and death.

The Bible gives us many warning signs. Rather than reacting like it's a false alarm, we need to listen intently. Second Peter 1:3 tells us, "His divine power has given to us all things that pertain to life and godliness." God gives us everything we need to walk with Him. Today as you read Scripture, pray to recognize the warning bells going off and be alert and ready for action.

Lift Up ...

Lord, I often get caught up with the things of this world. Help me to see those lies and hear and heed the warnings You have given. I want to conform to Your world, not this one, because this world is not my home. In Jesus' name. Amen.

Look At ...

Yesterday, we saw John talk to the "young men," believers who are strong in the Word and fighting to overcome the enemy. Overcoming Satan requires that we know the Father and are forgiven of our sins. We must be strong and have His Word hidden in our hearts. Looking at the reality of spiritual warfare and how often God talks about it in His Word helps us see the need to armor ourselves each day.

2 Love

The Greek word for *love* in this verse is *agab*, meaning to breathe after or to love sensually. *World* refers to the spiritual system of evil dominated by Satan. "Pure and undefiled religion before God and the Father is this ... keep oneself unspotted from the world" (James 1:27).

Barbara Mandrell once sang, "(If Loving You Is Wrong) I Don't Want to Be Right." Today, John speaks clearly about the wrong kind of love: the love of the world. God clearly told us that friendship with the world is enmity with Him. If we make friends with the world, we make an enemy of God (see James 4:4). Beware of getting too cozy with this world; it will all destruct in the end.

Read 1 John 2:15.

Do not love the world or the things in the world. If anyone loves the world, the love of the Father is not in him. 1 John 2:15

1. What two words signify a command is being given?

2. What are believers commanded not to do?

3. What else are we not to love?

4. Who is John applying this to?

5. What is missing from the life of the believer who loves the world?

6 Live

In this verse, the word *in* denotes a fixed position. People who delight in worldly values and possessions prove God's love is not fixed in them. "No one can serve two masters; for either he will hate the one and love the other, or else he will be loyal to the one and despise the other" (Matt. 6:24).

7 Hate

Hate is an intense hostility and aversion usually deriving from fear, anger, or sense of injury. People tend to hate what they are afraid of. Jesus handpicked us as "a chosen generation, a royal priesthood, a holy nation, His own special people, that you may proclaim the praises of Him who called you out of darkness into His marvelous light" (1 Pet. 2:9).

9 Abstain

Pilgrim means alien or sojourner and describes believers who realize heaven is their homeland and they are mere visitors on earth. "Beloved, I beg you as sojourners and pilgrims, abstain from fleshly lusts which war against the soul" (1 Pet.2:11).

6. In your own words, explain what John says about these people.

7. Read John 15:19 and answer the following questions.

a. How would the world react if we were "of" it?

b. What has Jesus done to ensure we are not of the world?

c. What is the result?

Live Out ...

8. *World* can refer to one of three things: (1) the spiritual system of evil dominated by Satan on earth, (2) the physical world, the earth, or (3) the human world or humankind. Get a newspaper and read the headlines and determine whether they reflect Satan's values or God's values.

a. Record one that reflects God's values.

b. Record one that reflects Satan's values.

c. Write a prayer of praise for the one that reflects God's values. Then read 2 Chronicles 7:14–15 and write a prayer that this nation will turn back to God.

If My people who are called by My name will humble themselves, and pray and seek My face, and turn from their wicked ways, then I will hear from heaven, and will forgive their sin and heal their land. Now My eyes will be open and My ears attentive to prayer made in this place.

9. As believers, we physically live in the human world, but we do not belong to the spiritual world that opposes God. This world is not

our home: "For our citizenship is in heaven" (Phil. 3:20). Read the verses below and answer the following questions.

a. Hebrews 11:13. What does this verse say about believers?

b. First Timothy 6:20–21. What are we to avoid as we sojourn on earth? Why?

11 Idolize

Loving people is not wrong, until we place them first in our lives, before God. By doing this, we adopt a worldly attitude and serve them as idols. "So these nations feared the LORD, yet served their carved images" (2 Kings 17:41).

10. John commanded believers not to love the world. So what are we to love? Read the following verses to discover the kind of love God desires of us.

Scripture	What We Are to Love
Psalm 119:140	
Matthew 5:44	
Matthew 22:37–38	
1 Peter 1:22	

11. Worldliness is the matter of the heart. To the extent that we love the world and the things in it, the love of the Father is not fixed in us. Examine your life. What in the world competes with God for your love?

- ☑ Family
- ❑ Friends
- ❑ Job
- ❑ Entertainment/social
- ❑ Possessions
- ❑ Time
- ❑ Pets
- ❑ Money
- ❑ Other: _____

12. In your journal write a prayer thanking God that His love outshines everything in this world. Thank Him for blessing you with the people and possessions in your life. Ask Him to help you guard your heart and mind against worldliness that compromises your walk in the light.

Over 715,000 Americans have heart attacks every year, resulting in 600,000 deaths. That's one in every four deaths.[9] The Center for Disease Control and Prevention believes that knowing the early warning signs and symptoms of a heart attack is the key to preventing death, but a 2005 study showed that of 70,000 people surveyed, only 31 percent knew all five early warning signs:

1. Pain or discomfort in the jaw, neck, or back
2. Feeling weak, lightheaded, or faint
3. Chest pain or discomfort
4. Pain or discomfort in the arms or shoulders
5. Shortness of breath[10]

Someone suffering a heart attack has a much better chance of survival if treatment is sought immediately.

Just as we should know the warning signs of a heart attack, we should be able to recognize the Bible's warning signs that the world is bearing down on us and squeezing God out. Ask the Holy Spirit to show you warning signs in your life, and respond to His loving grace with immediate action.

Listen To ...

Knowing the truth concerning the deep workings of the evil spirit helps the individual not only to overcome sins but to eliminate unnecessary afflictions as well.

—*Watchman Nee*

DAY 4

Avoiding the World

Over 3.2 million American adults suffer from the debilitating panic disorder of agoraphobia.[11] This phobia manifests in symptoms such as fear of crowded places or fear of places where it may be difficult to leave, like an elevator or train. The impact of this disorder can be devastating. Some people find themselves essentially housebound.

The web is full of stories of agoraphobics who haven't left their home in years. One thirty-four-year-old woman had not stepped outside her front door in seven years. Twenty-one-year-old Jemma Pixie Hixon has become famous without leaving the walls of her home. Using a makeshift recording studio to record music videos with a microphone, a webcam, and her Apple Mac, she is a household name in China with over twelve million Internet views.[12]

While God doesn't want us to lock ourselves away in fear, He does give us strong cautions about how to live in the world. We should be alert to the temptations that could wreak havoc in our lives.

Lift Up ...

Father, I don't want to be caught up in the things of this world. I want to be focused on Your world, Your Word, and Your glory. Help me each day to walk worthy of the calling of salvation. In Jesus' name. Amen.

Look At ...

Yesterday we saw that God warns us that being consumed with the world leaves no room for Him to dwell within us. We must decide whether to allow Satan to derail us or to walk boldly in the light of Christ. The choice to be worldly minded or heavenly minded is up to each one of us.

3 Lust For

Lust is a longing for what is forbidden and a strong desire for evil things. Desires and plans that are shaped by our impulses, whether physical or emotional, are not of the Spirit of God. "Let us walk properly, as in the day, not in revelry and drunkenness, not in lewdness and lust, not in strife and envy" (Rom. 13:13).

4 Rival For

Flesh refers not to skin but to human nature with its moral frailties and passions.[13] Our sin nature is rebellious and in opposition to God, but "those who are Christ's have crucified the flesh with its passions and desires" (Gal. 5:24).

5 Desire For

Satan strategically uses the eyes to provoke our wrong desires. The saying "Feast your eyes on this" reminds us that the eyes can have an appetite for pleasures that gratify the sight and mind. "When I saw among the spoils ... I coveted them and took them" (Josh. 7:21).

Today we will see that God pinpointed the three things Satan uses to devastate our lives: the lust of the flesh, the lust of the eyes, and the pride of life. These distractions and deceptions are designed to pit us against God's will by blinding our hearts. Today, search your life and let the light of the Son shine on any areas Satan is using to deceive or mislead you.

Read 1 John 2:16.

For all that is in the world—the lust of the flesh, the lust of the eyes, and the pride of life—is not of the Father but is of the world. 1 John 2:16

1. What inclusive word does John use to signify what he is about to address?

2. All these phrases refer to what main issue?

3. What word does John use to describe Satan's tactic?

4. How does Satan use our misplaced desires?

5. What is the next window through which lust can trap us?

6. What is the final window Satan uses to ensnare us?

7. Where does all that is in the world *not* originate?

8. In your own words, explain where it does originate.

Live Out ...

9. Worldly things that dominate our fascination and attention can lead to ruin.

    a. A common example of these three sins is found in the story of Eve. Read Genesis 3:6.

        1. How does Eve's story illustrate the lust of the flesh, the lust of the eyes, and the pride of life?

        2. Match the verse that corresponds with the worldly lure that has enslaved all of humankind.

        "The woman saw that the tree was good for food"   The lust of the eyes

        "That it was pleasant to the eyes"   The pride of life

        "A tree desirable to make one wise"   The lust of the flesh

    b. Another example is Jesus. Read Matthew 4:2–11 and answer the following questions.

        1. How did Jesus respond when tempted with the lust of the flesh?

        2. How did He respond when tempted with the lust of the eyes?

        3. How did He respond when tempted with the pride of life?

    c. How do you think Eve could have responded differently to temptation?

10. Turn on your television and watch the commercials for a few minutes. Record what products the ads are selling, how the ads appeal

---

6 Show For

Pride means boasting and self-confidence. In the Greek, the word described a braggart who tried to impress others with his or her importance. People who outspend others and overextend themselves are usually in it for the bragging rights. "My soul shall make its boast in the LORD" (Ps. 34:2).

9 Trade For

God tells us what sinful things we should put off in order to replace them with holy things. "But put on the Lord Jesus Christ, and make no provision for the flesh, to fulfill its lusts" (Rom. 13:14). Put off the things of this world and slip into the safety of Jesus.

to the flesh and to the eyes, and how they could encourage bragging rights.

Product	Appeals to Flesh	Appeals to Eyes	Encourages Pride of Life

11 Fight For

God gives us the Holy Spirit to alert us when we are walking in the flesh. "Walk in the Spirit, and you shall not fulfill the lust of the flesh" (Gal. 5:16). By keeping a close relationship with the Spirit, we overturn Satan's plans.

11. Satan operates by appealing to normal appetites and tempting us to satisfy them in forbidden ways. God gave us certain desires that are good, but when the flesh controls and perverts them, they become sinful lusts. Listed below are some God-given desires. Beside each good desire, write the perversion of that desire.

Hunger   *gluttony*   Thirst _____

Weariness _____   Sex _____

12. Scripture tells us that when we say "yes" to a new life in Jesus Christ, we should then say "no" to our old life with "its passions and desires" (Gal. 5:24). What worldly temptation do you struggle with?

☑ Food   ☐ Alcohol/drugs   ☐ Tobacco

☐ Gambling   ☐ Intellectualism   ☐ Shopping

☐ Other: _____

Write in your journal about the boxes you checked. Is their source the lust of the flesh, the lust of the eyes, or the pride of life? How will you endeavor to "walk in the Spirit, and ... not fulfill the lust of the flesh" (Gal. 5:16)? How will you consciously put on the new nature of Christ (see Gal. 5:22–23)?

_____

Hermits are those who live in seclusion from society. One of the most famous hermits in history is Valerio Ricetti, an Italian Australian, born in 1898. He lived in a cave in New South Wales, Australia, for twenty-three years. In the cave that stretched over half a mile, he carved out a kitchen, chapel, landscaping, pathways, terraced gardens, cisterns for his water supply, stone walls, and stairs.

Ricetti left his cave only because he needed medical attention for a broken leg suffered after a fall. He never returned to his cave life, and he is now listed on the New South Wales State Heritage Register.[14]

As believers, we cannot go into hiding in an effort to escape the world. As much as we might like to get away, God did not call us to retreat. Rather, we are called to walk in the light and be an example to the world. God knows we are entering dangerous territory, and He supplies us with the armor needed to "quench all the fiery darts of the wicked one" (Eph. 6:16). By being aware of the lust of the flesh, the lust of the eyes, and the pride of life, God teaches us to "be sober, be vigilant; because your adversary the devil walks about like a roaring lion, seeking whom he may devour" (1 Pet. 5:8). Don't be prey for the taking. Be on guard!

Listen To ...

Pride is the oldest sin in the world. Indeed, it was before the world.
—*John Charles Ryle*

Remaining in God's Will

While vacationing in Italy, famed actor James Gandolfini passed away at the age of fifty-one. When his will was read, errors in the planning of his estate were discovered, resulting in what was called a "tax disaster" for the family. As a result, his estate was subject to a 55 percent death tax, which means approximately thirty million of his estimated seventy-million-dollar estate must go to pay taxes. According to Gandolfini's lawyer, "The government doesn't accept the fact that it's difficult to come up with the money you owe."[15]

In Hollywood, where death is big money, the media frenzies over fighting families and contested wills. Even outside of Hollywood, we hear stories of family disputes and long, bitter battles, all for the love of money and possessions.

Being in God's will is a fact for believers; however, Satan and his demons will contest our inheritance any chance they get. They will fight to strip us of every crown and treasure Jesus wants to bestow on us. Satan doesn't care what it costs. He wants it all.

Thankfully, God has power over our enemy: "Behold, I give you the authority to trample on serpents and scorpions, and over all the power of the enemy, and nothing shall by any means hurt you" (Luke 10:19). Stand firm in the knowledge that your inheritance is safe with God.

Lift Up ...

Father, thank You for the promise of Your coming kingdom and for both the encouragement and warnings from Your Word. I know my position as a joint heir with Christ is uncontestable in Your heavenly courts. In Jesus' name. Amen.

Look At ...

Yesterday we learned the three pathways through which Satan has access to our hearts and minds: the lust of the flesh, the lust of the eyes, and the pride of life. Through these avenues, Satan causes the destruction of people, nations, and—his biggest conquest—the world.

Today we learn that while Satan will temporarily have his way in this world, ultimately, this world will pass away and God will reign. What are you fighting for in this life? Is it something that will stand the test of eternal fires or something that will perish in judgment? Matthew 6:19–21 warns, "Do not lay up for yourselves treasures on earth, where moth and rust destroy and where thieves break in and steal; but lay up for yourselves treasures in heaven, where neither moth nor rust destroys and where thieves do not break in and steal. For where your treasure is, there your heart will be also." Think about your earthly treasures—are they treasures or worldly trash?

Read 1 John 2:17.

And the world is passing away, and the lust of it; but he who does the will of God abides forever. 1 John 2:17

1. What does John say is happening to the world?

2. What is passing away along with it?

3. Considering what you learned yesterday, what do you think this means?

4. Who does John focus on?

3 Going Away

One day, the world's system, with its proud philosophies and its godless materialism, will vanish. One day, this world will be replaced by "a new heaven and a new earth, for the first heaven and the first earth" will pass away (Rev. 21:1).

4 Learning to Obey

Obedience to God's Word and His commands pleases the Lord. The more we obey Him, the better able we are to find and follow His will. Do you want to be a friend of Jesus? Then obey Him. "You are My friends if you do whatever I command you" (John 15:14).

5. What does John say will happen to those who do God's will?

6. In your own words explain what you believe this means.

Live Out ...

5 Getting to Stay

Forever means time without end. This world is temporary. Those who do God's will live as His people forever. "While we do not look at the things which are seen, but at the things which are not seen. For the things which are seen are temporary, but the things which are not seen are eternal" (2 Cor. 4:18).

7 Passing Away

The world is cursed because of Adam and Eve's original sin. When Jesus returns, "creation ... will be delivered from the bondage of corruption" (Rom. 8:21) "and God will wipe away every tear from their eyes; there shall be no more death, nor sorrow, nor crying. There shall be no more pain, for the former things have passed away" (Rev. 21:4).

8 Giving Way

The process of knowing God's will begins with surrender. Surrendering your life and will to God allows the Holy Spirit free access to your heart and mind. Through prayer, the Spirit will guide you, but always check what you've heard against the Word of God.

7. Read Isaiah 24:1–6 and answer the following questions.
   a. Who has complete power over the earth?
   b. What will He do with it?
   c. Who else will this affect?

8. One of the benefits of salvation is the privilege of knowing God's will. Read the following verses then record how you can know God's will for your life.
   a. Romans 12:1–2
   b. Psalm 119:105

9. Today we learned that the things of this world are vain, for one day they will vanish. Read Revelation 21:4–5. Write in your journal about the comfort you receive from this verse. How are you encouraged to persevere in your life until Jesus returns?

10. John compared the world with the will of God. Fill in the chart below to see what the following scriptures say about God's will.

Scripture	The Will of God
Romans 8:27	
Romans 12:2	
Philippians 2:13	
1 Thessalonians 5:18	
1 Peter 2:15	

Not long ago, a six-year-old boy fell into a sand dune in the Indiana Dunes National Lakeshore Park along Lake Michigan. As his family tried to dig him out, the dune collapsed, burying the child in eleven feet of sand. When the emergency responders arrived, they began digging by hand and were joined by a crew with excavation equipment. As the crew worked for over three hours, they began prodding the sand and discovered an air pocket where the boy was. Eventually, they dragged him out and rushed him to the hospital, where doctors called his survival a miracle.[16]

Sometimes we are trapped in a situation out of our control, but God keeps us in a protective bubble to preserve us. We walk in this world, surrounded by danger that could cave in on us at any moment. At the same time, God has promised us victory over our enemies.

John gave us clear warning signs of what to watch out for, how to behave, and what *not* to rely on. What we will find in the world is war, but God is readying us for the battle. "Blessed be the LORD my Rock, who trains my hands for war, and my fingers for battle" (Ps. 144:1).

Listen To ...

All heaven is waiting to help those who will discover the will of God and do it.
—*J. Robert Ashcroft*

Lesson Four

Nothing but the Truth

1 John 2:18–27

"Pilate therefore said to Him, 'Are You a king then?' Jesus answered, 'You say rightly that I am a king. For this cause I was born, and for this cause I have come into the world, that I should bear witness to the truth. Everyone who is of the truth hears My voice.' Pilate said to Him, 'What is truth?' And when he had said this, he went out again to the Jews, and said to them, 'I find no fault in Him at all'" (John 18:37–38).

This was Pilate's moment of truth. Jesus had just told him that He had come into the world to bear witness to the truth. This statement prompted Pilate to ask the right question to the right person. "What is truth?" Little did Pilate know that standing before him was the very answer to his question. Would Pilate fall to his knees in confession and faith? Sadly, no, he would only claim that he could find no fault in Jesus.

This week's lesson is about accepting and embracing nothing but the truth. God has revealed Himself to us through His Son, Jesus Christ, and given us a divine tutor—the Holy Spirit. As the Spirit teaches us the truth of God's Word, we are able to discern false doctrine and recognize deception. Unlike Pilate, we know the answer to the question "What is truth?" If we know Jesus, we know He is the Truth. "My sheep hear My voice, and I know them, and they follow Me" (John 10:27).

Day 1: 1 John 2:18–19 **Days of Deception**

Day 2: 1 John 2:20–21 **Detecting the Lies**

Day 3: 1 John 2:22–23 **Deity Denied**

Day 4: 1 John 2:24–25 **Depending on Truth**

Day 5: 1 John 2:26–27 **Directed by God**

Days of Deception

Lift Up ...

Lord, thank You for the truth of Your Word. I am so grateful for the faith and hope I have in You. In the coming days of deception, light my way so that I may help those who walk in the darkness of deceit. In Jesus' name. Amen.

Look At ...

In our study of 1 John, we have considered what God says about light and darkness as well as His perspective on love and hatred. Last week we were reminded that ultimately, God reigns, and Satan will pass out of our reality. In the meantime, we looked at the necessity for obedience in our pursuit of the will of God.

This week we will begin to look at God's direct warning to the believer about abiding in truth versus error. It is vital for believers to walk in the light and to walk in love, but they must also walk in truth. This week we will study how we must be mindful and watchful in following the Shepherd. There are wolves that want nothing more than to lead us astray with counterfeits of the gospel and promises that are lies. God wants us to be well informed and to follow His Word in wisdom.

Read 1 John 2:18–19.

Little children, it is the last hour; and as you have heard that the Antichrist is coming, even now many antichrists have come, by which we know that it is the last hour. They went out from us, but they were not of us; for if they had been of us, they would have continued with us; but they went out that they might be made manifest, that none of them were of us. 1 John 2:18–19

1. What familiar term of endearment does John use to address the readers?

2. What time is it according to John?

3. What warning had these believers heard before?

4. What evidence does John present to prove "that it is the last hour"?

5. What did these false teachers do? Why?

6. Explain how you know they were not true believers.

7. What purpose was served by their departure from the fellowship?

Live Out ...

8. John knew he was living in the last hour, yet two thousand years have passed since he wrote this epistle. Read 2 Peter 3:3–4, 8–9 and answer the following questions.

   a. What will scoffers say concerning Christ's return?

   b. How is God's timetable different than ours?

   c. Why has His coming been delayed?

9. John revealed that antichrists, or false teachers, would abound during the end times. Check the boxes below that indicate false teachings you're aware of in society today.

   ☒ If you claim it, you'll get it.

   ☒ Jesus was a profound prophet—not God.

2 Watchful

"The last hour" refers to the last days and includes all time between the first and second comings of Jesus Christ. It is a *kind* of time rather than a *duration* of time.[1] "The end of all things is at hand; therefore be serious and watchful in your prayers" (1 Pet. 4:7).

3 Warning

Antichrist, used only in the epistles of John, means against or instead of Christ. The term identifies a specific "man of sin ... who opposes and exalts himself above all that is called God or that is worshiped, so that he sits as God in the temple of God, showing himself that he is God" (2 Thess. 2:3–4).

4 Wolves

John used the term *antichrist* to describe false teachers who had arisen within the congregations. Jesus predicted the arrival of "false prophets, who come to you in sheep's clothing, but inwardly they are ravenous wolves" (Matt. 7:15). Paul warned that "from among yourselves men will rise up, speaking perverse things, to draw away the disciples after themselves" (Acts 20:30).

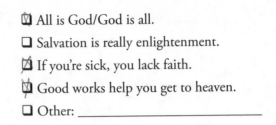

☑ All is God/God is all.

☐ Salvation is really enlightenment.

☑ If you're sick, you lack faith.

☑ Good works help you get to heaven.

☐ Other: _____

9 Withstand

False teachers usually arise from within Christian fellowships and then depart, leading others astray when their teachings are challenged by God's Word. "There are some who trouble you and want to pervert the gospel of Christ. But even if we, or an angel from heaven, preach any other gospel to you than what we have preached to you, let him be accursed" (Gal. 1:7–8).

10 Walk

The word *continued* comes from the same Greek word used for abide. In contrast to believers who are united with God and each other, John distinguishes false teachers as having abandoned the gospel of Jesus Christ. The test of a true believer is simple: Have you abandoned or do you abide?

10. The false teachers left because they were not really members of the body of Christ. What signs do you see in your own life that prove you are "of us"?

_____

Today we can hear the teaching of the Word of God through many avenues. From our local church to online teaching and radio broadcasts, we can hear Scripture taught twenty-four hours per day. We must remember to test what we hear according to God's perfect Word (see 1 Thess. 5:21).

Acts 17:11 tells us that the Bereans had the right attitude about knowing the truth: "They received the word with all readiness, and searched the Scriptures daily to find out whether these things were so." Honorably, the Bereans didn't simply believe everything that was being told to them. They were diligent to study and verify God's Word together as a body, and on their own, every day!

In a world inundated with false teaching, we must be like the Bereans and consider how we receive truth. Scripture reveals to us that a healthy view of the truth flourishes when we diligently and daily seek to rightly divide the word of truth (see 2 Tim. 2:15). Consistent study of God's Word, and abiding in His truth, will protect us from the many false teachers who live and speak as wolves in sheep's clothing (see Matt. 7:15).

Listen To ...

I am resolved never to do anything which I should be afraid to do if it were the last hour of my life.

—*Jonathan Edwards*

Detecting the Lies

In Florence, Italy, the Gallery of the Accademia di Belle Arti houses one of the world's most renowned masterpieces: Michelangelo's original statue of David. Towering at seventeen feet tall, this marble sculpture is a splendid sight to behold. Thousands travel from around the world each year to get a glimpse of this breathtaking work of art. Unfortunately, a number of tourists leave Florence thinking they have seen *David*, but they are sadly mistaken. They have seen and snapped pictures of a stone replica of David that stands a few blocks away in the Piazza della Signoria. While it is impressive, it cannot equate with the beauty of Michelangelo's marble creation.[2]

The Bible often warns about religious imposters and false teachers, who try to pass off deceptive beliefs as spiritual truths. Second Peter 1:20–21 tells us that the true Word of God came directly from the Father, through the Holy Spirit. Teaching that originates from anywhere else is a counterfeit. Unfortunately, counterfeits can look deceptively real. This is why you must test all things against the truth of the Scriptures and rely on the person of the Holy Spirit, who will "guide you into all truth" (John 16:13).

Lift Up ...

Dear God, thank You for sending Your Spirit to guide me into all truth. I rest firmly on the foundation of your unchanging Word of truth. I want to know You in all truth and authenticity. In Jesus' name. Amen.

Look At ...

Yesterday we read John's urgent warning. As predicted, false teachers had arisen from within the body of Christ. We found that our walk is not a passive belief in ideas and philosophies but an active, watchful life that seeks to abide with Christ and withstand the deceiver. We learned that false prophets are strategic in their approach, focusing on areas that appeal to our desires, pride, and points of spiritual weakness.

Today John reminds all believers just how to distinguish truth from lies: we are to rely not on our own discernment but on the insight that comes from the resident Holy Spirit, who affirms the truth and prompts us to suspect imposters who might lead us astray. John felt this admonition was vital to enable believers to grow in their walk with the Lord.

4 Perspective

Every believer is anointed with the Holy Spirit and given special insight into God's Word. "Now it is God who makes both us and you stand firm in Christ. He anointed us, set his seal of ownership on us, and put his Spirit in our hearts as a deposit, guaranteeing what is to come" (2 Cor. 1:21–22 NIV).

5 Person

Christians have a built-in lie detector: the Holy Spirit. He will always spotlight Jesus and confirm the doctrines found in the Bible. "Hold fast the patern of sound words which you have heard from me, in faith and love which are in Christ Jesus. That good thing which was committed to you, keep by the Holy Spirit who dwells in us" (2 Tim. 1:13–14).

Read 1 John 2:20–21.

But you have an anointing from the Holy One, and you know all things. I have not written to you because you do not know the truth, but because you know it, and that no lie is of the truth. 1 John 2:20–21

1. What two key words does John use to address the believing reader and distinguish them from the false believers?

2. John reminds these believers that they have what?

3. Who does the anointing come from?

4. How does the anointing affect the mind of the believer?

5. The Holy Spirit is not a force; *He* is a person. John 16:13–14 describes personal actions taken by Him on our behalf.

    a. In what ways does He help us know all things?

    b. Can any teaching that disagrees with Jesus' words come from the Holy Spirit? Why or why not?

7 Imposters

"What does it say about Jesus?" is the most important question to ask when discerning whether a teaching is true or false. The person who denies *any* part of the truth about Jesus denies the *whole* truth because "no lie is of the truth" (1 John 2:21).

9 Presence

In the Old Testament, kings and priests were anointed for service. The Holy Spirit came upon Saul and David during this ceremonial act (see 1 Sam. 10:1 and 16:13). In the New Testament, anointing signifies the presence of the Holy Spirit in a believer's life.

c. What evidence do you see in these verses that the Holy Spirit will not seek to draw attention to Himself? Who will He magnify instead?

6. Summarize the reasons John gives for writing about these things.

7. How does John emphasize that any doctrine deviating from God's Word is false?

Live Out ...

8. Last week we learned that *Christ* means Anointed One. Read Luke 4:18–19, where Jesus declares that He is the Christ.

a. List the six things Jesus was anointed to do.

b. Describe how Jesus has done one or more of these things in your life. (*Example: "I was spiritually poor, but now I have a rich inheritance."*)

9. Just as priests and kings were anointed, or set apart for service, Jesus, "who loved us and washed us from our sins in His own blood … has made us kings and priests to His God and Father" (Rev. 1:5–6).

a. How is God calling you to serve in His kingdom?

- ☑ In my family
- ❑ At my church
- ❑ At my job
- ❑ At my school
- ❑ Other: _____

b. Use Hebrews 13:20–21 to write a prayer asking God to anoint you as you serve in your family, at church, at work, or at school.

May the God of peace … equip you with everything good for doing his will, and may he work in us what is pleasing to him, through Jesus Christ,   to whom be glory for ever and ever. Amen. (NIV)

10 Prompted

Ask God for wisdom. His wisdom looks like Jesus. "If any of you lacks wisdom, let him ask of God … and it will be given to him" (James 1:5). "The wisdom that is from above is first pure, then peaceable, gentle, willing to yield, full of mercy and good fruits, without partiality and without hypocrisy" (James 3:17).

10. John told us that through the Holy Spirit, we can know all things. First Corinthians 2:12 says, "Now we have received, not the spirit of the world, but the Spirit who is from God, that we might know the things that have been freely given to us by God."

a. What have you learned from this Bible study that you didn't know before?

b. Describe something you still don't understand.

c. Write a prayer in your journal, asking God for spiritual wisdom in this area.

d. Now look up a verse in your Bible to help you gain understanding.

Discerning truth from the many lies around us can be simple if we use the power of the light of the Word to illuminate the darkness of deception. Do you need to know if the doctrine you are hearing is true? Hold it up to the light of the Word.

Have you ever held a dollar bill up to the light? When doing so, the discerning eye can see details and intricacies that have been embedded inside the cash to identify the real from the counterfeit.

The United States Treasury has placed these safeguards within our currency with the intention that illumination will give the key distinction in authenticating real cash. Likewise, the illumination of the Word of God is a shining light to lead us on the path of life (see Ps. 119:105).

As we will see tomorrow, the deity of Jesus Christ is the central point of deviation for false teachers. We can protect ourselves from error and deception by knowing and relying on the Light of the World: Jesus Christ.

Listen To ...

The book seems made of gold leaf; every single letter glitters like a diamond. Oh, it is a blessed thing to read an illuminated Bible lit up by the radiance of the Holy Spirit.
—*Charles Spurgeon*

DAY 3

Deity Denied

Who is Jesus? On a college campus, a group of students was asked this question. Their responses included a great teacher, a wise scholar, a man of great morals, a philanthropist, a carpenter, a fraud, and a world-changer. Very few recognized him as God incarnate—the Jesus of the Bible.

When He walked among us, Jesus asked His disciples what people were saying about who He was. They responded, saying, "Some say John the Baptist, some Elijah, and others Jeremiah or one of the prophets" (Matt. 16:14). These answers were all inadequate. Jesus then turned to His disciples and asked, "But who do you say that I am?" Peter was correct when he said, "You are the Christ, the Son of the living God" (see Matt. 16:15–16).

The great assertion of the faith that sets Christianity apart from others is this: Jesus Christ is God come in the flesh.[3] Don't be deceived by false descriptions of Jesus that you read, see, or hear about. Trust in and know the Bible. Then when people try to minimize His identity, you will have the knowledge to tell them who the real Jesus is!

Lift Up ...

Lord Jesus, thank You for paying my ransom and reconciling me to God the Father. Make me mindfully aware that Jesus is undermined at every turn in our society, and I must be ready to distinguish my faith and myself. Strengthen me to stand strong in the face of antichrist forces. In Jesus' name. Amen.

Look At ...

Last week we considered the role of the Holy Spirit to reveal the truth of God's Word to the believer. We detailed the devices used to deceive the believer and undermine our understanding

1 Refuse Recognition

To *deny* is to reject or refuse to recognize someone. The false teachers denied that Jesus was God in human flesh—Christ, the Messiah come to save the world from sin. These teachers lied about who Christ was. But John and the true believers "did not cease teaching and preaching Jesus as the Christ" (Acts 5:42).

2 Deliberate Substitution

To deny Jesus Christ is to deny God the Father. Jesus put it this way: "I and My Father are one" (John 10:30). Someone who is anti-Christ seeks a substitute for the only true Savior, but *there is only* "one Lord Jesus Christ, through whom are all things, and through whom we live" (1 Cor. 8:6).

4 Exact Representation

Acknowledge means to confess. Someone who acknowledges Jesus Christ agrees with God about who He is. "God, who at various times ... has in these last days spoken to us by His Son ... and the express image of His person, and upholding all things by the word of His power" (Heb. 1:1–3).

of the person of the Holy Spirit. Of utmost importance, we determined to always uphold the deity of the Lord Jesus Christ in our own minds and hearts.

Today, in just two verses, John challenges us to be ready to stand strong in our faith. He reminds us that there is no shortage of ways to cloud the clarity of the triune God. Denial of Jesus, or a refusal to adhere to scriptural truth, is an issue of the heart that must be searched out and addressed. If we allow a lie to penetrate our relationship with God, we will miss the glorious security of being right with God.

Read 1 John 2:22–23.

Who is a liar but he who denies that Jesus is the Christ? He is antichrist who denies the Father and the Son. Whoever denies the Son does not have the Father either; he who acknowledges the Son has the Father also. 1 John 2:22–23

1. Define a liar according to this verse.

2. Who does John describe as antichrist?

3. What does the person who denies the Son lack?

4. What does the person who acknowledges the Son have?

5. What do your answers to questions 3 and 4 tell you about the relationship between the Father and the Son?

6. How does John 14:6 prove that anyone who denies Jesus Christ can't really know God?

7. To acknowledge the Son is to agree with everything revealed about Him in the Bible. Match each scripture below with the truth it reveals about the Son, Jesus Christ.

a. He was born to a virgin and conceived by the Holy Spirit.   _a_ Matthew 1:20–21

b. He was fully human.   _d_ Mark 16:6, 9–15

c. He was fully God.   _c_ Mark 16:19

d. He died, rose again, and appeared to many.   _b_ John 4:6

e. He ascended into heaven to sit at God's right hand.   _f_ John 14:3

f. He will come again.   _c_ John 14:9

9 Confessed Association

In Psalm 139:23–24, the psalmist cried out, "Search me, O God, and know my heart ... and lead me in the way everlasting." May the cry of your heart be like the psalmist's. Allow the Lord to search your heart and open your mind to follow His beautiful life-changing purposes today.

Live Out ...

8. Antichrists are those who deny the Son, Jesus Christ. Read Matthew 16:24 and answer the following questions.

a. What *did* Jesus tell us to deny?

b. What do you think it means to take up your cross and follow Him?

c. What will you deny yourself of this week to follow the Son?

9. The false teachers denied that Jesus was the Son of God. Jesus said, "Whoever confesses Me before men, him the Son of Man also will confess before the angels of God. But he who denies Me before men will be denied before the angels of God" (Luke 12:8–9). Examine your heart; in which of these ways have you denied Him?

10 Divine Cooperation

The Bible teaches that there is one God manifest in three distinct persons. This mind-boggling concept can be compared to a symphony. The composer is the Father, the first-chair violinist is the Son, and the conductor is the Holy Spirit. As we cooperate with the Triune God, we become instruments in this symphony and complete a "four-part harmony."[4]

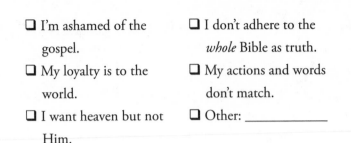

- ❑ I'm ashamed of the gospel.
- ❑ My loyalty is to the world.
- ❑ I want heaven but not Him.
- ❑ I don't adhere to the *whole* Bible as truth.
- ❑ My actions and words don't match.
- ❑ Other: _____

10. In this week's text, John gives us a beautiful picture of the Trinity. When we confess the Son, we have the Father, who gives us the anointing of the Holy Spirit. Each member of the Trinity blesses the believer in unique ways. Look up the verses below to discover the specific blessings that come from each in this package deal.

    a. 2 Corinthians 13:14

    b. 2 Thessalonians 2:13–14

    c. Jude 20–21

_____

A man was sound asleep when suddenly he was awakened by a loud noise, jolting him out of bed. Thick smoke was pouring into his room. He immediately jumped out of bed and tried to run toward the front door, but as he headed down the hall, he soon realized the front of the house was engulfed in flames. He tried to turn back but was surrounded by flames, and he quickly became disoriented and lost sense of which direction he was headed. He sank to the floor, yelling for help, coughing, and trying to stay conscious. He was trapped. There was no way out. Just as a sense of desperation and panic set in, he saw a figure. "Help me," the man gasped as a fireman picked him up and carried him to safety. There was a way out, but in the chaos and confusion, he simply couldn't find it.[5]

Jesus said, "I am the way, the truth, and the life. No one comes to the Father except through Me" (John 14:6). There is only one path to God, and it is found by placing our trust in Jesus Christ for the forgiveness of our sins. His work on the cross made the satisfying payment that reconciled us to the Father. When we surrender our lives to Jesus, the crucified and risen Savior, we are on the only way that will bring us home to our Father in heaven.

Listen To ...

My Father, I will anchor myself, my thoughts and my will in these facts: You are. You rule in heaven and on the earth. You call me righteous because I am in Jesus. No matter what it may seem, I will stand firm forever.

—Amy Carmichael

DAY 4

Depending on Truth

Abraham Lincoln, the sixteenth president of the United States, had the right perspective on truth. He carried the heavy burden of leading our country through a civil war but was determined to stand and fight for what he believed in: the abolition of slavery. With a New Testament in his hand and tears in his eyes, Lincoln spoke these words: "I know there is a God, and that He hates injustice and slavery. I see the storm coming, and I know that His hand is in it. If He has a place and work for me—and I think He has—I believe I am ready. I am nothing, but truth is everything."[6]

Lincoln's belief in the truth that God created all men equal prompted him to a life of action. He depended on the unchanging truth of God as motivation for a glorious purpose.

As you depend on and cling to the truth of God's Word, be challenged and strengthened to take a stand against false teaching and carry the light of freedom of the true gospel of Jesus Christ to this world. "You shall know the truth, and the truth shall make you free" (John 8:32).

Lift Up ...

Dear God, I am so grateful for unchanging truth. You know how easily I am influenced by the opinions of others and susceptible to clever arguments. I want to be so entwined and rooted in Your Word that I stand strong in Your strength, no matter how strong the winds of change. In Jesus' name. Amen.

Look At ...

Yesterday we learned that it is impossible to have a right relationship with God unless we confess Jesus Christ as Savior and Lord. It is a matter of heart examination that can only be accomplished when we are willing to allow the Holy Spirit to guide and correct us. The Father, Son, and Holy Spirit are one. Denial of one is denial of all.

Today we learn the importance of clinging to the truth of the gospel. The young believers needed the reminder that they could trust what they heard from Christ and the apostles. Others would attempt to plant doubt in their minds and try to weaken their faith. Yet John reminded them that the words of God are worthy of remembering, digesting, repeating, and pondering. The promises of God are good as gold and will carry us through eternity.

Read 1 John 2:24–25.

Therefore let that abide in you which you heard from the beginning. If what you heard from the beginning abides in you, you also will abide in the Son and in the Father. And this is the promise that He has promised us—eternal life. 1 John 2:24–25

1. What word does John use to connect verse 24 to yesterday's text?

2. Yesterday's lesson ended with "He who acknowledges the Son has the Father also" (1 John 2:23). What word in verse 24 indicates that we are allowed to choose what we *do* concerning what we've heard?

3. What do you think "that … which you heard from the beginning" refers to?

4. What must you *let* "that … which you heard from the beginning" do?

5. Explain the result of letting God's Word abide in us.

1 Link to …

When you see a "therefore" in Scripture, a good rule of thumb in Bible study is to find out what it's there for. *Therefore* links what has been said with what is about to be said. "I believed and therefore I spoke" (2 Cor. 4:13).

3 Think on …

John tells the young believers to recall the teachings of Jesus and all His apostles. False teachers will attempt to pervert the truth, "but you must continue in the things which you have learned and been assured of … the Holy Scriptures, which are able to make you wise for salvation through faith which is in Christ Jesus" (2 Tim. 3:14–15).

4 Sink in …

We should "desire the pure milk of the word" (1 Pet. 2:2). As we grow in Him, we seek "solid food" (Heb. 5:14). But we don't eat just for the sake of eating. We eat to be "nourished in the words of faith and … good doctrine" (1 Tim. 4:6). When we let the truth abide in us, it's like consuming nutritious food and drink.

9 Feast on ...

God invites us to feast on His Word and allow it to change us. "For the word of God is living and powerful, and sharper than any two-edged sword, piercing even to the division of soul and spirit, and of joints and marrow, and is a discerner of the thoughts and intents of the heart" (Heb. 4:12).

10 Count on ...

Eternal life describes the abundant life enjoyed by the believer on earth and the reality of being with God for eternity. In contrast, the person who rejects God in this life chooses to be separated from Him forever. A believer has the "promise of the life that now is and of that which is to come" (1 Tim. 4:8).

6. What action has God taken because we abide in Him and in His Son?

7. What exactly has He promised us?

Live Out ...

8. We've compared letting Scripture abide in us to the physical acts of eating and drinking. When the body needs food and water, it sends out cries for help—sensations of hunger and thirst. As spiritual beings, we need consistent spiritual nourishment.

a. Which one of these selections best describes your spiritual eating habits?

❑ Small bites once a week

❑ Sweets only (promises, not commands)

❑ Feast or famine

☑ Regular, frequent, balanced meals

b. How can you tell when you're starving for God's Word, time in prayer with Him, or fellowship with other believers?

9. We found that John's use of the word *let* implies an action on our part. God is faithful to satisfy those who hunger for Him. "Blessed are you who hunger now, for you shall be filled" (Luke 6:21). But we have to reach out and take the bread He offers.

a. How will you let His Word fill you?

☑ Read the Bible   ☑ Attend Bible study

❑ Memorize Scripture   ☑ Make God's Word my standard
                                                   of truth

☑ Listen to praise music   ❑ Other: _____

b. Pick the item from the list above that is most lacking in your life. What specific action will you take this week to make it a reality?

10. God promises eternal life to those who confess His Son and abide in Him. What else does He promise as a result of this relationship?

Scripture	God's Promises
Acts 2:38–39	
Hebrews 10:36–37	
2 Peter 1:3–4	
2 Peter 3:13	

———————————

Today we discovered what it means to abide in Christ and His Word. Setting aside time daily to draw close to Jesus in His Word is essential for our spiritual growth. In Matthew 9:20, we meet a woman with a bleeding issue who had sought healing from many doctors over many years. Scripture gives up a snapshot of a life-changing moment for this woman: when she reached out to touch the hem of Jesus' garment and was completely healed. Jesus met this woman's deepest need. As we reach out to Jesus, He is always there waiting for us with a word from His Scripture, which meets us where we are and carries us further on.

Amy Carmichael said, "God's way of passing by, of letting His 'hem' come near us, is to take some single word in His Book and make it breathe spirit and life to us. Then, relying upon that word, meditating, feeding our soul on it, we find it is suddenly possible to go from strength to strength."[7] May we reach out to Jesus and feel His beautiful touch on our lives.

Listen To ...

The unattended garden will soon be overrun with weeds; the heart that fails to cultivate truth and root out error will shortly be a theological wilderness.

—A. W. Tozer

Directed by God

Lost and frustrated, Sarah picked up her phone and cried out, "Siri, where in the world am I?" Siri robotically but politely responded with Sarah's exact location. "Now, how do I get to the 405 freeway?" was Sarah's next question. With a map showing point A to point B, Sarah was now on her way in the right direction.

Navigational systems have been lifesavers for all of us, at one time or another. A proper GPS will direct us to our intended destination in an instant.

As Christians, we are equipped with an internal navigational system. The Holy Spirit Himself lives within us to guide us into all truth (see John 16:13). Jesus further assured His disciples that they wouldn't be left without the teaching and leading: "But the Helper, the Holy Spirit, whom the Father will send in My name, He will teach you all things, and bring to your remembrance all things that I said to you" (John 14:26). If you are in need of direction in your life, be assured of the divine power of the Holy Spirit within you. He will surely lead you in the right direction. "Trust in the LORD with all your heart, and lean not on your own understanding; in all your ways acknowledge Him, and He shall direct your paths" (Prov. 3:5–6).

Lift Up ...

Dear Lord, I am so grateful for Your presence and your guidance. Thank You for holding my hand and leading me through life on earth and into glory. Make me mindful that You have anointed me for Your truth and Your purposes. In Jesus' name. Amen.

Look At ...

Yesterday, we considered the importance of consciously abiding in God's truth. John compelled the believers (and us) to consider the validity of the words of Jesus and His apostles and the certainty that their faith would be challenged. When we feast on His Word and linger on truth, we will be securely connected to God for eternity.

In today's lesson, John summarizes his warning about false teachers and reminds us of our anointing. The need to get ready for spiritual warfare is as important as preparations for a military battle. We must know the enemy's tactics and the vulnerabilities we possess. Similarly, we must understand our strengths and hold the victory uppermost in our minds. As soldiers/believers, we have been covered by our God, who never leaves or forsakes us.

2 False Teachers

Deceive describes an attempt to seduce someone from the truth. Years earlier, Paul warned the church about "false apostles, deceitful workers, transforming themselves into apostles of Christ" (2 Cor. 11:13).

3 Clever Persuaders

False teachers cleverly use "persuasive words … philosophy and empty deceit, according to the tradition of men, according to the basic principles of the world, and not according to Christ" (Col. 2:4, 8). Some teaching is false because it's unbalanced, overemphasizing one area of Scripture to the neglect of teaching the Bible as a whole.

Read 1 John 2:26–27.

These things I have written to you concerning those who try to deceive you. But the anointing which you have received from Him abides in you, and you do not need that anyone teach you; but as the same anointing teaches you concerning all things, and is true, and is not a lie, and just as it has taught you, you will abide in Him. 1 John 2:26–27

1. What action has John taken to protect these believers from false teaching?

2. So far John has called false teachers "antichrists" and "liars." How does he describe them now?

3. Read 2 Corinthians 11:14–15.
    a. Who is the mastermind behind spiritual deception?
    b. Why are so many people fooled by false teaching?
    c. What is the ultimate fate of these charlatans?

4. Describe our relationship with the anointing—the Holy Spirit.

5 False Dependency

John is not refuting the need for teachers in the body of Christ, because the Lord calls some to be "evangelists, ... pastors and teachers, for the equipping of the saints for the work of ministry, for the edifying of the body of Christ" (Eph. 4:11–12). However, it is *our* responsibility to be spiritually discerning when listening to *any* person's teaching.

8 Rock Solid

A genuine Holy Spirit anointing will continue to reveal those things that have been revealed "from the beginning." If we cling to the rock of God's truth as the waves of false doctrine beat against us and refuse to deviate from God's Word, we will not "be carried about with various and strange doctrines" (Heb. 13:9).

5. In comparison to the importance of being taught directly by the Holy Spirit, whose teaching do we *not* need?

6. Which anointing teaches us? How many things can we be taught?

7. John probably used the defining phrase "the same anointing" because false teachers often claimed to have a "new" anointing or revelation from God. But a counterfeit anointing will produce false teaching.

    a. How can we be sure this anointing is trustworthy?

    b. Describe the end result of being sensitive to the teaching of the Holy Spirit.

Live Out ...

8. This week we've discovered the importance of recognizing deceptive teaching, but sometimes we deceive ourselves. Knowing the truth found in God's Word allows us to "take captive every thought to make it obedient to Christ" (2 Cor. 10:5 NIV) and replace lies with truth. Look up each verse below and record the truth that will counteract deception.

Deceptive Thinking	Scripture	God's Truth
I can't forgive myself for past sins.	Psalm 103:12–14	
I'm not qualified to serve God.	1 Corinthians 1:27–29	
I need to prove I'm right.	1 Peter 5:5–6	
I have so many burdens to carry.	1 Peter 5:7	

9. Today we learned that the anointing abides *in us*. Close your eyes and picture God anointing you with priceless ointment—His Holy Spirit. Which of the following areas of your spiritual body need His touch most?

☐ My head (thoughts)   ☐ My heart (emotions, desires)

☐ My eyes (spiritual awareness) ☐ My hands (reaching out to others)

☐ My ears (listening ability) ☐ My feet (staying on the path)

☐ My lips (words)   ☐ Other: _____

Write a prayer to God, surrendering these "body parts" to His Holy Spirit.

9 Fully Covered

Anoint means to smear or rub with ointment. This practice was common in the East for many reasons, such as cleansing, refreshment, illness, preparation for burial, and showing hospitality. "Mary took a pound of very costly oil of spikenard, anointed the feet of Jesus, and wiped His feet with her hair. And the house was filled with the fragrance of the oil" (John 12:3–4).

10. The Holy Spirit often moves through human beings to impart spiritual knowledge. Think about someone who has been a teacher to you in the things of God. Name some things this person has taught you.

Stop now and write a note or email to let this person know how his or her example has blessed you.

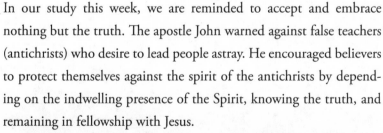

In our study this week, we are reminded to accept and embrace nothing but the truth. The apostle John warned against false teachers (antichrists) who desire to lead people astray. He encouraged believers to protect themselves against the spirit of the antichrists by depending on the indwelling presence of the Spirit, knowing the truth, and remaining in fellowship with Jesus.

In these days of deception, may we individually, and as the body of Christ, be able to detect the lies, exalt Jesus, depend on the truth, and lead lives directed by the Holy Spirit.

As Charles Spurgeon eloquently said, "May God give you to know the truth in your hearts! May the Spirit 'guide you into all truth'! …

'And you shall know the truth, and the truth shall make you free'. 'And if the Son has made you free, you shall be free indeed'. For he says, 'I am the way, the truth, the life'. Believe on Jesus thou chief of sinners; trust his love and mercy, and thou art saved. For God the Spirit gives faith and eternal life."[8]

Listen To ...

God hath but three things dear unto Him in this world, His saints, His worship, and His truth; and it is hard to say which of these is dearest to Him.

—*Thomas Goodwin*

Anchor of Hope

1 John 2:28—3:3

In the novel *Life of Pi*, author Yann Martel tells the fantastic adventures of Pi, a young man who is swept to sea by a tsunami. He survives 227 days, stranded in a boat adrift on the ocean with only a few life-sustaining items on board. And oh, yes, a Bengal tiger! Pi drifts along at the mercy of storms, winds, and currents, dealing with dangers both inside and outside the boat. He has no idea if he will survive.

Most of us won't ever have to deal with a tsunami or being up close with a tiger, but even Christians can find themselves adrift and beset with sudden storms and tribulations. Thankfully, the Lord promised to be with us as we navigate the currents of life. No matter where we are, we are steadied and hopeful because of our Anchor, Jesus Christ.

Hebrews 6:19 assures us of God's purpose in Christ: "This hope we have as an anchor of the soul, both sure and steadfast." Without continuous fellowship with Him, even a small wave can carry us into dangerous waters. The strong and trustworthy promises of God serve to calm our fears and hold us steady in the midst of the uncertainties of life.

Christians must persevere, knowing that the Lord gifts us with sustainable hope in His promise to return. This week we will study five aspects of our hope of eternity with Him.

Day 1: 1 John 2:28	**Hope Sustains Faith**
Day 2: 1 John 2:29	**Hope Produces Habits**
Day 3: 1 John 3:1	**Hope Is Strengthened by Love**
Day 4: 1 John 3:2	**Hope Rests in Christ**
Day 5: 1 John 3:3	**Hope Promotes Purity**

Hope Sustains Faith

Lift Up ...

Lord, the hope of a future with You sustains me in my walk today. I am Your child, and I'm so thankful that You are my Heavenly Father. I want to grow in grace, obedience, and wisdom so I can stand unashamed before You on that great day. In Jesus' name. Amen.

Look At ...

Last week we studied the methods the Enemy uses against us. He is a clever deceiver who uses false teachers, illusions of independence, and deceptive thinking to lead us off course. False prophets, like wolves, are determined to prey on the Shepherd's sheep. As followers of Jesus Christ, we must maintain an attitude of watchful discernment. The Word of God is the definitive Word.

Today we study our relationship to God and the way it manifests both inwardly and individually and outwardly and publicly. The Holy Spirit lives in us and teaches us the truth—our job is to consistently abide in Him. John reinforced his message of our hope in Jesus Christ by reminding us of our relationship to God, our priority to abide in Him, and our perspective on this present life and the future. As believers, we have every reason to be confident and hopeful.

Read 1 John 2:28.

And now, little children, abide in Him, that when He appears, we may have confidence and not be ashamed before Him at His coming. 1 John 2:28

1. Looking back at last week's text, why are we commanded to abide in Him "now"?

2. Who are the "little children"?

3. What does the word *abide* mean to you?

4. This passage uses the pronouns *Him, He,* and *His.* Who do they refer to?

5. To what event does John draw his readers' attention?

6. What two feelings can we expect to experience at the time of the Lord's appearance?

7. Where will we be at the time of His coming?

2 Stand Fast

When we have experienced the indwelling of the Holy Spirit, we strive to stand and obey the Lord's commandments. By our steady obedience born out of love, we show others that we are His children. Jesus Himself "became obedient to the point of death" (Phil. 2:8).

3 Stand With

Abide means to stand fast and remain. Maintaining fellowship with Jesus by continually walking in His light enables us to overcome trials and our susceptibility to false teachers. We abide in the Holy Spirit within.

5 Stand Aside

We know that the second coming promises vindication (God will judge unbelievers) and salvation (He will gather all His children). This knowledge serves as inspiration for godly living and is the "blessed hope" not only of the early church but also of Christians today.

Live Out ...

8. Believers are instructed to abide in the Lord. We are to manifest God in our actions. When your life is properly focused, God is manifested in it! Reflect on what your actions say about you to
   a. Your family
   b. Your friends
   c. Your coworkers or casual acquaintances
   d. Your Lord

9. We hear a lot about the importance of self-confidence. How does self-confidence differ from Savior-confidence?

9 Stand Back

When we follow Christ's example, we fall into a natural humility. John the Baptist said it perfectly: "He must increase, but I must decrease" (John 3:30). By maintaining fellowship with God, believers will enjoy a genuine confidence when they meet the Lord.

10 Stand Corrected

Shame is the pain we feel as a result of improper behavior. Sin is improper behavior. If we confess our sin and shame, 1 John 1:9 tells us that "He is faithful and just to forgive us our sins and to cleanse us from all unrighteousness."

Self-Confidence	**Savior-Confidence**
a. Allows me to speak to others about my accomplishments in Him	Allows me to speak to others about His accomplishments in me
b.	
c.	
d.	

10. a. Recall your behavior this week, and list three actions that might be considered shameful.

     1. I was sarcastic with my husband.

     2.

     3.

b. Read Psalm 103:12 and describe what happens to our shameful deeds if we give them up to God.

c. Now express what you can do to clean your slate before the Lord.

d. Finally, write a simple prayer that will help you remember to confess, repent, and ask for forgiveness for the inevitable shameful actions of the day. Memorize this prayer and use it daily.

The concept of sustainable living has taken on new popularity as people become aware of global warming. Sometimes, the environmental news is alarming, and we wonder how we can exist under rapidly changing circumstances. A "sustainable" life is based on the premise that everything we need to survive and live well depends on our natural environment. When we create and maintain conditions under which humans and nature can exist in harmony, life is more easily sustained. Actions that support this ideology include measures like conscientious recycling, using reclaimed materials for home building, or collecting rainwater to water the garden.

In a world that appears to be on a path of diminishing resources, it is reassuring to have confidence in our Savior and His promise to return. Without faith, we are adrift; with faith, we are hopeful as we journey through both good and bad times. He walks alongside us and provides for our needs.

Hope in His return keeps us focused on the reliability of God and puts earthly matters into a divine perspective. Our hope is a witness to unbelievers. "Christ in you, the hope of glory" (Col. 1:27). This is our sustaining hope.

Listen To ...

In God alone is there faithfulness, and faith is the trust that we may hold to Him, to His promise, and to His guidance. To hold to God is to rely on the fact that God is there for me and to live in this certainty.

—*Karl Barth*

DAY 2

Hope Produces Habits

Did your family encourage you to become excellent in activities such as playing an instrument, participating in sports, or studying in school? If so, you're familiar with practice. Practice involves repeating something over and over until you can do it comfortably and proficiently.

Eric Liddell, a gold medalist in track at the 1924 Olympic Games, exemplified the potential of passion plus practice. In the 1981 movie *Chariots of Fire*, his character directly related his success on the track to his relationship with the Lord: "I believe God made me for a purpose but He also made me fast. And when I run, I feel His pleasure."[1] Liddell's strong faith led to habits that supported and propelled him through his athletic and missionary life until he died in a Japanese prison camp in 1945.[2]

In order to achieve the desired results, practice must become a habit. God is pleased with us when we develop the routine of practicing our faith through prayer, study, and service. He places a high priority on His people's knowledge of Him: "I desire mercy and not sacrifice, and the knowledge of God more than burnt offerings" (Hos. 6:6). This kind of knowledge requires both habitual and devoted commitment to learning. Without a doubt, understanding God is the most complex subject we will ever undertake.

Lift Up ...

Lord, I want to live a holy and righteous life, but first and foremost, I want to know You. Eric Liddell had a passion for running and for You. I, too, want to feel Your pleasure in my efforts. In Jesus' name. Amen.

Look At ...

Yesterday we were reminded that if we abide in Christ, we will have confidence to stand before Him on the day of His return. Like children, we sometimes try to *appear* obedient rather than genuinely bowing to God's authority, but there are no shortcuts to the obedience of abiding. We also studied the seductive influence of false teachers that can lead us away from the Word and were reminded that others observe our actions. Most importantly, so does our Father.

Today we will learn that, as with any love relationship, we must develop habits that deepen our devotion to God. John told us that we don't come to righteousness without the intention to be righteous. He made sure we understood that we are born into the capacity for righteousness when we become God's children. John stressed that the closer we are to Jesus, the closer we are to righteousness, as Jesus *is* righteousness.

Read 1 John 2:29.

If you know that He is righteous, you know that everyone who practices righteousness is born of Him. 1 John 2:29

1. Why do you think John starts this sentence with the word *if?*

2. How do you come to know God?

3. What constitutes righteous behavior?

4. Knowing God's standard of righteousness, how can we gauge others who claim fellowship with Him?

2 Know Him

J. I. Packer wrote about the high pursuit of knowing the Savior: "How can we turn our knowledge about God into knowledge of God? The rule for doing this is simple but demanding. It is that we turn each Truth that we learn about God into a matter for meditation before God, leading to prayer and praise to God."[3]

3 Seek Him

Simply put, being *righteous* means doing right. Jesus tells us to "seek first the kingdom of God and His righteousness" (Matt. 6:33). Put His interests first in your life, and He will guarantee your future. With unshakable confidence, you can trust that He will provide.

4 Imitate Him

Again, practice is what we do repeatedly in order to learn or become proficient. Righteous behavior arises from practicing righteous acts. "For to this you were called, because Christ also suffered for us, leaving us an example, that you should follow His steps" (1 Pet. 2:21).

7 Be Like Him

We are changed from within through the work of the Holy Spirit. He gives us understanding as well as the ability to seek opportunities to do righteous acts that demonstrate our love of God to others. "But as He who called you is holy, you also be holy in all your conduct" (1 Pet. 1:15).

5. Everyone who practices righteousness is therefore recognized as being what?

6. Think about the phrase "is born of Him." What does that mean to you?

Live Out ...

7. Animals are born after their own kind. Kittens are born only of cats, bunnies are born only of rabbits, and Christians are born only of God. Once birthed in the Lord, we begin a relationship with Him that is evident in common characteristics with our Father. Are you confident that you have been born of God? Would you like to rededicate your life to the Lord? If you have any doubts, take this moment to pray the following prayer, given out to every visitor upon exiting the Billy Graham Library in Charlotte, North Carolina:

> Jesus, You died upon a cross
> And rose again to save the lost
> Forgive me now of all my sin
> Come be my Savior, Lord, and Friend
> Change my life and make it new
> And help me, Lord, to live for You.

If you have received Jesus Christ as your Lord and Savior, express your feelings in writing about this new commitment.

8. We cannot attain personal righteousness on our own. Paul tells us in Romans 4:13 that it is through faith that we receive God's righteousness. Hebrews 11:1 reminds us that "faith is the substance of things hoped for, the evidence of things not seen." Because of our sin

nature, we can never be 100 percent righteous. Nonetheless, we must practice righteousness every day. Ask yourself, What practices, habits, or thoughts are pulling me toward unrighteous behavior?

Now match the righteous behaviors below with their unrighteous counterparts. Then add two or three of your own behavior couplets to the bottom of the lists.

9 Pursue Him

The things we do frequently and repetitively eventually become habits. So, make it a daily habit to pursue your Savior. Strive to make prayer, Bible study, and worship as regular as your morning cup of coffee or daily exercise.

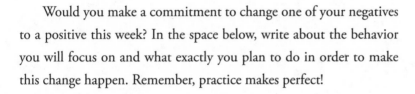

Righteous	**Unrighteous**
a. Generosity	a. Whining about your life
b. Peaceful nature	b. Selfishness
c. Accepting what comes	c. Argumentative
d.	d.
e.	e.

Would you make a commitment to change one of your negatives to a positive this week? In the space below, write about the behavior you will focus on and what exactly you plan to do in order to make this change happen. Remember, practice makes perfect!

9. Our love of God produces a desire to have a life of good habits. Good habits lead to righteous behavior; bad habits can lead you astray.

a. Below, list three of your good habits:

1.

2.

3.

b. Now list three habits that need correcting.

1.

2.

3.

c. What will you do in order to turn your bad habits into good habits?

———————

Throughout our lives we've heard the admonition "Practice makes perfect." However, an online *Wall Street Journal* article by Doug Lemov describes how practice is useful for more than simply doing well in public performances or for proficiency in sports. Adhering to a repetitive routine allows us to execute a task while using diminishing amounts of brain processing. Practiced activities become automatic, freeing up our brains for new or more complex tasks.[4]

What drives mastery is performing an action the right way over and over. When learning any behavior, it is important to repeat it until it is ingrained in our minds. Similarly, we are able to make a habit of our faith—and that faith becomes manifest through the actions of prayer, Bible study, and service. Habitual practice of our faith leads to righteous behavior.

Although we can be forgiven for unrighteous behavior, if we make that a habit, we will be in trouble. We know that "godliness is profitable for all things, having promise of the life that now is and of that which is to come" (1 Tim. 4:8).

Listen To ...

> *How many Christians think that in the morning and evening they ought to come into the company of Jesus, and may then give their hearts to the world all the day: but this is poor living; we should always be with Him, treading in His steps and doing His will.*
>
> —*C. H. Spurgeon*

DAY 3

Hope Is Strengthened by Love

In the 1970 tearjerker movie *Love Story*, the story unfolds of Oliver and Jenny. Oliver is from a rich family of Harvard graduates, and Jenny is a smart Radcliffe grad from a working-class family. They marry without the blessing of Oliver's father, who severs ties with them and withdraws his financial support of Oliver's continuing studies at the Harvard Law School. Despite coming from different social backgrounds, the couple loves each other deeply, and they work together to achieve their goals. However, when the time comes to start a family, they are unsuccessful and eventually learn the reason: Jenny is gravely ill.

In the aftermath of Jenny's death, Oliver's father asks for forgiveness from his heartbroken son, who repeats the statement he heard so often from his young wife: "Love means never having to say you're sorry."[5]

Life is not like the movies, and as believers, we know that our love for God and for others often means acknowledging a wrongdoing with an apology. Immense value and healing come from asking for and receiving forgiveness.

Even when we make mistakes, our hope is rooted in God's provision for His flawed children and in His promise never to leave us: "I am with you always, even to the end of the age" (Matt. 28:20). No matter what happens, God will never disown us or leave us without hope. What a wonderful love story.

Lift Up ...

Lord, I'm amazed when I think about Your unfailing love that saved me from eternal death. What a blessing to be Your child—misunderstood by the world but secure in Your everlasting love. In Jesus' name. Amen.

1 Behold the Lamb

When someone tells us, "Behold," the speaker wants our undivided attention. It is the word John the Baptist used to draw attention to the Savior of the world: "Behold! The Lamb of God who takes away the sin of the world!" (John 1:29).

2 Beyond Our Expectations

Our Lord loves us so much, He adopted us. Without the blood of Jesus that paid our penalty, our sinfulness would separate us from Him for eternity. Instead, His great love brought us into the family of God, "having predestined us to adoption as sons by Jesus Christ to Himself, according to the good pleasure of His will" (Eph. 1:5).

4 Bestowed Love

To *bestow* is to give as one would give a present. The Lord presents us with the gift of His love, the love we hold dearest in our hearts. This abounding love has the power to fill the empty spaces within us and diminish our fears or doubts.

Look At ...

Yesterday we learned our relationship with the Lord deepens in proportion to our active and habitual pursuit of Him. Righteousness, we discovered, is an inherited trait from our Father in heaven to His children. It is based on the righteousness of Jesus rather than any pure goodness generated on our own merit.

Today we will discover the depth and width of God's love. John wanted believers to consider God's love from the standpoints of His deity and our humble humanity. To help us grasp this, He reminded us that the love of Christ can only be understood through the person of Christ. We can't earn His love, and God knows that. So, He gave us His love freely at great cost to Himself.

Read 1 John 3:1.

Behold what manner of love the Father has bestowed on us, that we should be called children of God! Therefore the world does not know us, because it did not know Him. 1 John 3:1

1. What word is used initially to spark your interest?

2. In this passage, John asks us to behold something special. What?

3. What is our status in the family of God?

4. In what way is God's love given to us?

5. The Lord desires that we call ourselves by what phrase?

6. Because we are loved by God, who doesn't know us?

7. Read John 15:18–21. Why doesn't the world accept and understand us?

Live Out ...

8. When we regard children as well-behaved, what are they doing? Below write out three examples of a child's good behavior.

1.

2.

3.

Now list three examples of a child's poor behavior.

1.

2.

3.

Through their good conduct, children show their love and respect for their parents. In the same way, through our obedience, we demonstrate our love of God. Reflect on this and write in your journal about one area of disobedience God is asking you to replace with loving obedience to Him.

9. We bestow our love on others.

a. Did you bestow love on someone this week? What were the circumstances?

b. Now ask yourself, What typically sidetracks me from loving others? Write in your journal about a time this week when you should have given love but didn't.

c. Jesus teaches us in Matthew 19:16–19 that if we want to enter into eternal life, we are to keep the commandments, one of which is to love your neighbor as yourself. Examine your heart and then write

8 Behavior That Honors

Philippians 2:14–15 instructs us to "do all things without complaining and disputing, that you may become blameless and harmless, children of God without fault in the midst of a crooked and perverse generation, among whom you shine as lights in the world." That says it all.

10 Broaden Our Perspective

Jesus gave us a perspective of welcoming love and how we are to regard nonbelievers in Matthew 28:19: "Go, therefore and make disciples of all the nations, baptizing them in the name of the Father and of the Son and of the Holy Spirit."

a prayer asking God to use you this week to bestow His love on someone—even if it is difficult.

10. The world does not know or understand God's children because they do not know or understand God. Similarly, many Christians grapple with fear of that which is foreign to them. Countless people from other nations would like to move to the United States. How do you feel about this? Please check the boxes that fit your view.

❑ Allow everyone in—we are a nation of immigrants.

❑ Allow only certain groups in—the highly educated or wealthy.

❑ Allow in only people who are from countries I like.

❑ Allow only well-behaved people.

What if we applied those same considerations or restrictions to people who desired to immigrate into the family of God?

Romans 13. 1 - 7

_____

Several hymns written in the nineteenth century by Dr. Robert Lowry are still sung today. In 1876 he penned the words to "Nothing but the Blood."

> For my pardon, this I see,
> Nothing but the blood of Jesus;
> For my cleansing this my plea,
> Nothing but the blood of Jesus.[6]

Jesus gave His lifeblood so that we could be "heirs of God and joint heirs with Christ" (Rom. 8:17). This is the way "God demonstrates His own love toward us, in that while we were still sinners, Christ died for us" (Rom. 5:8). Without the strong love of God, we might give up, fall under the spell of the world, and gravitate toward sin. With His love and through our hope in the promises of Jesus, our love is strengthened, and we are able to be children of God throughout eternity. Pray and thank the Lord for expressing His love by giving Jesus to die for you. There was no other way.

Listen To ...

God has the right to be trusted; to be believed that He means
what He says; and that His love is dependable.

—*A. J. Gossip*

DAY 4

Hope Rests in Christ

When the time came to release Karyn Williams' beautiful song "Rest in the Hope," a year had passed since her father's diagnosis of multiple myeloma. Later, in an interview, she was asked how she felt about this piece of music. She said it was born directly out of the trial of dealing with her dad's illness. During that time, she felt dazed and she wrestled with God while trying to understand these difficult circumstances. She eventually "got to the place where [she] had to trust, and rest, knowing that this diagnosis did not come as a surprise to the Lord, [as] everything that happens to us goes through Him first."[7]

> *You are the truth that never changes*
> *You are the love that came to save us*
> *Even through all my fear and sorrow*
> *Facing a new unknown tomorrow …*
> *I'm gonna rest in the hope that I'm Yours*[8]

Satan wants us to feel discouraged and defeated, but God walks with us through all our struggles, providing a sanctuary of peace and rest. The author of Hebrews stressed that when we are in need, we should turn to our loving Father: "Let us therefore be diligent to enter that rest" (Heb. 4:11). Are you weary? Climb up on your Father's lap and rest.

Lift Up …

Lord Jesus, I look forward to the day when, by Your mighty power, I am changed into Your likeness. Sometimes my circumstances dominate my thinking, and I am tired. As I wait for that glorious time, help me to trust and rest in You. In Jesus' name. Amen.

Look At ...

Yesterday we looked at the vast scope and power of God's love as personified in Jesus Christ. His love was a perfect gift, and our understanding of its value is evidenced in our behaviors toward others. God loves us so much, He reached from heaven to make us His children through the blood of His Son, Jesus.

Today we will examine another amazing aspect of the believer's hope: the transformation into Jesus' likeness at His return. There is great mystery involved in becoming like Christ while still being fully loved and accepted for ourselves as individuals. We have every reason to feel hopeful, ready, humbled, blessed, and loved as we wait for our Savior.

Read 1 John 3:2.

Beloved, now we are children of God; and it has not yet been revealed what we shall be, but we know that when He is revealed, we shall be like Him, for we shall see Him as He is. 1 John 3:2

1. What tender word does John use to reach his readers?

2. Collectively, who are we now?

3. What are we waiting to find out?

4. How will we find out what we shall be?

5. What do we know is going to happen next?

6. In what way will His revelation change us?

7. What will we see?

1 Be Loved

Do you struggle with accepting love? Don't! Be loved! To *be* is to stay and to exist, so allow yourself to stay and reside in the love of the Lord. What could be better? "The beloved of the LORD shall dwell in safety by Him, who shelters him all the day long" (Deut. 33:12).

3 Be You

In heaven, we will probably possess our own distinct appearances, but we will finally be like Jesus in that we will be free from sin, sorrow, sickness, and Satan. In this earthly life, "let your light so shine before men, that they may see your good works and glorify your Father in heaven" (Matt. 5:16).

4 Be Enlightened

Revelation means a disclosure of what was previously unknown. The Lord reveals Himself through His Word so that we can build a relationship with Him. Jesus told Peter, "Flesh and blood has not revealed this to you, but My Father who is in heaven" (Matt. 16:17).

9 Be Like

Shamelessly copy Jesus. Want above all else to be a mirror reflecting His nature into the world, conforming to the likeness of the One who is the perfect image of the invisible God.

10 Be Hopeful

We often see ourselves as falling short of God's desire for us, but we should not be dismayed. He sees us not only as we are but also as we will be. Jesus will appear, we will see Him, and we will be changed into His image. Hallelujah!

Live Out ...

8. Do you know that you are beloved by God? Look up the following verses. How does each Scripture make you feel?

  Psalm 63:3

  Psalm 89:33

  Isaiah 38:17

  John 14:21

  Romans 5:8

Scripture enables us to glimpse God's love.

9. Children grow up wanting someone they can look up to. For example, they might try to be like a parent, a pastor, a teacher, or an athlete. When you were a child, who did you want to be like? What attracted you to this person? And now? Have you changed the center of your attention to another? Why?

Let's aspire to be like Jesus Christ.

10. Is it difficult for you to see things as they are? Do you err on the side of being an always-sunny optimist or a perpetually gloomy pessimist? Examine this by answering the questions below.

  a. Areas of my life that look bright to me are:

  b. Areas of my life that look dark to me are:

  c. Based on your answers above, circle the one you most resemble:

    Optimist   Pessimist

Darkness and light, blindness and sight are fundamentals in this world of contrasts. Through faith, prayer, and obedience, you can see a brightening of any darkness in your life. Eventually, when we see the Lord as He is, we will witness the most brilliant experience of our lives.

When passing by a mirror, do you cast a glance to check yourself out? According to a 2010 study done for *The Today Show*, the average woman checks her appearance in a mirror as many as eight times a day.[9] Does that ring a bell with you? What would happen if we took that self-fascination and turned it toward looking at our Lord?

Helen Lemmel wrote a hymn about that very thing. She urged us, "Turn your eyes upon Jesus, look full in His wonderful face, and the things of earth will grow strangely dim in the light of His glory and grace."[10]

Scripture tells us, "For now we see in a mirror, dimly, but then face to face" (1 Cor. 13:12). This addresses the truth that for now we can only see a dim and partial image of our glorious Jesus, but upon His return, our image will match His. We will be enveloped in a light that surpasses anything we can imagine.

What is the result of looking to God? "They looked to Him and were radiant, and their faces were not ashamed" (Ps. 34:5).

It is a good idea to occasionally check our appearance to make sure we are beautifully reflecting the nature of Christ in our words and demeanor. Let's be sure to keep the mirror of our lives smudge-free in order to reflect God's glory.

Listen To ...

The Christmas message is that there is hope for a ruined humanity—hope of pardon, hope of peace with God, hope of glory—because at the Father's will, Jesus Christ became poor, and was born in a stable so that thirty years later He might hang on a cross.

—J. I. Packer

Hope Promotes Purity

Purity means to contain nothing that does not properly belong and to be spotless and stainless. In America we take for granted that our water is pure. In other parts of the world, pure water is not a given. The United Nations stated in 2010 that over four million people die every year from dirty water, half of those being children. Impure water kills more people than wars and other violence![11]

Those who love God strive for personal purity. In the Old Testament, God's chosen people were required to follow a multitude of rules and regulations. No matter how hard they tried, they were not able to purify themselves sufficiently to achieve an intimate relationship with God. It is only through Christ that we can be made pure.

So, what does a pure life look like? Titus wrote that believers should be "denying ungodliness and worldly lusts, [and] we should live soberly, righteously and godly in the present age" (Titus 2:12). Thankfully, the writer did not put the burden for purity solely on our efforts and goals but reminded us of the hopeful perspective that enables a pure life: "Looking for the blessed hope and glorious appearing of our great God and Savior Jesus Christ" (Titus 2:13). Pure gold.

Lift Up ...

Lord, You've shown me the path to purity through the example of Your life and through Your Word. Thank You that I can live a pure life in Your eyes because You live in me. In Jesus' name. Amen.

Look At ...

Yesterday we looked forward in hope to our transformation into Jesus' likeness on the day of His return and discussed the mystery of being loved for who we are while also being changed

by love. We cultivated hope in the atmosphere of humility, proper perspective, and evidence of a reliable Savior and God.

Now, at the end of this week of study, we explore the believer's hope: Christ's return. His love for humankind brings us the assurance of our acceptance. We find a solid hope in His purity rather than the inconsistency of our own efforts. We will learn that we should face steadily forward in our focus. God's righteousness will be accounted to those who put their faith in Him.

Read 1 John 3:3.

And everyone who has this hope in Him purifies himself, just as He is pure. 1 John 3:3

1. John now speaks of an inclusive group consisting of whom?

2. Everyone has something. What is it?

3. In whom do they hope?

4. Based on our study so far, what do they hope for?

5. In reaction to this hope, what does everyone do?

6. Who else is pure? How do we know He is pure?

7. Why is it important to be pure?

1 Inclusive Love

Saving faith is not limited to one special group. We are assured that God "desires all men to be saved and to come to the knowledge of the truth. For there is one God and one Mediator between God and men, the Man Christ Jesus" (1 Tim. 2:4–5).

2 Unshakeable Hope

Hope is only as meaningful as that in which we place our hope. "Blessed be the God and Father of our Lord Jesus Christ, who according to His abundant mercy has begotten us again to a living hope through the resurrection of Jesus Christ from the dead" (1 Pet. 1:3).

6 Undefiled Purity

Scripture tells us Jesus Christ is pure, for we are "redeemed with ... the precious blood of Christ, as of a lamb without blemish and without spot" (1 Pet. 1:18–19). Such a standard of purity exceeds our human perspective, and when understood, brings us to our knees.

Live Out ...

8. Unlike Jesus when He walked this earth, none of us will be perfect in our flesh. However, Philippians 3:12–14 gives us a pathway to purity.

8 Unstoppable Faith

"But those who wait [hope] on the LORD shall renew their strength; they shall mount up with wings like eagles, they shall run and not be weary, they shall walk and not faint" (Isa. 40:31). Determine to walk until you can run, and run until you can fly.

9 Uncontested Righteousness

A sin of weakness is different than a sin that is willful and habitual. We all sin and fall short. A righteous person may have occasional sins of weakness yet still be pure. It is habitual, unconfessed sin that makes us impure.

a. Read these verses and explain what the apostle Paul did to model Christlike perfection.

b. Based on your study this week, write a couple of changes you have decided to make in your life that will move you toward being pure like Christ.

   1.

   2.

c. Thank the Lord for what He has revealed to you.

9. As a sinner, how can you rest your hope on Jesus?

a. First, ask yourself what sin you are willing to confess to right now.

b. Next, is this a sin you have committed frequently or only once?

c. Finally, do you think this sin will keep you from eternal rest with Jesus? In your journal write a prayer asking the Lord to forgive you and, by so doing, purify you. Reference Psalm 51:10 for inspiration.

10. For more help regarding the process of purification, read the verses below and answer the following questions.

a. Psalm 51:1–2. Who can purify us? How is this done?

b. Hebrews 10:19. How are we purified?

c. 1 John 1:9. What is our part?

d. Psalm 119:9, 11. How can we remain pure?

———————

This week we learned that through God's abiding love and the Holy Spirit's guidance, we are able to live in obedience, practicing righteousness. Our greatest incentive to godly living is the hope of Christ's return. Until then, we persevere in our efforts to live a pure life. Remember, we are passing through here on earth, and heaven is our final home. We will arrive there safely as long as we anchor our hope in Christ.

Rainer Maria Rilke once wrote that you can "believe in a love that is being stored up for you like an inheritance, and have faith that in this love there is a strength and a blessing so large that you can travel as far as you wish without having to step outside it."[12] How reassuring to know we cannot escape the enveloping love of God.

Listen To ...

He came to deliver us from our sinful dispositions, and create in us pure hearts, and when we have Him with us it will not be hard for us. Then the service of Christ will be delightful.

—D. L. Moody

Family Tree

1 John 3:4–15

Certain words in the English language may elicit an unexpected reaction. A case in point is *outlaw*. An outlaw is someone who chooses to live outside of the parameters of the law, so logically and morally we should be offended by his or her behavior. But interestingly, history and society often elevate outlaws and bestow on them a curious level of admiration.

Consider Jesse James. For sixteen years he robbed trains. He was clever, so he was never arrested or brought to trial. Ultimately, a member of his own gang gunned him down.[1] To this day, the story of Jesse James is recounted with a touch of respect for his record and disdain for his betrayer.

Bonnie and Clyde are another example of infamous people who captured the fascination of the public. As a young couple during the Depression, they not only went on a bank-robbing spree; they murdered innocent people along the way. Their lives on the run were chronicled in the newspapers and followed by a spellbound population. Their violent lives ended in equally violent deaths that are still romanticized and remembered today.

Beware! Although our culture may celebrate lawlessness, God does not. We begin this week by learning that sin is lawlessness and lawlessness is sin. There is no leeway to glamorize or minimize this truth. We are all sinners that deserve the harshest punishment. There is only one hope for a lenient judgment: the sacrifice of a sinless Savior.

Day 1: 1 John 3:4–5   **Sinless Sacrifice**

Day 2: 1 John 3:6–8a   **Spotlight on Sin**

Day 3: 1 John 3:8b–9   **Second Nature**

Day 4: 1 John 3:10–12   **Sons and Siblings**

Day 5: 1 John 3:13–15   **Signs of Life**

DAY 1

Sinless Sacrifice

Lift Up ...

Lord, You are a God of unwavering truth and justice. Please help me recognize and label my sin as sin and allow your saving grace to cleanse and restore me. In Jesus' name. Amen.

Look At ...

We finished last week on a high note: rejoicing in the hope that comes with knowing we will one day see the Lord, and on that day we will be like Him (1 John 3:2–3). What an awesome promise! What a glorious hope!

Now, John brings us back down to earth. We find ourselves forced to make some important choices in light of some harsh truths. We must decide: Who do we belong to, and who do we trust and live for? This week we will study and compare sin with righteousness; the Devil with the Son of God; and love with hate. Our Lord stands at every crossroad, instructing, encouraging, and pointing us to our future and our hope. "For I know the thoughts that I think toward you, says the LORD, thoughts of peace and not of evil, to give you a future and a hope" (Jer. 29:11).

Read 1 John 3:4–5.

Whoever commits sin also commits lawlessness, and sin is lawlessness. And you know that He was manifested to take away our sins, and in Him there is no sin. 1 John 3:4–5

1. In this text John is speaking about people who do what two things?

2. What verb does John use to reveal the crucial relationship between sin and lawlessness?

3. Record the words John uses to indicate that those who commit sin and those who commit lawlessness are one and the same.

4. What phrase indicates that John is restating a truth his readers have already heard?

5. Who is John referring to when he says "He/Him"?

6. What two truths about "Him" does John express?

Live Out …

7. John describes the person who practices sin as a lawless person, an outlaw. Habitual sin originates in a rebellious heart. Search your heart for any of these rebellious attitudes.

❑ I decide what is right for me.   ❑ When they change, I'll change.

❑ My circumstances are unique.   ❑ Everyone else does it.

❑ I'm not hurting anybody.   ❑ I'm not as bad as they are.

❑ I'm just watching out for me.   ❑ I'm just trying to fit in.

Write a prayer in your journal, asking God to convict you of any sinful attitudes. Ask Him to forgive you and to help you rid them from your heart. "Blessed are those whose lawless deeds are forgiven, and whose sins are covered" (Rom. 4:7).

8. Jesus came to take away sin.

a. Read John 1:29 and record whose sin Jesus takes away.

b. Now note whose sin Jesus takes away in 1 John 3:5.

c. Explain the distinction between *the sin of the world* and *our sins*.

1 Habitual Sin

The verb *commit* is translated from a Greek verb that implies habitual behavior.[2] John refers to engaging in a lifestyle of sin as opposed to occasionally falling into sin. "Shall we continue in sin that grace may abound? Certainly not! How shall we who died to sin live any longer in it?" (Rom. 6:1–2)

3 Wandering Sin

Sin is defined as missing the mark or wandering from the path, while *lawlessness* is defined as intentional disobedience. John does not separate the two but implies that both come from a heart of willful rebellion against God. "Whoever commits sin also commits lawlessness" (1 John 3:4).

6 Exposed Sin

Manifest means to shine upon, to make visible, or to reveal. Jesus, the light of the world, came in order to expose and dispose of our sin. He tells us, "I am the light of the world. He who follows Me shall not walk in darkness, but have the light of life" (John 8:12).

7 Disposed Sin

Jesus came to reveal and to take away our sin. Ask Him daily to do just that. "Search me, O God, and know my heart; try me, and know my anxieties; and see if there is any wicked way in me, and lead me in the way ever-lasting" (Ps. 139:23–24).

8 Forgiven Sin

Jesus came as the only perfect sacrifice that could reconcile a sinful world to a holy and righteous God. He is the Savior of the world, and His death offers us eternal salvation. But His sacrifice also allows us to receive daily forgiveness for our sinful attitudes and behaviors.

d. How are both purifications necessary and personal in our Christian lives?

9. We read in 1 John 3:5 that "in Him there is no sin." He was sinless but willing to die for our sin so that we could live forever in His presence. Look at the following verses and note the aspects of this truth that are meaningful to you. Thank the Lord for His undeserved sacrifice.

Isaiah 53:5

Romans 5:8

2 Corinthians 5:21

Ephesians 1:7

1 Peter 2:24

———————————

Perhaps the most highly esteemed outlaw of all time is the legendary Robin Hood. His goal and purpose were to "rob from the rich and give to the poor."[3] His success is attributed to cunning, scheming, and his remarkable archery skills. He lived in England in an area called the Sherwood Forest and was assisted by his fellow outlaws, the "Merry Men."

Although Robin Hood seemed to be motivated by a generous heart and an unselfish spirit, he was still obligated to abide by the law of the land. Each time he rebelled and did things his way, he found himself further from the standards set by the law.

The same is true for us. We are all sinners. In Romans 3:23 we read, "All have sinned and fall short of the glory of God." No matter how noble our motives, when we choose to do things our way, we choose sinfulness and lawlessness.

Frank Sinatra's signature song "My Way" shows the attitude of a person dedicated only to himself:

> *For what is a man, what has he got?*
> *If not himself, then he has naught*
> *To say the things he truly feels and not the words of one who kneels,*
> *The record shows I took the blows and did it my way!*
> *Yes, it was my way!*[4]

Being a person after God's heart means striving to live life God's way so you might glorify Him. Don't let your way interfere with His way!

Listen To ...

Sinfulness is not wrong doing, it is wrong being, deliberate and emphatic independence of God.
—Oswald Chambers

Spotlight on Sin

Sergeant Joe Friday, a fictional police detective renowned for his no-nonsense demeanor, was known for this statement: "Just the facts, ma'am." This intense and unsmiling officer did his best work with the cold, hard facts; anything extra got in his way.

Joe Friday's technique is in direct opposition to another famous fictional sleuth, Sherlock Holmes. Holmes is famous for his keen powers of observation and his ability to draw accurate conclusions from seemingly insignificant details. He once chastised his friend and companion, Dr. Watson, for not recalling how many steps they had just climbed to the door of his home. "Watson, he said, "there are seventeen steps; you see but you don't observe."[5]

In this letter, John utilizes these two methods to impart his message. At times he states the truth as a factual reality. Other times, he allows his audience to listen and to observe. He then reaffirms the truth of the gospel to them.

Today's lesson is a "fact" day. John leaves no room for misinterpretation. He clearly defines and differentiates a follower of God from a follower of the Devil. No nonsense! No debate!

Are you prepared to hear it? "He who has ears to hear, let him hear!" (Matt. 11:15). Prepare your heart to dive into this deep, straightforward truth as John presents "just the facts, ma'am."

Lift Up ...

Lord, prepare my heart for the truths You have for me today. Draw me close and keep me from being deceived by the Enemy of this world or by my own prideful heart. In Jesus' name. Amen.

Look At ...

Yesterday's lesson laid the groundwork for a frank discussion on sin. In his letter, John defined sin as lawlessness and confirmed that we are a sinful, lawless people. Thankfully, he balanced that sad realization with the promise of Jesus, a sinless Savior.

3 Acutely Aware

To *see God* is to be completely aware of His presence in your life. He may be invisible, but He is not unseen. "Blessed are the pure in heart, for they shall see God" (Matt. 5:8). "Pursue peace with all people, and holiness, without which no one will see the Lord" (Heb. 12:14).

In today's study John again utilizes this comparison approach. He contrasts the righteous person with the sinner and encourages us to assess our status. When everything is clearly presented, the truth becomes obvious and our choices evident.

Dwight L. Moody helps to clarify this approach: "The best way to show that a stick is crooked is not to argue about it or to spend time denouncing it, but to lay a straight stick alongside it."[6] John lays it all out, and we can see the straight truth for our lives. "And you shall know the truth, and the truth shall make you free" (John 8:32).

Read 1 John 3:6–8a.

Whoever abides in Him does not sin. Whoever sins has neither seen Him nor known Him. Little children, let no one deceive you. He who practices righteousness is righteous, just as He is righteous. He who sins is of the devil, for the devil has sinned from the beginning. 1 John 3:6–8a

1. John begins by introducing and contrasting which two groups of people?

     a. Whoever_____

     b. Whoever_____

2. What behavior is to be expected from those who abide in Him?

3. What level of familiarity do those who sin have with the Lord?

4 Open-Hearted

In this letter John often refers to his audience as "little children." This is an expression of the love and responsibility he felt for God's people. Jesus valued a childlike heart. "Unless you are converted and become as little children, you will by no means enter the kingdom of heaven" (Matt. 18:3).

7 Active Avoidance

"All sin of whatever degree is satanic in nature. This is because the devil has been sinning from the beginning. Sin originated with Satan and is his constant practice. To take part in sin is to take part in his activity.'" (Read also Eph. 6:12.)

8 Devoted Dwelling

Jesus honors us with this invitation in John 15:4: "Abide in Me, and I in you." He is telling us to abide, dwell, and remain in Him, and He will do the same for us. "He is the One who goes with you. He will not leave you nor forsake you" (Deut. 31:6).

4. How does John address his listeners, and what warning does he give?

5. How does John define a righteous person?

6. Who do we emulate when we practice righteousness?

7. What does John say about the one who practices sin, and what fact does he reference to emphasize his position?

Live Out ...

8. To *abide in Christ* is to live in intimate fellowship with Him, to faithfully remain in His presence and His promises. John tells us that "whoever abides in Him does not sin" (1 John 3:6). Read the following verses and record some of the other blessings we receive when we abide.

Scripture	Blessings of Abiding
John 15:4	
John 15:7	
John 15:9	
1 John 4:13	

9. We read today that "He who practices righteousness is righteous." According to Philippians 3:9, "not having my own righteousness, which is from the law, but that which is through faith in Christ." Righteousness is a gift bestowed upon us. Carefully read 2 Corinthians 5:21 and, in your own words, explain whose righteousness we receive and the price that was paid for our gift.

> For He made Him who knew no sin to be sin to be sin for us, that we might become the righteousness of God in Him. (2 Cor. 5:21)

10. John boldly acknowledges the influence and the tactics that the Devil uses in our lives.

> a. Read John 8:44 and list some more facts and schemes that you learn about the Devil.

> b. Do you recognize that the Devil has a desire to manipulate and deceive you personally? Be assured and confident of the truth found in 1 John 4:4: "You are of God, little children … He who is in you is greater than he who is in the world." Write a short prayer thanking God for His sovereign power against this enemy.

9 Wholly Righteous

Righteousness is holy and upright living in accordance with God's standard. It comes from a root that means "straightness," an unbending standard.[8] God's character is the definition and source of all righteousness; therefore our righteousness is defined in terms of God's.

———————————

Today's text contains some convicting facts about sin and the sinner: "Whoever sins has neither seen Him nor known Him" (3:6) and "He who sins is of the devil" (3:8). These words not only are difficult to hear but can lead to some confusion when we recall the words in 1 John 1:8: "If we say that we have no sin, we deceive ourselves." In 1 John 1:10, we see a greater consequence: "If we say that we have not sinned, we make [God] a liar."

At a glance these could appear to be contradictory truths, but they are not. Reading 1 John 3:6 in the NIV translation helps shed some light on its meaning: "No one who lives in him *keeps on* sinning. No one who *continues to* sin has either seen Him or known Him" (emphasis added). We are all sinners, but if we willfully practice sin, or continue in habitual sin, it may indicate that we belong to the Devil and not to the Lord. Warren Wiersbe sums it up well: "It is clear that no Christian is sinless, but God expects a true believer to sin less."[9]

These are the cold, hard facts! Examine your heart, your motives, and your sin. Ask the Lord to forgive you and to draw you close. Tell Him that you want to abide in Him and Him alone.

Listen To …

The devil is a better theologian than any of us and is a devil still.

—A. W. Tozer

Second Nature

Recently a newspaper published this headline: "Giving Away Shoes to Homeless Man Is Second Nature to Good Samaritan." The story told of a bus driver, Kris Doubledee, who stopped his bus to speak with a homeless man walking shoeless in cold weather. After a brief conversation, the bus driver took off his own leather shoes and gave them to the man. He then completed his shift in his stocking feet. When asked why he stopped, Mr. Doubledee answered, "It's kind of a thing with me. I see somebody with a need, I try to take their pain away or pray they find relief. It was cold and he was barefoot. I had to help him. Anyone would have done it."[10]

Known for having a heart that reaches out to help strangers, Kris Doubledee does it without thinking. It is a decision and a habit that has become ingrained in his character; it has become *second nature*. He naively believes that all people would react as he does.

This generous bus driver responds on a human level but is inspired on a spiritual level. Mr. Doubledee does have a second nature, but it is more than a learned reaction; it is evidence of the Spirit of God living in Him.

We all want to think that we would take off our shoes and give them to a homeless person. But, would you? Consider this question as we study the true second nature: God's nature in us!

Lift Up ...

Lord, thank You for delivering me from the Evil One and for giving me a new life and a new nature. Please guide me as I learn to walk in You and in Your Word. In Jesus' name. Amen.

1 Destroyed Power

The word *destroy* in (v. 8) does not mean Satan is annihilated. In this context, *destroy* means to "render inoperable, to rob of power." So, while Satan is definitely still at work today, his power has been reduced and his weapons have been impaired. He is no match for the power of God."

Look At ...

Our lesson yesterday ended with a cliffhanger. As we closed, John stated, "He who sins is of the devil" (1 John 3:8a). Today we find out that God doesn't leave us at that point—the Son of God has plans to deal with the Devil and his influence on us.

We do not want to underestimate the role of the Devil throughout the Word of God. We meet him in Genesis as the "serpent," and he is still around in Revelation, where he is called the "accuser of the brethren." In between, we know the Devil by other names: Satan, wicked one, enemy, father of lies, god of this world, ruler of darkness, and more.

Though ominous, these names are just that, names only! *Yahweh*, the name of your heavenly Father, is the name above *all* names. Still, there is a choice to be made: In whom do you place your trust?

Read 1 John 3:8b–9.

For this purpose the son of God was manifested, that He might destroy the works of the devil. Whoever has been born of God does not sin, for His seed remains in him; and he cannot sin, because he has been born of God. 1 John 3:8b–9

1. a. According to this text, for what purpose was the Son of God manifested?

b. Look back at 1 John 3:5 and record for what other reason He was manifested.

2. Though the Devil will ultimately be destroyed, he is actively working in the world today. Look up the following verses and record the specific works of the Devil revealed in them.

Scripture	Works of the Devil
Acts 13:8–10	
2 Corinthians 4:3–4	
1 Thessalonians 2:18	
2 Thessalonians 2:9–10	

3. John turns his attention away from the Devil and focuses on whom?

4. What is the first reason John gives for the lack of habitual sin in the life of someone who has been born of God?

5. John 1:12–13 gives more insight into what it means to be born of God. Read and answer the following questions.

   a. To whom does Jesus give the right to become children of God?

   b. Those who meet these criteria were *not* born of:

   c. But *are* born of:

6. First John 3:9b reads, "He cannot sin, because he has been born of God." *Cannot* is a strong word. To gain further insight into the intent, read and compare this verse in other Bible translations. Then explain "cannot" in your own words.

Live Out ...

7. Being born of God produces in us a new nature often described as "living in the Spirit." The old nature is referred to as *the sin nature* or *the flesh*. Read the following scriptures and write the descriptions of the two opposing natures.

3 Second Birth

When people receive Jesus Christ as their Lord and Savior, they experience major spiritual changes. One powerful change is known as *regeneration* (*re* means "again," and *generation* means "birth"). A regenerated person is reborn into a new nature and a new family.

4 New Nature

God's seed represents the new nature received at salvation through the Holy Spirit. Just as seeds grow into mature plants, the new nature allows believers to grow into righteous disciples. "Having been born again, not of corruptible seed but incorruptible, through the word of God which lives and abides forever" (1 Pet. 1:23).

7 Spirit-Ruled

Those who belong to Christ, who allow the Spirit's nature to rule in their lives, have defeated the power of the flesh to rule over them. "For if you live according to the flesh you will die; but if by the Spirit you put to death the deeds of the body, you will live" (Rom. 8:13).

Scripture	Flesh	Spirit
Romans 8:5		
Romans 8:13		
Galatians 5:13		
Galatians 6:8		

9 Proof Positive

"The Spirit Himself bears witness with our spirit that we are children of God" (Rom. 8:16). When we are born into the family of God the Holy Spirit verifies it by the fruit He produces in us. The Spirit Himself is all the proof we need.

8. God's Word does not leave us wondering about the source of our thoughts, motives, or actions. "For the flesh lusts against the Spirit, and the Spirit against the flesh; and these are contrary to one another, so that you do not do the things that you wish" (Gal. 5:17).

   a. Read Galatians 5:19–21 and list what Paul calls the "works of the flesh."

   b. What warning does Paul give in verse 21?

   c. Now look at Galatians 5:22–23 and record the fruit of the Spirit.

9. Look back on the lists you created in question 8:

   a. Acknowledge the works of the flesh that are operating in your life.

   b. Review the fruit of the Spirit and select those you would like to substitute for your works of the flesh.

   c. Write a prayer in your journal, asking God to fill you with His Spirit and to exchange His supernatural fruit for your natural sin.

When we refer to actions being "second nature," we are speaking of our human character. Something becomes second nature to us when we begin to do it automatically, without questioning or thought. It can be an action, a habit, or even a skill that becomes part of who we are.

In many instances, these are admirable qualities—for example, firefighters who head into the fire as others are running out, soldiers who place themselves in danger to protect others, or mothers who know just how to lovingly comfort a hurting child. Their responses are second nature—other options are not even considered.

On a spiritual level, we can also respond by our second nature. Believers have a first nature, a sin nature. God's Word tells us "the heart is deceitful and desperately wicked" (Jer. 17:9) and that "all have sinned and fall short of the glory of God" (Rom. 3:23). But God does not want us to live in this state, so He willingly imparts His life and nature to us. "And he died for all, that those who live should no longer live for themselves but for him who died for them and was raised again" (2 Cor. 5:15 NIV).

Let your new nature in Christ become "second nature" to you. Pray for the Lord to fill you with His Spirit. Ask him to "create in you a clean heart … and renew a steadfast spirit within [you]" (Ps. 51:10).

Listen To ...

If you have love you are not only going to think no evil; you are going to take your tongue and have it nailed to the cross so that you bless instead of curse.

—*Billy Graham*

DAY 4

Sons and Siblings

In the world of sports we find examples of "deliberate practice." According to research, "The important thing is not just practice, but practice focused on self-evaluation and examination of weaknesses rather than the glorification of strengths. Deliberate practice is, relentlessly focusing on our weaknesses and inventing new ways to root them out."[12]

When the basketball legend Michael Jordan first entered the NBA, his jump shot didn't measure up to the league. He spent his off-season practicing hundreds of jump shots a day until it was acceptable. Jordan's coach, Phil Jackson, writes that "Jordan's defining characteristic wasn't his talent, but having the humility to know he had to work constantly to improve and to be the best."[13]

It is humbling to admit and focus on our weaknesses, but this is exactly what John is asking us to do in our text today. He doesn't sugar-coat anything; he tells us that unless we practice righteousness, we do not belong to God. Practicing righteousness is the deliberate practice of living out God's holy righteousness in our lives. This is definitely an assignment in self-evaluation and humility, but it is one worth doing to the best of our ability.

Lift Up ...

Lord, my weakness can only be overcome by your strength. Today, please help me to be more like You than I have ever been before. In Jesus' name. Amen.

Look At ...

Yesterday we were reassured to know that Jesus came to destroy the works of the Devil. The deceiver tries to draw us into his family, but we don't have to oblige because we are born of God, and He is the head of our household.

In today's lesson John takes that relationship a little deeper. We are born of God, so we are children of God, and along with that title comes some behavioral requirements. Our earthly parents expect our words and actions to honorably represent our family, and God expects the same. People will know about our family by our actions and decisions. Today we critique our behavior. Are we proving our status as children of God, or are we displaying tendencies that link us with the Enemy and his family?

Read 1 John 3:10–12.

In this the children of God and the children of the devil are manifest: Whoever does not practice righteousness is not of God, nor is he who does not love his brother. For this is the message that you heard from the beginning, that we should love one another, not as Cain who was of the wicked one and murdered his brother. And why did he murder him? Because his works were evil and his brother's righteous. 1 John 3:10–12

1. Which two families does John contrast?

2. Those who *do not* belong to God's family reveal their identity by *not* doing what two things?

3. a. To what foundational message is John referring?

   b. How long has this message been shared?

4. John refers to an Old Testament figure, Cain, as a negative example. Who was Cain "of" and what sin did he commit?

5. According to this text, why did Cain murder his brother?

1 Family Is Fundamental

"Only two kinds of families exist in the world, children of God and children of Satan. No one can belong to both families simultaneously. Either one belongs to God's family and exhibits his righteous character or one belongs to Satan's family and exhibits his sinful nature."[14]

3 Love Is Paramount

Message here means to proclaim a word or news. The word *beginning* implies something of importance or worth, from the first.[15] This statement then refers to the foundational gospel message summed up as God's love for us, our love for God, and the demonstration of that love for others (Matt. 22:37–40).

6 Truth Is Vital

God attempted to instruct Cain before he went too far. He does the same for us. "Let every man be swift to hear, slow to speak, slow to wrath; for the wrath of man does not produce the righteousness of God....But be doers of the word and not hearers only, deceiving yourselves" (James 1:19–20, 22).

7 Sin Is Sin

We cannot justify our sin by comparing our sin with others. Dietrich Bonhoeffer says, "If my sinfulness appears to me to be in any way smaller or less detestable in comparison with the sins of others, I am still not recognizing my sinfulness at all."[16] Sin is sin; it is not measured by degrees.

9 Christ Is Righteousness

As believers, Christ sees us as righteous. Therefore, we desire to be "righteous, just as He is righteous" (1 John 3:7). We learn today that the practice of righteousness must include the practice of love (v. 10). "Pursue righteousness, faith, love, peace with those who call on the Lord out of a pure heart" (2 Tim. 2:22).

6. Read the account of Cain and Abel in Genesis 4:1–10, then answer the following questions.

    a. What emotions was Cain experiencing that led up to the murder?

    b. How did God encourage Cain to choose righteousness over sin?

    c. How do you know Cain was unrepentant even after the murder?

Live Out ...

7. We read that the reason Cain murdered Abel was because Cain's works were "evil" and Abel's were "righteous" (v. 12). Cain compared himself with his brother, and that comparison resulted in pride, envy, and murder. What warnings do we receive from the following verses concerning envy and pride?

    Proverbs 14:30

    Proverbs 28:25

    Psalm 10:4

    1 Corinthians 3:3

    James 3:16

8. Paul's words in Philippians 2:3 instruct us on how to avoid the sins of pride and envy. Rewrite this verse to show how we can accomplish that. Then answer the follow-up questions.

> Let nothing be done through selfish ambition or conceit, but in lowliness of mind let each esteem others better than himself. Let each of you look out not only for his own interests but also for the interest of others. (Phil. 2:3–4)

a. Is the Lord prompting you to esteem a particular person more than yourself?

b. Whose interest do you need to place above your own?

c. Pray specifically asking God to direct your next step with these individuals.

9. John tells us that we must practice righteousness to be "of God." If righteousness is the condition that makes us acceptable to God, how exactly can we practice righteousness?

———————

Deliberate practice is not for the weak. It is hard work. Part of the process involves the strength and resolve to stick with it. To coin an old phrase, we have to "keep on keeping on." So keep on striving for improvement and perfection. Vladimir Horowitz, the famous pianist, supposedly said, "If I don't practice for a day, I know it. If I don't practice for two days, my wife knows it. If I don't practice for three days, the world knows it."[17]

In order to keep moving forward, we must have an objective and a goal we want to reach. John offers us just such a purpose. He proposes an end result so magnificent that any hard work required is transformed into a desire rather than a duty. If we want to be recognized as children of God, we must *practice* righteousness.

The goal is to be known as God's child—His pride and joy. We do that by serving Him in the ways He has instructed. Make the Lord your focus, and steadfastness will be an added blessing. Make your choice, set your goal. Follow the example of Joshua when he said, "Choose for yourselves this day whom you will serve … But as for me and my house, we will serve the LORD" (Josh. 24:15).

Listen To …

It is not love that produces jealousy, it is selfishness.

—*Justice Wallington*

DAY 5

Signs of Life

It is said that love is the universal language. While that may be true, definitions of love vary greatly. Nothing is more convicting and endearing than the definitions and descriptions of love offered by a group of four- to eight-year-old children.

> "When my grandmother got arthritis, she couldn't bend over and paint her toenails anymore. So my grandfather does it for her all the time, even when his hands got arthritis too. That's love."
>
> "When someone loves you, the way they say your name is different. You know that your name is safe in their mouth."
>
> "Love is what makes you smile when you're tired."
>
> "Love is what's in the room with you at Christmas if you stop opening presents and listen."
>
> "If you want to learn to love better, you should start with a friend who you hate."
>
> "You really shouldn't say 'I love you' unless you mean it. But if you mean it, you should say it a lot. People forget."[18]

These children exhibit an amazing grasp of both the simplicity and the depth of love. So, do we love God and belong to Him, or do we love the world? The answer is based on God's definition of love. Why do you love? How do you love? Who do you love?

Lift Up ...

Lord, I want to love like You love. Help me follow Your example of love, not the world's example. Give me a heart to love the people that You love, even if the world doesn't understand. In Jesus' name. Amen.

Look At ...

Yesterday we looked at the children of God versus the children of the Devil. No one likes to think that anyone, much less a child, belongs to the Devil, but as we learned last week, we all have that DNA lurking in our family tree. John reminded us of this with his reference to the story of Cain and Abel. Both brothers presented offerings to the Lord, but that was the end of their resemblance. Cain appeared to be a member of the family of God, but his heart apparently belonged to the Devil. He resented his believing brother, Abel, enough to kill him.

We learn today to be careful in this world. Those who don't love and worship the Lord will hate those who do. But we are in the best of company, because Jesus reminds us that we will be hated for His namesake, but whoever endures to the end will be saved (Mark 13:13).

Read 1 John 3:13–15.

Do not marvel, my brethren, if the world hates you. We know that we have passed from death to life, because we love the brethren. He who does not love his brother abides in death. Whoever hates his brother is a murderer, and you know that no murderer has eternal life abiding in him. 1 John 3:13–15

1. We have seen John call his audience various terms of affection.

a. What term of affection and relation does John use to address his audience in this passage?

1 Common Ground

In this context, the word *brethren* refers to a community of people based on a common identity. It is used to denote a group united by a shared calling,[19] in this case, believers in Jesus Christ. "But when you thus sin against the brethren, and wound their weak conscience, you sin against Christ" (1 Cor. 8:12).

2 Worldly Outcast

We should not *marvel*, or be surprised, shocked, or dismayed, if we are hated by unbelievers or those with anti-Christian values. "If you were of the world, the world would love its own. Yet because you are not of the world ... therefore the world hates you" (John 15:19).

4 Brother-Love

Loving our brothers and sisters in Christ is a matter of life or death. Genuine love is the most compelling sign to the world that Christianity is real. "By this all will know that you are My disciples, if you have love for one another" (John 13:35).

8 Forever-Life

God's Word is clear on the path to everlasting life. "For God so loved the world that He gave His only begotten Son, that whoever believes in Him should not perish but have everlasting life" (John 3:16). "He who has the Son has life; he who does not have the Son of God does not have life" (1 John 5:12).

b. Why do you think he chose this family term?

2. What is the anticipated reaction of the world toward believers?

3. What do we know if we love the brethren?

4. How does John describe someone who does not love his brother?

5. To whom does John equate someone who hates?

6. What do we know about a murderer?

7. What does Jesus teach about murder in Matthew 5:21–22, and how does it help explain John's statement?

Live Out ...

8. John mentions two signs that prove we have passed from death to life: (1) the world hates us, and (2) we love fellow believers. So let's look back to be sure we understand what is required to make this transition from death to life. Read John 5:24 and list the steps to life.

He who

hears _____

believes _____

has _____

shall not _____

has passed _____

If you are certain that you have passed into life, take a moment to praise the Lord for His provision. If you are uncertain of your status between death and life, pray to Jesus expressing your desire to hear, to believe, to have everlasting life, to bypass judgment, and to pass from death into life.

10 Other-Love

When the Pharisees asked Jesus what was the greatest commandment, He answered, "You shall love the LORD your God with all your heart, with all your soul, and with all your mind ... And the second is like it: 'You shall love your neighbor as yourself'" (Matt. 22:37, 39).

9. Jesus gave us instructions to love others in two ways. Look up the following references and (1) state how we are to love others, and (2) give some practical examples of how to love the people in your lives.

> John 15:12
>
> Matthew 22:39

10. In its simplest form, Jesus stated that the greatest commandment is to love God and love others. For us to love others means more to God than the many activities to which we ascribe great value.

> a. Read 1 Corinthians 13:1–3 and summarize what these verses are saying.
>
> b. Ask God to replace your priority with His priority of love in one specific area of your life (home, work, ministry, hobbies, talents, spiritual gifts).

———————————

We have spent this week evaluating subjects of the heart: sin and righteousness, flesh and spirit, and hate and love. In John's writings, love is the overwhelming theme. This comes as no surprise, since he is known as "the disciple whom Jesus loved." John walked beside Jesus, who was the ultimate example and teacher of love. John wants nothing more than for us to love one another.

In our text today, the word used for *love* is the Greek word *agapao*, or agape love. This describes the divine love of God for Jesus and for humankind. It is God's will that we also embrace that definition and our love for one another. This kind of love is not predicated on feelings but seeks to do good toward all people, especially fellow believers. It is an others-oriented, unselfish love that gives and expects nothing in return.

There is a story about a four-year-old girl who lived next door to an elderly gentleman whose wife had recently died. The child loved him, so she went to visit and talk with him. When she came home, her mother asked what she had said to the neighbor, and the little girl answered, "Nothing, I just sat in his lap and helped him cry."[20]

There is no substitute for loving and caring. "My little children, let us not love in word or in tongue, but in deed and in truth" (1 John 3:18).

Listen To ...

> *Satan separates; God unites; love binds us together.*
>
> —*D. L. Moody*

All We Need Is Love

1 John 3:16–23

It was known as "The Summer of Love." The year was 1967, and a countercultural revolution was under way in America. Young people—disillusioned with the war in Vietnam, racial unrest, and pressure to conform—flocked from all corners of the country to the Haight-Ashbury crossroads in San Francisco, California. The "hippies," as they came to be known, were easy to identify: they had long hair, wore loud clothes, spoke a rhetoric of love and peace, and reacted to social conventions and authority with clear rebellion.[1]

In the same year, on the other side of the "pond," the Beatles were reaching a zenith of popularity. The BBC asked them to write a song containing a message that would be understood and supported by everyone. The resulting song captured the heartbeat of a generation: "All You Need Is Love." When asked to comment about the song, Brian Epstein, the Beatles' manager, said, "The nice thing about it is that it cannot be misinterpreted. It is a clear message saying that love is everything."[2]

The lyrics assured us that in spite of our tendency to overcomplicate, love, at its core, is "easy."

Sounds nice, but love is not always easy. Christian love is not a vague feeling of affection but a condition of the heart that prompts us to actively seek the welfare of others. It is true that in this world we need love, but in our hearts, we first need Jesus.

Day 1: 1 John 3:16–17	**Sacrificial Love**
Day 2: 1 John 3:18–19	**True Love**
Day 3: 1 John 3:20–21	**Confident Love**
Day 4: 1 John 3:22	**Obedient Love**
Day 5: 1 John 3:23	**Faithful Love**

Sacrificial Love

Lift Up ...

Lord, thank You for the supreme sacrifice of Your life that separated us from the power of sin and death. Praise You, Lord, for Your example of love, by which I can gauge my motives and actions in this life. In Jesus' name. Amen.

Look At ...

Last time, we looked in the mirror of God's Word and learned to differentiate between genuine and artificial believers. John helped us discern the validity of a person's claim of belonging to the family of God. We concluded that we must be wise and observant in this world. Those who don't love and worship the Lord will hate those who do. Yet even being hated for our love of Christ is an honor because the world hated Him before it hated us (see John 15:18).

This week John will introduce to us another test of salvation: the outward working of love that reflects the presence of God in a believer's heart. Our actions speak louder than our words. We can't be in pursuit of the treasures of the world without losing our focus and our witness to others.

Read 1 John 3:16–17.

By this we know love, because He laid down His life for us. And we also ought to lay down our lives for the brethren. But whoever has this world's goods, and sees his brother in need, and shuts up his heart from him, how does the love of God abide in him? 1 John 3:16–17

1. By whose example and standard can we measure and know true love?

2. On whose behalf was this selfless act performed?

3. Read John 10:11, 18, and answer the following questions.

a. What title does Jesus give Himself (v. 11)?

b. What did He sacrifice? For whom did He make that sacrifice (v. 11)?

c. Was Jesus' action voluntary or involuntary (v. 18)? Why?

d. What did Jesus receive from His Father, and what was His active response (v. 18)?

4. On whom does John refocus his attention?

5. Next, who does John turn his attention to?

6. Explain what this type of professing Christian sees and does.

7. What does it prove when a person is hard-hearted toward the needs of others?

Live Out ...

8. Jesus' sacrificial act of death on the cross was the ultimate demonstration of His love for us.

a. What is the most sacrificial act you have ever done for another person?

b. What is the most sacrificial act someone has ever done for you?

9. With Jesus as our example of love, what should we also be willing to do and for whom?

2 He Divested Himself

The phrase *laid down* speaks of stripping oneself of something.³ "Let this mind be in you which was also in Christ Jesus, who, being in the form of God, did not consider it robbery to be equal with God, but made Himself of no reputation, taking the form of a bondservant, and coming in the likeness of men. And being found in appearance as a man, He humbled Himself and became obedient to the point of death, even the death of the cross" (Phil. 2:5–8).

3 He Risked Himself

A shepherd becomes a living door of a sheepfold. He curls up in the doorway of the pen, or the entrance of a cave, and willingly places his body between the flock and ravenous animals or thieves. Jesus willingly laid down His life to save us from the thief who comes "to steal, and to kill, and to destroy" (John 10:10).

6 He Shared Himself

Shut up means to close. The word *heart* is translated from the word *bowels*, meaning sympathy, inward affection, and tender mercy. "Command those who are rich in this present age ... [to] do good, that they be rich in good works, ready to give, willing to share" (1 Tim. 6:17–18).

10. If God is nudging you to act in sacrificial love to those around you, how will you allow yourself to be used in order to act on behalf of others?

————————

8 He Sacrificed Himself

Ought means to owe or be indebted. Jesus died to prove His love for us, and as His followers, we owe it to Him to selflessly sacrifice for our brothers and sisters in Christ. "For I have given you an example, that you should do as I have done to you" (John 13:15).

9 He Reached Out

Jesus did more than talk; He took action. The Greek word for *reach* indicates the kind of stretching that would occur when extending a hand to help someone over an obstacle or to pull him or her out of the water and into a boat. We, too, are to love others practically and visibly, extending ourselves to help those who are in need.

Business managers are often analytical types who delve into finances, projections for the future, the corporate bottom line or net worth, and various internal systems. While they excel in these areas, they may come up short on the human side of management. Efficiency often fails on this level, resulting in a dissatisfied population of employees. The manager may say all the right things, but something's lacking. Most often it comes down to this motto: "They don't care what you know unless they know that you care."

There is a vast difference between hearing people talk about loving others and observing actions that either verify their statements or negate them. In this passage of Scripture, John sets the standard high for believers with the example of the sacrificial life and death of Jesus. Often, we opt out of involvement with others on the basis of our circumstances or our personalities. We tell ourselves we are shy or overwhelmed or consumed by work or self-oriented interests. Yet no matter how we couch our reasons and excuses, a closed heart is an offense to God, who kept nothing back from us.

Listen To …

Such was God's original love for man that He was willing
to stoop to any sacrifice to save him; and the gift of a
Saviour was the mere expression of that love.

—*Albert Barnes*

DAY 2

———

True Love

In *Mortal Lessons: Notes on the Art of Surgery*, Dr. Richard Selzer writes with scalpel-like precision about being in the presence of true love:

> I stand by the bed where a young woman lies, her face postoperative, her mouth twisted in palsy, clownish. A tiny twig of the facial nerve, the one to the muscles of her mouth has been severed. She will be thus from now on. The surgeon had followed with religious fervor the curve of her flesh; I promise you that. Nevertheless, to remove the tumor in her cheek, I had to cut the little nerve. Her young husband is in the room. He stands on the opposite side of the bed and together they seem to dwell in the evening lamplight, isolated from me, private. Who are they, I ask myself, he and this wry mouth I have made, who gaze at and touch each other so generously, greedily? The young woman speaks, 'Will my mouth always be like this?' she asks. 'Yes,' I say, 'it will. It is because the nerve was cut.' She nods and is silent. But the young man smiles. 'I like it,' he says, 'It is kind of cute.' All at once I know who he is. I understand and I lower my gaze. One is not bold in an encounter with a god. Unmindful, he bends to kiss her crooked mouth and I am so close I can see how he twists his own lips to accommodate to hers, to show her that their kiss still works.[4]

Lift Up ...

Lord, when I think of Your twisted body hanging on the cross—for me—I am not only humbled; I am filled with wonder. Such love! True love transcends mere words. I want to live in such a way that my words confirm my love for You and for others. In Jesus' name. Amen.

Look At ...

Yesterday, John helped us see the value and necessity of the outward love that testifies to our inward beliefs. At times, *love* involves giving up our own comforts in the best interest of others. As evidence of God's love in our lives, our hearts and hands must be open to those in need. We are known by our actions, just as Christ allowed us to know Him through His love and sacrifice.

Today, we go even deeper into self-examination. When our outward actions contradict our words, we will see that our character is devalued and God is robbed of glory. Empty words mean nothing and accomplish even less. If God abides in our hearts, our actions will verify and honor that truth. John tells us that living out the truth of God's abiding presence brings confidence and certainty.

Read 1 John 3:18–19.

My little children, let us not love in word or in tongue, but in deed and in truth. And by this we know that we are of the truth, and shall assure our hearts before Him. 1 John 3:18–19

1. Describe how Christians are commanded *not* to love.

2. In your own words, explain what Ezekiel 33:31 says about loving in this manner.

3. According to 1 John 3:18, how are we commanded to love?

4. John commands us to live out the love of God in our hearts by contrasting two ways in which Christians love: false love versus genuine love.

    a. Take the first part of the first phrase of John's command in verse 18 and combine it with the first part of the second phrase of his command:

        "Let us not love __ _____, but __ _____."

    b. Now take the last part of the first phrase and combine it with the last part of the second phrase:

"Let us not love __ _____, but __ _____."

5. If we love in deed and in truth, then what do we know?

6. Read the following verses, and record other truths about our heavenly Father.

Scripture	Other Truths about God
Exodus 34:6	
Deuteronomy 32:4	
Psalm 25:10	
Psalm 96:13	
Psalm 111:7–8	

7. What else does loving other believers in deed and truth produce?

Live Out ...

8. We learned today that actions speak louder than words. Loving people with "lip-service" not only hurts them but calls into question whether a believer is truly in fellowship with God. In what way or ways will you commit to put your love into action and provide for another's needs?

- ❏ Disciple a new believer
- ❏ Volunteer time at a shelter
- ❏ Commit to pray with someone
- ❏ Visit someone in the hospital
- ❏ Cook a meal for a family in crisis
- ❏ Babysit for a new/overworked parent
- ❏ Grocery shop for an elderly neighbor
- ❏ Other: _____

4 Loving In Deed

Loving "in word" means simply to talk about the needs of others. But loving "in deed" means meeting those needs. Loving "in tongue" means to love others insincerely. But loving "in truth" means we love them from our hearts.[5] "Therefore, as we have opportunity, let us do good to all, especially to those who are of the household of faith" (Gal. 6:10).

5 Loving in Truth

Truth is a moral and personal characteristic of God the Father, God the Son, and God the Holy Spirit. Our obedience to God's command to put His love in action verifies that we genuinely are born again. Jesus said, "Everyone who is of the truth hears My voice" (John 18:37).

7 Loving with Assurance

Assure means to have confidence, trust, or set at rest. *Heart* means the inner self that thinks, feels, and decides. Loving others is one thing we can pursue in life with absolute confidence that God is pleased and present in our efforts.

Write a prayer to the Lord, asking Him to help you remain faithful to the commitment you checked above.

Father …

10 Love That Glorifies

Good works glorify our Father in heaven, just as an obedient, kind child glorifies his earthly father and mother. "That you may with one mind and one mouth glorify the God and Father of our Lord Jesus Christ" (Rom. 15:6). Our good works should sift through the sieve of our love.

11 Loving *for* Assurance

Obediently placing God's love into action allows us to come confidently before Him at any time with a clear conscience. "Let us draw near with a true heart in full assurance of faith, having our hearts sprinkled from an evil conscience and our bodies washed with pure water" (Heb. 10:22).

9. John taught that we are to love "in deed and in truth."

a. Read Matthew 6:1–4 and record under the appropriate column what these verses say about how we are and are not to perform our deeds.

How We Are to Perform Deeds   How We Are Not to Perform Deeds

b. What does Jesus promise those who follow these instructions?

10. According to Matthew 5:16, what should be our main motive for good deeds?

11. One of the blessings of love in action is the assurance it gives our hearts before the Lord of truth. Read Romans 2:6–10. In your own words, describe what these verses say God will do when all of humanity stands before Him.

Romans 2:6

Romans 2:7, 10

Romans 2:8–9

John tells us throughout this entire book that our words are simply not enough. When our deeds verify our love for others, they are not only assured of our character and love, they see through us to see the image of Christ. The bonus here is that when we behave in this way, *we* also are assured that our beliefs are genuine.

It's true that God hates sin, but He loves sinners with a consuming passion. When the Samaritans did not receive Jesus, James and John looked for retaliation: "'Lord, do You want us to command fire to come down from heaven and consume them, just as Elijah did?' But He turned and rebuked them, and said, '… the Son of Man did not come to destroy men's lives but to save them'" (Luke 9:54–56).

The litmus test of our love for God is compassion and love for others.

Listen To …

Genuine faith that saves the soul has for its main element trust—absolute rest of the whole soul—on the Lord Jesus Christ to save me, whether He died in particular or in special to save me or not, and relying, as I am, wholly and alone on Him, I am saved.

—*Charles Spurgeon*

Day 3

Confident Love

You're sitting in the movie theater. The lights go down, the cell phones click off, the bag of popcorn on your lap is hot and buttery. You snuggle down in your chair. Now, picture this movie trailer of coming attractions (make sure you're imagining the announcer's deep, resonant voice):

> In a world … that had never heard the roar of thunder, or seen a jagged flash of lightning split the sky, or felt a single drop of rain, one man stands alone as a testimony of courage, determination, and trust in God. His name? Noah.
>
> Living in the perilous trenches of an earth saturated with sickening wickedness and constant violence, this good man not only hears the voice of God; he bravely obeys it: "Make yourself an ark of gopherwood; make rooms in the ark, and cover it inside and outside with pitch."
>
> Year after year, against all odds, the six-hundred-year-old Noah tirelessly labors amid the threats and jeers of neighbors and strangers. He builds a vessel of monumental proportions, not knowing its purpose or God's plan. Until …
>
> The sky darkens, the thunder rumbles, the sky ruptures.
>
> The rains have begun.

Even the overdramatized hype of Hollywood could not match the true drama of Noah and the great flood.

Noah was "just a man" who "walked with God" (Gen. 6:9). Even as evil swirled all around him, Noah's love and confidence in the Lord pleased God, and he found "grace in the eyes of the Lord" (v. 8)—even in the face of catastrophic disaster.

We, too, can confidently follow God through the rising waters of everyday life. Even our doubts can be subdued when we confidently obey and love the Lord.

Lift Up ...

Thank You, Lord, for the assurance and peace I have even in this dangerous world. Help me grow in love and confidence, both in my relationship with You and in the way I treat others. I know I can do this because You were the one who closed the doors of the ark, and You secured my future through Your sacrifice. In Jesus' name. Amen.

Look At ...

Yesterday John taught us that *talking* about true love is very different from *living* it out. When we love others, the evidence supports it. Our deeds demonstrate love, our confidence banishes doubt, our faithfulness means we are above reproach, and our lives give glory to God. We are assured we can stand before men and God.

Today we will look deeply at our inward lives before the Lord. At times we are fraught with uncertainty or doubt and we become confused about our lives. If we look to others for assurance concerning our actions, we can be left in confusion and despair. John showed us that God has provided a way for us to assess ourselves and our actions so we can stand confidently before Him.

Read 1 John 3:20–21.

For if our heart condemns us, God is greater than our heart, and knows all things. Beloved, if our heart does not condemn us, we have confidence toward God. 1 John 3:20–21

1. Having assured us that we belong to the truth, what does John say our hearts or consciences might try to do?

2. What does Jeremiah 17:9 say about our hearts?

3. Read the verses below, and answer the following questions.

3 Not Guilty

Condemnation is a judicial term that means to declare a person guilty and worthy of punishment. Christians who repent and trust in Jesus' forgiveness may be accused but are not condemned. "There is therefore now no condemnation to those who are in Christ Jesus, who do not walk according to the flesh, but according to the Spirit" (Rom. 8:1).

4 All-Knowing

Omniscience is a theological term that refers to God's superior knowledge, wisdom, and power to know all things. Only the all-knowing and all-powerful God can guarantee our freedom from sin and condemnation. "Now the Lord is the Spirit; and where the Spirit of the Lord is, there is liberty" (2 Cor. 3:17).

6 God-Confidence

True Christians know they will sin. They also know that sin, if confessed, is not a barrier to a confident approach to God. Even when our hearts do condemn us, we can come boldly to God because of our "Advocate with the Father, Jesus Christ the righteous" (1 John 2:1).

a. Job 1:7. Who sees our deeds and has an audience with God?

b. Revelation 12:10. What is another name for this character?

4. If we do self-condemn, of what can we be certain?

5. Our loving Father knows us better than we know ourselves. Read the following Scriptures, and record what these verses say about our all-knowing God.

Scripture	Omniscient God
Psalm 139:1–2	
Psalm 139:3–4	
Psalm 139:5–6	
Isaiah 40:13–14	

6. What is the result of our hearts not condemning us?

Live Out ...

7. A self-condemning heart is put at rest based on God's knowledge of our sin and His greatness in forgiving it. In other words, God knows all about us and loves us anyway! With this in mind, list some biblical characters who had every right to have guilty, self-condemning hearts, and explain how God proved that His love was greater than their sin.

8. Obedience to show God's love to others proves we stand uncondemned before God. On the other hand, our disobedience affects our fellowship with others and with Him.

a. Has God ever asked you to help someone in need and you didn't obey?

b. Who was the person, and what were the circumstances?

c. How did this hurt your witness for Jesus and your fellowship with Him?

9. Self-condemnation robs us of the peace Jesus freely gives to all believers. But God judges "righteously, testing the mind and the heart" (Jer. 11:20).

a. Read Matthew 26:33–35. Briefly describe Jesus' and Peter's conversation.

b. Skim Matthew 26:69–75, concentrating on verse 75. What was Peter's response to his own behavior?

c. Read John 21:15–17. What did Jesus do for Peter after his fall, and what declaration did Peter make?

10. We can be our own worst enemy, but Satan stands in line to throw punches at us too. Read Micah 7:8–9. Rephrase these two verses into your own confident response to your archenemy about your Almighty God.

Do not rejoice over me, my enemy; when I fall, I will arise; when I sit in darkness, the LORD will be a light to me. I will bear the indignation of the LORD, because I have sinned against Him, until He pleads my case and executes justice for me. He will bring me forth to the light; I will see His righteousness. (Mic. 7:8–9)

8 Self-Condemnation

Confident love banishes self-condemnation. Paul wrote to assure believers that in those cases when we are guilty, the goodness of God leads us to repentance (see Rom. 2:4). Confess and ask God to forgive you. Ask Him to show you how you can serve that person or someone else today. Father, forgive me …

9 Restoration

Peter's heart condemned him, but Jesus was greater than Peter's heart. Knowing all things, Jesus gave Peter the assurance he needed to confidently serve God's people. "He who believes in Him is not condemned" (John 3:18).

Our society has a particular aversion to the word *sin*. Politicians spin their sinful antics with phrases like "Mistakes were made." While this may somewhat soften the public's reaction to bad behavior, it leaves out an important component: the offender's own conscience. In the quiet place of their interior lives, they may suffer in silence, knowing they are truly guilty. There is no way out.

In this lesson, the apostle peeled back the layers of believers' anxiety over their sin. In so doing, he exposed the glorious state of freedom from condemnation for those who live in the Spirit. Even when we find ourselves perplexed before God, He graces us with confidence to trust Him to forgive us and allow us to go forward in peaceful freedom.

As believers, we know we will sin. But Christ is our Advocate, praying for us, loving us, and restoring us to fellowship with Him and other believers. How can we resist loving Him in absolute confidence?

Listen To ...

> *The true confidence which is faith in Christ, and the true difference*
> *which is utter distrust of myself—are identical.*
> —*Alexander MacLaren*

DAY 4

Obedient Love

The place was London, England, and the year was 1554. A nineteen-year-old man by the name of William Hunter was engaged in work as a silk weaver. He was a Protestant living under the reign of the newly crowned Mary Tudor following the death of her brother, Edward VI. Queen Mary was determined to restore England to the authority of the Catholic Church. A time of persecution of Protestants began.

Following an edict to attend mass, young William was noticeably absent and was subsequently relieved of his position. Shortly thereafter, he was found reading the Bible for himself, which was forbidden. He was arrested and interrogated. After nine months of imprisonment, on March 26, 1555, he was burned at the stake for refusing to obey the Catholic Church and steadily obeying and following his faith in Christ.[6]

Obedient love is not a passive, warm feeling but a tenacious, obedient clinging and adhering to the Word of God.

Christ demonstrated the pinnacle of obedient love. "And being found in appearance as a man, He humbled Himself and became obedient to the point of death, even the death of the cross" (Phil. 2:8). Loving obedience cost Him everything. "Therefore God also has highly exalted Him and given Him the name which is above every name, that at the name of Jesus every knee should bow, of those in heaven, and of those on earth, and of those under the earth" (vv. 9–10).

Lift Up ...

Lord, I know You see and hear everything I think, do, and say. Thank You, Lord, for loving me even when my focus shifts away from You and at the times my obedience falters. Help me continue walking in obedient love. In Jesus' name. Amen.

1 Ask

The word *ask* means to call or pray for something needed or desired. Believers who demonstrate love for others and are committed to God's will and Word have freedom to boldly pray for their needs and the needs of others.

3 Abide

Scripture assures all believers that God is personal, living, loving, and active in our lives. We know that our heavenly Abba can hear our prayers and wants to "grant [us] according to [our] heart's desire, and fulfill all [our] purpose" (Ps. 20:4).

Look At ...

Yesterday we delved into the prayerful introspection that sets our hearts and minds at ease. We found that Jesus, through His work on the cross, enabled us to stand uncondemned before the Father. We learned that while we can be confident in God's all-knowing nature, we can also come to a place of peaceful self-confidence if we are unnecessarily condemning ourselves.

Today we will examine a second benefit of an obedient life of love—answered prayer. We see that the effectiveness of our prayer conversations with God are not random shots in the dark but a laid-out path of fellowship, faith, and obedience with our Lord, who longs to bless us. John articulates God's plan that guides us ever closer to Him.

Read 1 John 3:22.

And whatever we ask we receive from Him, because we keep His commandments and do those things that are pleasing in His sight. 1 John 3:22

1. Standing uncondemned and confident before God, what privilege does John say we have?

2. What will we receive from Him?

3. What prerequisites do the following verses say we must fulfill to receive answers to our prayers?
    a. John 15:7
    b. John 16:23–24

4. What is the first reason John gives for us receiving answers to our prayers?

5. Read the verses below, and answer the following questions.
   a. Romans 13:8. What command are believers given and why?
   b. Romans 13:9. What relationships do these commands affect?
   c. Romans 13:10. What is the fulfillment of the law?

6. According to 1 John 3:22, what is the second reason we receive answers to our prayers?

Live Out ...

7. What does Hebrews 13:20–21 say God accomplishes for us and in us? Do you feel peaceful confidence that you are living in the fullness God has planned for you? Why or why not?

8. Today we learned that when we keep God's commands and are obedient to do what He asks of us, we can ask for whatever we need and we will receive it from Him. Read the verses in the table below and record what inner needs are met through prayer.

Scripture	What We Receive from Prayer
Psalm 138:3	
Joel 2:32	
Luke 11:13	
Philippians 4:6–7	

4 Keep

Keep means to hold fast or fulfill a command. A commandment is a law or statute, specifically, one of the Ten Commandments given by God through Moses. "You shall walk after the LORD your God and fear Him, and keep His commandments and obey His voice; you shall serve Him and hold fast to Him" (Deut. 13:4).

6 Obey

Obedience is carrying out or *doing* the will of God. It is a positive, active response to what we hear and learn from God's Word about what He desires. Obedience is a key to receiving God's blessing and favor. "Behold, to obey is better than sacrifice" (1 Sam. 15:22).

7 Peace

The Hebrew word *shalom* carries many meanings, but the basic idea is that of being whole or full. When we see God's faithful protection of His children, we can legitimately lie down every night in peace and rise up every morning in hope.

9 Immediate

When something happens *immediately*, it occurs in an instant, quickly, or swiftly. We love immediate answer to prayers, but we are often slow with immediate obedience. God is not so much about giving us the desired result of our prayers as He is about seeing our immediate response to His leading.

9. Have you ever asked God for something and received it immediately or soon after? Record your prayer request in your journal and how God answered you.

10. Read Isaiah 58:9–11. Under the appropriate columns, list the Lord's commands for us and our blessings for obedience.

Then you shall call, and the LORD will answer; you shall cry, and He will say, "Here I am." If you take away the yoke from your midst, the pointing of the finger, and speaking wickedness, if you extend your soul to the hungry and satisfy the afflicted soul, then your light shall dawn in the darkness, and your darkness shall be as the noonday. The LORD will guide you continually, and satisfy your soul in drought, and strengthen your bones; you shall be like a watered garden, and like a spring of water, whose waters do not fail. (Isa. 58:9–11)

The Lord's Commands	Blessings for Obedience

11. Read 1 John 3, and write a prayer asking God to help you have a heart that is right before Him and men. Ask Him to use you to be an encouragement and help to others.

Heavenly Father …

———————

Obedience is a high call and persuasive evidence of a life hidden with Christ in God.

A steady, obedient walk with the Lord can manifest in extraordinary ways for ordinary people. Loving obedience takes us out of the comfort of home and into often-hostile mission fields; it humbles us to ask for forgiveness when we ourselves have been wronged; it prompts us to open our mouths to share the gospel despite our fears.

Obedience prompted Christ to leave the glory and harmony of heaven to come to a contentious earth to save and redeem the people He loved. There can be no love without obedience or meaningful obedience without love.

Listen To ...

Our Lord told His disciples that love and obedience were organically united. The final test of love is obedience.
—A. W. Tozer

Faithful Love

In 1924 a Japanese man by the name of Hidesamuro Ueno moved to Tokyo to teach in the agriculture department at the University of Tokyo. Every morning when the professor left for work, his dog Hachiko saw him off at the front door, and every day when he returned on the train, his dog was waiting for him at the station.

Sadly, after a year and a half, Hidesamuro died, but Hachiko never wavered from his routine. Every day, at precisely the same time, the dog faithfully waited for his master at the train station.

Initially, the nearby vendors assumed the dog was waiting for someone else, but eventually they realized this loyal dog was waiting for his master—a master who would never arrive. For eleven years, Hachiko waited. He became an icon of faithfulness to the community. He was so admired that a statue of Hachiko was erected at the train station and is still a popular meeting point for travelers.[7]

We may not be aware of it, but when we follow Jesus, our faithful love is observed by others. We too wait for the return of our Master, and we will not be disappointed.

Lift Up ...

I praise You, Lord, for the life of faith and hope I have in the midst of a faithless and hopeless world. Grow me toward a greater obedience to Your Word so that I can love others, and point them toward the glorious hope that is You. In Jesus' name. Amen.

Look At ...

Yesterday we learned that a lifestyle of obedient love leads to confident prayer and pleases God. We found that the key to answered prayer is also the key to a peaceful and fruitful life.

There are no magic phrases or prayer postures, just the authentic life of abiding with Christ and knowing Him so well that our prayers reflect His will.

We close this week with the culmination of a life of love, faith toward God, and love toward mankind. In today's lesson, John reiterates the high points of being a believer. We are to follow God's commands and demonstrate them through our actions. We are reminded that our belief is in none other than the Son of God and manifested to the children He loves by the children He loves.

1 Commanded to Act

When Jesus *commands* us to action, we can assume He is giving us the direction and emphasis that a commanding officer in the army would give his soldiers. To disregard a command is to dismiss God's purpose for our life.

Read 1 John 3:23.

And this is His commandment: that we should believe on the name of His Son Jesus Christ and love one another, as He gave us commandment. 1 John 3:23

2 Believe on the Name

Believe means to have faith and trust. Believing on Jesus' name means taking God at His word and trusting Jesus for our salvation and spiritual well-being. "He who believes in the Son has everlasting life" (John 3:36).

1. What do you think John means when he tells us that Jesus commanded us to love one another?

2. What is the first part of this twofold command?

5 Choose to Love

Choosing to love the unbelieving, unlovable, undeserving, and unnoticed resonates with the pure love of God. "For God so loved the world that He gave His only begotten Son, that whoever believes in Him should not perish but have everlasting life" (John 3:16). Loving others bears witness to God's love and our trust in Him.

3. Read Ephesians 2:4. Based on this verse, whose commandment do you think John is referring to in verse 23?

4. What is the second part of God's commandment?

5. Everything John has said about love this week hinges on what one thing?

6. Read Matthew 22:37–39. What are the first and second great commandments, and how does Jesus compare them?

Live Out ...

7. The royal law, "love your neighbor as yourself," has been twisted like everything else by the world. What are some ways the world tells us to love ourselves?

7 The Royal Law

The "royal law" commands that we practice meeting the physical and spiritual needs of the people in our lives with the same intensity and concern with which we meet our own needs. "Let each of you look out not only for his own interests, but also for the interests of others" (Phil. 2:4).

9 The First Love

Praying for the salvation of the unsaved is an act of love. Even those who seem dead to the message are not beyond the love of God. "But God, who is rich in mercy, because of His great love with which He loved us, even when we were dead in trespasses, made us alive together with Christ (by grace you have been saved)" (Eph. 2:4–5).

8. Today we learned about God's single greatest command—believing on His Son's name and loving our neighbors. Read the scriptures below, and record why these verses say we should believe on the name of Jesus Christ.

Scripture	Why We Should Believe on Jesus' Name
Acts 16:31	
Romans 5:1	
Romans 5:9	
Ephesians 2:7	

9. We learned this week that if we keep God's commands and do what pleases Him, then we can confidently approach Him with our prayers and requests. Is there someone in your life who does not believe on the name of Jesus Christ?

a. Write the person's name here:

b. In your journal write a prayer for this person. Ask God to give him or her "a new heart and put a new spirit within [them]" and to "take the heart of stone out of [their] flesh and give [them] a heart of flesh" (Ezek. 36:26–27). Remember, He loves this individual even more than you do.

Lord …

10. In light of what you have learned this week, what do you think "love your neighbor as yourself" means biblically?

_____

We cannot escape God's command to manifest His love by loving others. Jesus has chosen to make Himself known through those who believe in Him. We are *commanded* to love others rather than given the discretion to find someone whom we deem worthy of the honor.

It is a fine reminder of our own condition before we were saved. And lest we come to believe we are saved out of some inner goodness, we are humbled knowing our belief in God hinges on the knowledge of our absolute unworthiness and Christ's absolutely sufficient worthiness and love that were manifested on the cross.

Christ is the capstone of faithful love—indeed of *all* love. For while we were yet sinners, He died for us. Such love does not end when the Master is temporarily out of sight. We obediently believe, wait, love, and serve until He comes to take us home.

Listen To …

I want the love that cannot help but love; loving, like God, for the very sake of love.

—*A. B. Simpson*

Lesson Eight

Spirit Savvy

1 John 3:24–4:6

One of Aesop's Fables called *The Birds, the Beasts, and the Bat* goes like this: The birds waged war with the beasts, and each was by turns the conqueror. A bat, fearing the uncertain issues of the fight, always fought on the side he felt was winning. When peace was proclaimed, his deceitful conduct was apparent to both combatants. Therefore, being condemned by each for his treachery, he was driven forth from the light of day and henceforth concealed himself in dark hiding places, flying always alone and at night.[1]

The early church was experiencing a similar problem with false prophets. "Bats" were making their way into the Christian ranks, spreading false teachings. Apparently, they were difficult to detect, so John felt he needed to write to the church and give them some tools to test whether these teachings were of God. They could then assess for themselves whether the teachings were true.

John wanted to banish these false teachers. He reminded the early Christians of the strength and power of the Holy Spirit living in them that would guide them through their examination of these teachings.

Day 1: 1 John 3:24	**The Spirit in Us**
Day 2: 1 John 4:1–2	**The Spirits to Test**
Day 3: 1 John 4:3	**The Spirit of the Antichrist**
Day 4: 1 John 4:4–5	**The Spirit in the World**
Day 5: 1 John 4:6	**The Spirit in the Apostles**

DAY 1

The Spirit in Us

Lift Up ...

Heavenly Father, You have sealed and marked me as Your own. It is still important to hear with discernment and determine to be sensitive to the leading of Your Holy Spirit. Thank You for standing by me, making me stand firm, and guaranteeing my future. In Jesus' name. Amen.

Look At ...

Last week's lesson revealed the benefits of keeping God's commandments and living a life of love.

John patiently gave us the specifics of how we can live the Christian life in a way that glorifies God and draws nonbelievers. We found that there were no shortcuts or meaningless catch phrases that could replicate a true follower of Jesus Christ.

This week we study John's reminders of yet another blessing that comes from walking with God—the abiding presence of His Holy Spirit. As we analyze the biblical uses of the word *spirit,* we will discover that there are only two sources from which all spirits originate. John is straightforward in pointing us to evidence of our spiritual condition. It is found as close as our hearts.

Read 1 John 3:24.

Now he who keeps His commandments abides in Him, and He in him. And by this we know that He abides in us, by the Spirit whom He has given us. 1 John 3:24

1. What key word ties verse 24 to last week's lesson, indicating that John has more to tell us about the benefits of obedience to God's Word? What does John instruct us to do?

2. Explain the result of keeping His commandments.

3. Read John 14:23. How does Jesus describe this abiding relationship?

4. How do we know God abides in us?

5. Read John 14:15–17.

    a. What two terms did Jesus use to describe this Spirit?

    b. What kind of relationship do believers have with the Spirit?

    c. Based on the verses above, do you think unbelievers have God's Holy Spirit living inside them? Why or why not?

6. Match the following verses with the type of Holy Spirit manifestation described above.

    a. John 16:8 — upon

    b. Acts 1:8 — with

    c. Romans 8:11 — in

7. The Holy Spirit's indwelling presence assures us that God abides in us. Look up the following scriptures to see what else the Spirit does in the life of a believer.

Scripture	Activities of the Holy Spirit
Romans 8:26–27	
1 Corinthians 2:10	
1 Corinthians 12:13	
Titus 3:5	
Hebrews 10:15	

1 Commandment Keeper

John continues the thought from verse 23 in last week's lesson. God's chief commandment is this: believe on His Son Jesus Christ, and love one another as Jesus commanded. If we do these two things, we will keep His commandments. "You are My friends if you do whatever I command you" (John 15:14).

4 Spirit Dwelling

Spirit is translated from the Greek word *pneuma*, which means breath or wind. In this verse it refers to God's Spirit, also known as the Holy Spirit. "In whom you also are being built together for a dwelling place of God in the Spirit" (Eph. 2:22).

5 With, In, and Upon Us

Scripture refers to the Holy Spirit using three Greek prepositions: *para* or with, *en* meaning in, and *epi* or upon. He is the voice of conviction *with* the unbeliever prior to salvation. He dwells *in* the believer at the moment of salvation, and He comes *upon* the believer to empower for service and bestow spiritual gifts.

8 Welcoming Love

When we walk in obedience, it demonstrates love for Jesus and results in intimate fellowship with Him and the Father. Jesus said, "Behold, I stand at the door and knock. If anyone hears My voice and opens the door, I will come in to him and dine with him, and he with Me" (Rev. 3:20).

9 Forever Abode

The Old Testament records instances where the Spirit of God indwelt certain people such as Saul, but the extent was temporary (see 1 Sam. 16:14). It is not until the New Testament that the Bible speaks of the Holy Spirit living within a believer forever (see John 14:16).

Live Out ...

8. Taking time to dine with others indicates a desire to get to know them and deepen relationships. How would you describe your dining relationship with Jesus?

☑ We linger over meals together daily.

❑ We have a weekly lunch date.

❑ He's at my table, but I rarely include Him in my conversations.

❑ I see others dining with Him, but I don't really know Him.

9. John wants us to know that God abides *in* us through the person of the Holy Spirit. Romans 8:9, 14, and 16 from *The Living Bible* are printed below. Circle or highlight the phrases that reveal the Holy Spirit's presence in a believer's life.

a. "You are controlled by your new nature if you have the Spirit of God living in you" (Rom. 8:9).

b. "For all who are led by the Spirit of God are sons of God" (Rom. 8:14).

c. "For his Holy Spirit speaks to us deep in our hearts and tells us that we really are God's children" (Rom. 8:16).

10. In which of the above ways have you experienced the Holy Spirit? Explain how it has assured you that God really lives *in you*.

The "Fifty Percent League" is a very exclusive club with only one rule: give away at least half your income. It was founded by Chris and Anne

Ellinger, who received an inheritance and decided to give away half of their money. Anyone can join the club. Members report the decision to join this group as being one of the best they've ever made and one of the most joyful.[2]

You can bet no one takes membership in this club lightly. It would take a lot of dedication and commitment to join such an elite group. John spoke about this kind of dedication and commitment when he described what it would take for Christians to abide with God and He in them. This abiding relationship is a secure intimacy facilitated by the Holy Spirit. There's one rule to join the ranks of the abiding: obedience. Through loving obedience, access to God and all the pleasures of knowing Him are enjoyed. Obedience, like giving money away, is not always easy, but just as with the generous people who share their wealth, the decision to obey God will be one of the best and most joyful ones you'll ever make.

Listen To ...

You can give without loving. But you cannot love without giving.

—*Amy Carmichael*

DAY 2

The Spirits to Test

There exists in nature a rather devious and ruthless bird called the cuckoo. Although mainly associated with the whimsical cuckoo clock, there's nothing charming about the real cuckoo, which is known for parasitism. Rather than building its own nest, it lays its egg in another bird's nest. The unsuspecting bird incubates and rears the baby cuckoo. In order to diminish the chances of its egg being rejected, the adult cuckoo will push one or more legitimate eggs from the nest. Equally horrifying, the baby cuckoo, once hatched, will eliminate competition by heaving the other eggs or nestlings out of the nest.[3] The mother bird, if she is unable to detect the imposter cuckoo egg, runs the risk of losing some of her own eggs or nestlings.

What a heartbreaking thought. It was with this kind of concern that John wrote to the early Christians about the false prophets making their way into the church. John urged the young believers to be watchful about new teachings being introduced. Even if a teaching had the appearance of truth, it was important to analyze it carefully, or it could very well hatch into trouble that would threaten the congregation.

While some might argue that the cuckoo is only following its natural instinct and therefore not really cruel, no such statement could be made about Satan. His plans are always deliberate and aimed at destroying God's work.

Lift Up ...

Dear Lord, protect Your church from the Enemy's lies and give our leaders discernment. Remind me to look to You alone for answers and to verify teachings against the truth of Your Word. In Jesus' name. Amen.

Look At ...

We've learned about the tremendous benefits of having God's Spirit living inside us. We considered the dilemma of finding evidence of the resident Spirit of God. John assured us that the evidence was not hidden from us but found in our obedience to God. Being filled with the Spirit is a condition that is all encompassing: He is with us, in us, and upon us.

Next, John warns against blindly receiving everyone who claims to be His spokesperson. He reminds us to actively be involved in what we hear by testing the validity of what we hear and the credibility of the one who speaks it.

Read 1 John 4:1.

Beloved, do not believe every spirit, but test the spirits, whether they are of God; because many false prophets have gone out into the world. 1 John 4:1

1. What does John lovingly warn these Christians *not* to do?

2. What does he admonish them to *do*, and for what purpose?

3. Why is it so important to test the spirits?

4. What does John emphasize about the number of false prophets? Why do you think this was important?

5. The "sheep's clothing" Jesus mentioned in Matthew 7:15 probably referred to the wool garments worn by shepherds. False prophets don't just pretend to be sheep; they impersonate shepherds.[5] Read 2 Peter 1:20–21, and answer the following questions.

a. Where does true prophecy originate?

1 Discern the Spirit

Spirit is used to describe the forces that guide and inspire teachers and doctrines. Behind every spiritual teacher is a spiritual influence, and it isn't always God's. "The Spirit expressly says that in latter times some will depart from the faith, giving heed to deceiving spirits and doctrines of demons" (1 Tim. 4:1).

2 Test the Teachings

Test is a word used to describe the process by which metals are evaluated for purity. All teachings should be tested. We know a teaching is of God if it agrees with "the words of the LORD [which] are pure words, like silver tried in a furnace of earth" (Ps. 12:6).

4 Watch for False Prophets

A *prophet* is one who exhorts, reproves, or foretells future events under God's influence, while a *false prophet* teaches false doctrine in God's name.[4] Satan uses "false prophets, who come to you in sheep's clothing, but inwardly they are ravenous wolves" (Matt. 7:15).

5 Look for Good Fruit

Jesus said false prophets
would be known by their
fruits. "A good tree can-
not bear bad fruit, nor can
a bad tree bear good fruit"
(Matt. 7:18). The char-
acter and lifestyle of the
prophet is as important as
his message.

8 Check the Source

The Thessalonians treated
Paul and Silas poorly, and
they were sent away to
Berea under the cover
of night. The Bereans
gave them a much better
reception and were more
open-minded and willing
to hear Paul and Silas, but
they were also diligent
to check their message
against Scripture.

b. Describe the character and lifestyle of a true prophet
of God.

6. Read 2 Timothy 1:13–14. How do we test every teaching according to Paul?

Live Out ...

7. Have you ever heard a teaching or read a "Christian" book that
didn't seem right? Sometimes it's difficult to distinguish between personal preference and true discernment. Which of the following are valid
criteria for judging whether the Spirit of God is behind a teaching?

❑ Unattractive presentation   ❑ Makes me uncomfortable

☑ Doesn't exalt Jesus Christ   ❑ Doesn't agree with my
                                       denomination's beliefs

☑ Contradicts Scripture   ☑ Overemphasizes one truth
                                      and neglects the whole

8. John links spirits that are not "of God" with false prophets. While
false teaching is often very persuasive, the apostle Paul said of himself,
"And my speech and my preaching were not with persuasive words of
human wisdom, but in demonstration of the Spirit and of power, that
your faith should not be in the wisdom of men but in the power of God"
(1 Cor. 2:4–5).

a. Read Acts 17:10–11. How did the Bereans respond
to Paul's teaching?

b. What do you learn from their example?

9. We've learned that the word *spirit* can refer to (1) God's Spirit or
(2) deceiving spirits who propagate false doctrine through false prophets.
It can also refer to our personal affections, emotions, and disposition.

Find verses that describe (1) a spirit upon which God looks favorably and (2) a spirit that displeases Him. *(Example: a patient spirit and a proud spirit in Eccles. 7:8.)*

Pleases God   **Displeases God**

Family traditions can be warm and wonderful, making us feel like we belong and share in special family wisdom and customs. Over time, we can blindly adhere to a family custom without thinking it through. For instance, one man cut two inches off a new broom handle because his family always did. To his embarrassment, he learned that a relative down the line had a short broom closet that necessitated the reduction. Then there was the bride who cut off the ends of a roast before baking it because her mother and grandmother did. She learned that grandma did it because her roasting pan was too small to accommodate a full roast.[6]

When it comes to accepting the opinions and teachings of others, we must constantly verify what we hear in light of the Word of God. When we blindly follow teachings without filtering them through the fine sieve of Scripture, we are on perilous ground. No tradition, custom, or ritual should ever take the place of digging through the Word for ourselves to see if what is being taught is truly godly. Don't follow any teaching without giving it thought and prayer.

Listen To ...

> *Discernment is not a matter of simply telling the difference between right and wrong; rather it is telling the difference between right and almost right.*
>
> —*Charles Spurgeon*

The Spirit of the Antichrist

Designer handbags cost a lot of money not only because they are well crafted but also because they are status symbols. A bag speaks of the owner's personal taste and is an indicator of her social and economic status. Because designer handbags are so popular and coveted, counterfeits flood the marketplace in an effort to cash in on a designer's reputation.

A discerning shopper can take measures to avoid getting ripped off. The surest way is to purchase the bag from a manufacturer's retail store, a reputable boutique, or a department store. As a rule of thumb, the genuine article won't be found at a flea market or from a street vendor.

There are also a few tip-offs to look for that might give away the fake. If the price is too good to be true, it probably is. A genuine designer bag usually carries a hefty price. Another indicator is the stitching: it should not be slanted or sloppy; quality stitching is a hallmark of a fine handbag. The bag should have the proper logo, charms, and attachments. If any of these are missing, it's a fake. The material, lining, and serial number of the bag are also signs of authenticity.[7]

Who knew buying a designer purse could be so difficult? Just as there are ways to detect a counterfeit bag, there are ways to test whether a spiritual teaching is godly or ungodly. Fakes among the body of Christ aren't always easy to detect, but through John's teachings, we learn that God has given us criteria to judge the authenticity of any spiritual message.

Lift Up ...

Lord, You hold the key to my salvation, and thankfully, that can never be taken away. Yet I want to be alert for those who might distort Your Word in the hope of creating confusion and doubt. Make me mindful that the deceiver delights in nothing more than sending imposters to imitate You. In Jesus' name. Amen.

Look At ...

Yesterday we learned that deception is one of the key weapons in Satan's arsenal. He especially loves to employ this device through people who claim to be shepherds of God's flock. John told us we have a sure process we can use. We can test the teachings, observe the fruits, and rely on the guidance of the Holy Spirit.

3 Who Is Jesus?

Today John gives us specific tools with which to test the spiritual validity of any teaching. We are to consider the source of the information and understand the cunning ways of Satan. Lies are often packaged in appealing ways and by appealing people. As important as understanding the Antichrist of prophesy, we are to be discerning of those who rise up against Christ today.

False teachers in John's day denied the simultaneous humanity and deity of Jesus Christ. They taught that Jesus only appeared to be human but did not suffer pain on the cross. Others taught that "the Christ" descended on Jesus at His baptism and departed before the crucifixion.

Read 1 John 4:2–3.

By this you know the Spirit of God: Every spirit that confesses that Jesus Christ has come in the flesh is of God, and every spirit that does not confess that Jesus Christ has come in the flesh is not of God. And this is the spirit of the Antichrist, which you have heard was coming, and is now already in the world. 1 John 4:2–3

1. What does John want us to know?

2. How can we discern whether a spirit is "of God"?

3. How can we know if a spirit is "not of God"?

4. According to 1 Corinthians 12:3, how does our confession about Jesus Christ determine whether we are of God?

5 Who Is the Imposter?

Antichrist means against or instead of Christ. The Antichrist who comes to power during the tribulation period (see Rev. 13) will be the "ultimate embodiment of all the antichrist spirits that have perverted truth and propagated satanic lies since the beginning."[8]

6 Who Perverts the Truth?

Satan's primary goal is to pervert the truth about Jesus Christ. John elaborated on "the spirit of the Antichrist" in 2 John 1:7: "For many deceivers have gone out into the world who do not confess Jesus Christ as coming in the flesh. This is a deceiver and an antichrist."

8 Who Is the Greatest?

First John 4:4 tells us that because we are of God, we have already overcome. "He who is in you is greater than he who is in the world." The way to overcome the spirit of the Antichrist is to abide in God.

5. If a spirit is not of God it must be the spirit of whom?

6. What prediction had these readers heard, and how was it being fulfilled during their lifetime?

Live Out ...

7. John contrasts the Spirit of God with the spirit of the Antichrist. The following verses identify the ways in which these two opposing spirits work. Summarize the verses under each column in your own words.

Spirit of God	Spirit of the Antichrist
a. John 16:13	a. Revelation 12:9
b. Romans 8:2	b. Luke 8:12
c. Ephesians 3:16	c. 1 Peter 5:8

8. Look at the characteristics of the spirit of the Antichrist as listed above. Now think about a situation where the spirit of the Antichrist is at work. Which of the following will you do to bring God's light and truth to that situation?

❏ Battle the Enemy's forces through prayer and/or fasting

❏ Share my testimony with the person involved at the risk of being vulnerable

❏ Offer practical help to the person who is suffering

❏ Other: _____

In your journal write a prayer asking God to reveal exactly how He wants to use the power of His Holy Spirit through you in this situation.

9. In the process of distorting the truth about Jesus Christ, the spirit of the Antichrist seeks to shift worship away from Him. Which of the following things have you been tempted to worship instead of Christ?

❏ Material things ❏ Social media ❏ Addictive substances

❏ My career ❏ Church activities ❏ Other: _____

If you have allowed any of the above to become your focus in life, confess it to God now. Renounce your dependence on these things in a prayer.

9 Who Are You Worshipping?

The enemy can be hard to identify. He will use seemingly innocent avenues to access our devotion. Be on guard as you "give unto the LORD the glory due to His name; worship the LORD in the beauty of holiness" (Ps. 29:2).

———————————

Certain vocations garner a lot of respect from Americans. Members of the Armed Forces are among them. The men and women serving the USA have earned the admiration of their fellow citizens because everyone knows it takes courage and commitment to wear the uniform. A lot of training, both physical and mental, is required. Military personnel must pass rigorous testing on and off the field. Those who have fought in conflicts were put in danger and risked their lives. Those in command put the lives of those under them on the line on a daily basis, often sending them into volatile situations. Sometimes they don't return or they return with the physical and emotional scars of war.

Hard work, persistence, and dedication go into serving the United States. If someone claimed to be a military person yet never received any training or served in any capacity, what kind of reception would this imposter receive if discovered? The immediate shock and outrage we feel toward anyone who falsely claims to serve our country in uniform should pale in comparison to our outrage toward a teacher of false doctrine.

Be on the lookout. If a teaching or person is found to be false, cast it out without a second thought. We should have no tolerance for false spiritual teachings or anyone delivering such messages.

Listen To ...

Every Christian is either a missionary or an imposter.
—*Charles H. Spurgeon*

The Spirit in the World

In a healthy family, there is a beautiful simplicity about how small children trust their parents. Without worrying about their parents' capacity to provide, infants will cry for food, comfort, and attention. As children grow, so does their awareness, and eventually they respond to a daily routine involving meals, play, and bedtime. Home becomes a place of safety and security, and parents a source of provision, love, and care. This sense of belonging contributes to healthy physical and mental development. Sadly, many children don't know this kind of security. Due to different circumstances, they find life to be a constant search for food, shelter, and safety—a battle for survival. It's a heartbreaking situation known everywhere in the world.

With these two contrasting images in mind, consider God's relationship with His children. He desires to be the provision and safety His children need. He is the strength and power that can overcome the world. He is willing and able to protect us. We are His, and we don't have to worry about His capacity to take care of us. Like little children, we need only put our trust in Him and wholly depend on His strength. We are not Fatherless.

Lift Up ...

Lord, I stand in awe of You. What a relief to know that even though the spirit of the Antichrist works *in* the world, You are sovereign *over* this world. I have the supreme privilege of being a child of the King. In Jesus' name. Amen.

Look At ...

Yesterday we contrasted the disparity between the Spirit of God and the spirit of the Antichrist. We found that Satan will pervert the truth, make false claims, cast doubt or confusion, and

2 Know Your Strength

Overcome is translated *niko*, from the Greek noun *nike*, which means victory. As believers, we are victorious over (1) the worldly spirit in our sin nature, (2) the opposition of the spirit in the world and those who yield to it, and (3) the world's ruler: Satan.[9]

4 Know the Enemy

Even though "we do not wrestle against flesh and blood, but against principalities, against powers, against the rulers of the darkness of this age, against spiritual hosts of wickedness in the heavenly places" (Eph. 6:12), believers need not fear, because the power of God is in us.

5 Know That You Know

In John's time, the Gnostics were among the intellectual giants of the day. They were well educated and tried to intimidate believers by appearing to have greater knowledge. John encouraged believers not to fall for this outward appearance but to rely on the power of God within them.

tempt us to worship false idols. He likes nothing better than to parade himself as godlike, but he is an imposter, a phony.

Today we look at the distinction between mere knowledge and godly certainty. John shows us that knowledge appeals to the world, while certainty speaks to the heart of the believer in Jesus Christ, even as we reside in a corrupt world. We must know what we believe, in whom we believe, and why we believe. The world is armed with lies, and we must be armed with the truth. Today John reminds us that as children of God, we are victorious over the schemes of the wicked one.

Read 1 John 4:4–5.

You are of God, little children, and have overcome them, because He who is in you is greater than he who is in the world. They are of the world. Therefore they speak as of the world, and the world hears them. 1 John 4:4–5

1. Whose children does John address?

2. John reminds these believers that they have overcome whom? (Hint: look back to v. 1.)

3. Children of God overcome the wicked one and his forces because of what relationship?

4. How does John compare "He who is in you" to "he who is in the world"?

5. Those who are not of God are of what?

6. Because of their origin, *how* and *with whom* do they communicate?

Live Out ...

7. John reminds us that we have overcome the spirit in the world by virtue of our position as God's children and the indwelling power of His Holy Spirit. Jesus said, "In the world you will have tribulation; but be of good cheer, I have overcome the world" (John 16:33). Look up the verses, and fill in the chart with the blessings that belong to those who overcome.

Scripture	Blessings Belonging to Overcomers
Revelation 2:11	
Revelation 3:5	
Revelation 3:12	
Revelation 3:21	
Revelation 21:7	

6 Know False from Truth

False prophets and teachers are human expressions of demonic spirits.[10] They speak like the world, not like God. Satan, the ruler of this world, has an agenda that is marked by the spirit of the Antichrist. Jesus said, "The ruler of this world ... has nothing in Me" (John 14:30).

8 Know the Victor

Scripture records that Elijah was able to see into the unseen spiritual realm of angels surrounding the city that was encircled by the Syrian army. "Do not fear, for those who are with us are more than those who are with them" (2 Kings 6:16).

8. John calls us "overcomers," and Paul reminds us that we are "more than conquerors through Him who loved us." He goes on to say, "For I am persuaded that neither death nor life, nor angels nor principalities nor powers, nor things present nor things to come, nor height nor depth, nor any other created thing, shall be able to separate us from the love of God which is in Christ Jesus our Lord" (Rom. 8:37–39).

In your journal write about a time when you conquered one of the hindrances listed above by abiding in God's love.

9. The spirit in the world speaks the world's language, but "we have received, not the spirit of the world, but the Spirit who is from God" (1 Cor. 2:12). Find a scripture that reflects God's truth for one or more of the worldly statements below.

a. "Believing in God is enough. You don't need to be a fanatic."

b. "God is a god of diversity. He accepts all religious views."

c. "If it feels right and makes me happy, God must be okay with it."

———————————

Galileo Galilei was born in Pisa, Italy, in 1564. He lived during a time of great intellectual activity and scientific discovery. He made contributions to the worlds of physics, mathematics, astronomy, and philosophy, including the invention of the thermometer and a military compass and the perfecting of the telescope. During his lifetime he championed the unpopular idea that the earth was not the center of the universe and that it rotated around the sun. This contradicted the church's teachings, and Galileo was accused of heresy and brought before the Inquisition. While he was not found guilty, he was censured from spreading this teaching.

Many years later Galileo wrote about this subject again and found himself before the Inquisition for a second time; this time he publicly confessed it was wrong for him to espouse this view and was allowed to live out his remaining years under house arrest.[11]

The world isn't always receptive to the gospel of Jesus Christ. It is unpopular with those who wish to live under their own rules. John wrote to the early church, asking them not to be discouraged that they carried an unpopular message but to be encouraged that God was greater than any opposition they would face. Interestingly, in 1989 NASA launched the Galileo spacecraft to Jupiter, and in 1992 the Vatican formally and publicly cleared Galileo of any wrongdoing.

One day, God will set all things right for those who believe in Him.

Listen To ...

Our God is greater, our God is stronger, God, You are higher than any other; our God is healer, awesome in power, our God, our God.
—*Chris Tomlin*

DAY 5

The Spirit in the Apostles

Advances in 3D technology have resulted in more film and television offerings with this feature. The process by which it works, amazingly, is not that complicated. Essentially, 3D films are captured using two lenses placed side by side, like your eyes. 3D movies are actually two films playing at the same time through polarized filters; one is meant for your right eye, the other for your left. The special glasses are also polarized, and they filter the images, giving each eye a slightly different perspective. Your brain combines both images to create the 3D effect.[12]

Have you ever been to a 3D movie and taken off your glasses to see what the screen looks like? The images appear blurred because without the polarizing filters, the brain can't combine the images.

The message of Jesus Christ as Savior was confusing to many during the time of the early church. They could not reconcile the person of Jesus Christ with His deity. As a result, many people would not or could not believe. John pointed out that those who were of God would believe the message that he preached because it was of God. These believers wore "glasses" that allowed them to see the true picture and full dimension of the gospel. Those who did not believe did not respond to the message of the gospel—to them, the "image on the screen" was a confusing blur.

Lift Up ...

Dear Lord, I want to see You with spiritual eyes and hear Your Word with spiritual ears. I pray that Your Holy Spirit will do its work in me. Then, as a body of believers, I pray that we are unified in our honor for You and that our unification can easily be seen and heard by the world. In Jesus' name. Amen.

2 Listen Closely

Hearing doesn't simply refer to the process of sound waves entering the ear to be interpreted by the brain. It means actually listening, giving heed to, and obeying what is said. "He who has ears to hear, let him hear" (Luke 14:35).

3 Align with Truth

The Spirit of truth refers to God's Holy Spirit, while the spirit of error is a deceiving spirit seeking to seduce by deceptive or fraudulent means.[13] Holy Spirit-inspired teaching aligns perfectly with Scripture.

5 Be Steadfast in Doctrine

The true church was known for their dedication to the message of the gospel as taught by the apostles and not by variations or new revelations. "And they continued steadfastly in the apostles' doctrine and fellowship, in the breaking of bread, and in prayers" (Acts 2:42).

Look At ...

Yesterday John helped us affirm what we know as children of God and be aware of what we are up against while we live in a world under the rule of Satan; it is important to be wise and alert, ready to assess the strategies of any force or person who is against Christ. John affectionately calls us "little children," but he does not want us to be gullible or defenseless.

Today we talk about the importance of having good hearing. The world hears the voice of Satan and responds to it. Believers possess the resident Spirit of God and recognize His voice when they hear it "spoken before by the holy prophets, and … the apostles of the Lord and Savior" (2 Pet. 3:2).

Read 1 John 4:6.

We are of God. He who knows God hears us; he who is not of God does not hear us. By this we know the spirit of truth and the spirit of error. 1 John 4:6

1. John described the false prophets as being "of the world" in verse 5.

> a. What contrasting phrase does he use to describe those who preach the unaltered message of Jesus Christ?
>
> b. What word in this passage lets you know John considers himself among the true prophets?

2. What test does he offer to determine who knows God and who is not of God?

3. What do we know based on the results of this test?

4. Based on what you've learned so far, contrast who you think is behind both (1) the spirit of truth and (2) the spirit of error.

5. *False teachers* are described in Jude 4 as "ungodly men" who "have crept in unnoticed." Read Jude's description of these teachers in Jude 12–13, 16–19, and answer the following questions.

      a. What picturesque words and phrases give you insight into the character of these false teachers?

      b. What symbolic language reveals that perverting the gospel message is serious business (v. 13)?

      c. Jude encourages true believers to remember whose words (v. 17)?

      d. What key phrase lets you know false teachers cannot be "of God"? (v. 19)

6. In striking contrast to the false prophets mentioned in Jude, Paul describes true apostles in the passage below. Circle the phrases that are *opposite* the description of false prophets and teachers.

For our exhortation did not come from error or uncleanness, nor was it in deceit. But as we have been approved by God to be entrusted with the gospel, even so we speak, not as pleasing men, but God who tests our hearts. For neither at any time did we use flattering words, as you know, nor a cloak for covetousness—God is witness. Nor did we seek glory from men, either from you or from others, when we might have made demands as apostles of Christ. But we were gentle among you, just as a nursing mother cherishes her own children. So, affectionately longing for you, we were well pleased to impart to you not only the gospel of God, but also our own lives, because you had become dear to us. (1 Thess. 2:3–8)

8 Be Christ-Wise

The world's wisdom comes from the spirit of error and appeals to those who don't know God; "the wisdom of this age ... [and] the rulers of this age ... are coming to nothing" (1 Cor. 2:6). In contrast, "Christ Jesus ... became for us wisdom from God" (1 Cor. 1:30).

9 Be Word-Filled

"The Bible contains God's final and complete written revelation to man (see Jude 3 and Rev. 22:18–19). Currently the Holy Spirit instructs and guides a believer, not by revealing newly inspired data, but by bringing illumination to God's already revealed Word."[14]

Live Out ...

7. Those who know God listen to scriptural suggestions, exhortations, and godly counsel. Think about someone who is of God and speaks the truth to you in love. Which of the following describe your usual reaction to this person?

❏ Anger   ❏ Embarrassment   ❏ Justification and excuses

☒ Thanksgiving   ☒ Humility   ❏ Other: _____

In your journal write a prayer asking God to give you a teachable spirit so that, even when someone gives you *unsolicited* advice with an *unbiblical* attitude, you can hear the truth and allow God to use it for good in your life.

8. John reminds us that those who know God heed the words of apostolic teaching. But the spirit of error seeks to deceive us into thinking there must be answers beyond those found in God's Word.

a. In which of the following places have you looked for answers, either *before* or *instead of* turning to God's Word?

❏ Women's magazines   ❏ Psychics   ❏ Secular psychology

☒ Advice of others   ❏ Talk shows   ❏ Other: _____

b. Describe how the answers found in these places distorted God's truth and led you astray.

9. According to 1 Corinthians 2:9–10, "'Eye has not seen, nor ear heard, nor have entered into the heart of man the things which God has prepared for those who love Him.' But God has revealed them to us through His Spirit. For the Spirit searches all things, yes, the deep things of God."

a. Write a prayer telling God what you long to see, hear, or understand.

b. Now thank God for giving you His "Spirit of truth [who] will guide you into all truth … and … tell you things to come" (John 16:13).

The compass, like any tool, is impartial to its user or the surrounding conditions. It does what it does regardless of circumstance. While there are various kinds of compasses, all do the same thing: a pointer aligns itself to the earth's magnetic poles and indicates where north is. From that true point, the navigator is able to determine a course to reach his destination.

A compass has no power to dictate or command action; it merely reflects a truth: north. Not knowing how to use the compass renders it useless. God's Word is our compass. Putting it into practice requires that we read it with comprehension. When we understand His Word, through the help of the Holy Spirit, we are able to make decisions about whether to accept or reject what we hear.

When we dedicate time and effort to studying God's Word, those trying to point us in the wrong direction will not draw us off course. God's Word won't *make* us do anything—taking action is up to us. But if we want to go deeper in our relationship with God, the study and application of His Word are essential. Jesus is our True North.

Listen To …

We must come back to the soul and to God who made it. We were made for Him, we are meant for Him, we have a correspondence with Him, and we will never come to rest until, like that needle on the compass, we strike that northern point, and there we come to rest—nowhere else.

—Martyn Lloyd-Jones

Love Defined

1 John 4:7–16

In 1984 pop icon Tina Turner released the song "What's Love Got to Do with It," which hit the top five in the United States and United Kingdom. It was ranked #309 on *Rolling Stone* magazine's list of "The 500 Greatest Songs of All Time" and #38 on Songs of the Century.

> *What's love got to do, got to do with it*
> *What's love but a sweet old fashioned notion*
> *What's love got to do, got to do with it*
> *Who needs a heart when a heart can be broken*

Human love is fickle and can change from day to day based on our emotions. God's love, however, is infinite and never changes. If you Google "What is love," you will find over four billion returns. From song lyrics to articles trying to characterize exactly what love is, we are all trying to define love. We live in a world where some celebrity marriages are shorter than the average person's vacation. *Merriam-Webster* defines *love* as "a feeling of strong or constant affection for a person."[1]

This week, we learn what God says love is. He simply defines it as Himself. God is love. Any other definition cannot adequately describe it. If we want to find true love, we have to find the One who created it and who *is* love, God Himself. We can be jaded by the lie of this world and ask ourselves, *What does love have to do with it?* God will show us this week that love has everything to do with it, because love is the answer. We don't have to continue questioning it or searching for it, because if we know God, we will know love.

Day 1: 1 John 4:7–8   **The Provider of Love**
Day 2: 1 John 4:9–10   **The Proof of Love**
Day 3: 1 John 4:11–12   **The Pattern of Love**
Day 4: 1 John 4:13–15   **The Proclamation of Love**
Day 5: 1 John 4:16   **The Picture of Love**

DAY 1

The Provider of Love

Lift Up ...

Dear Lord, thank You for allowing me to be Your beloved. Thank You for showing me what true love is by sending Your Son to die for my sins and give me eternal life. Help me to daily walk in that love and, in turn, pour it out on others. In Jesus' name. Amen.

Look At ...

Last week we learned about the Spirit of God. There is a defining standard, and we should test the spirits because some of them are false. These spirits are of the world and can deceive us if we aren't diligent in our faith. They speak and act just as the world. But we are not of this world; we are of God, who hears us and allows us to understand Him.

This week we learn that there is also a standard for the love of God: God Himself. Just as there are spirits of the world, there is love that is deceiving and can fool us into believing we have the real deal. Today we will read how to determine if we have the real-deal love. It's by knowing the real-deal God.

Read 1 John 4:7–8.

Beloved, let us love one another, for love is of God; and everyone who loves is born of God and knows God. He who does not love does not know God, for God is love. 1 John 4:7–8

1. How does John refer to the reader? What does this tell you about who he is speaking to?

2. John reminded his brethren to do what?

1 Be Loved

Beloved is being loved by God, Christ, and one another and is found over a hundred times in the Bible. John uses it five times in this epistle alone. John is speaking to fellow believers.

2 Be Brotherly

True love originates with God and flows from God. God makes this kind of love evident to us, for "concerning brotherly love you have no need that [anyone] should write to you, for you yourselves are taught by God to love one another" (1 Thess. 4:9). How well we love our neighbor reflects how well we know God.

6 Be Loving

John Walvoord writes, "Since God is love, intimate acquaintance with Him will produce love."[2] As we read God's Word, talk with Him in prayer, and follow the guidance of His Holy Spirit, we come to know Him more intimately, and the love, which He has poured out in our hearts by the Holy Spirit, becomes evident to everyone we meet.

3. Where does John say this demonstration of love begins?

4. List the two truths concerning everyone who loves.

5. When we love others, we prove we are members of God's family. We are His elect, His chosen ones. Read Colossians 3:12–13, and describe how we are to show love to others.

6. Can the person who does not love know God? Explain why or why not.

Live Out ...

7. Today we learned that God is the very definition of love. Look up the following scriptures, and match the references with other definitions of God.

God is a strong tower.   Deuteronomy 4:24

God is Spirit.   Psalm 61:3

God is a sun and a shield.   Psalm 84:11

God is light.   John 4:24

God is a consuming fire.   1 John 1:5

8. Living in the world today, we can get a distorted view of love. Looking into the Word of God, we can know the true definition of love. How has your definition of love changed as your life has changed?

a. Describe how you defined love before becoming a believer in Jesus Christ:

Before I was saved, I thought that love was ...

b. Now journal about how that definition changed after your salvation experience.

After I was born again, I knew that love was ...

9. In Lesson Six we learned there are only two spiritual families—God's and the Devil's. Those who do not love belong to the Enemy. Read 1 John 3:10. What are two evidences that someone is *not* of God?

10. Ask yourself this question: Have I ever professed to know God with my words but denied being His child by my actions? If the answer is yes, write a prayer of confession to the Father. Accept His forgiveness of your sin. Then tell Him what specific steps you will take to make certain that your words of faith are backed up by actions of faith. (*Example: If you failed to love your neighbor as yourself, make a plan to seek out that neighbor and do something to bless him or her this week.*)

Forgive me, Father …

My plan of action:

_____

9 Be Obedient

Love and obedience are twin evidences that we are of God. They cannot be separated or examined apart from one another. Jesus said, "If you love Me, keep My commandments" (John 14:15). It is only in obeying God that we demonstrate love, and it is only in loving God that we obey.

10 Be the Light

First John 2:15 says, "Do not love the world or the things in the world," but that doesn't apply to those in the world who are lost. As believers, we are to be like Christ, who came "to seek and to save that which was lost" (Luke 19:10).

"I Wanna Be Loved by You" is a song written by Herbert Stothart, Henry Ruby, and Bert Kalmar for the 1928 musical *Good Boy*. It was first released by Helen Kane, who became known as the "Boop-Boop-a-Doop-Girl" because of her baby-talk tagline in the song. It became her signature song, and two years later a cartoon character was created and named after Kane, known as Betty Boop. Marilyn Monroe also sang the song in the movie *Some Like It Hot* in 1959.[3]

I couldn't aspire to anything higher
and to feel the desire to make you my own.
I wanna be loved by you
just you and nobody else but you
I wanna be loved by you—alone.

So many in this world are looking to be loved, but they don't know the One who *is* love. We look to movie icons, money, jobs, and anything else we think will make us feel loved, but they are empty. Until we come into a relationship with the living God, we can't aspire to anything other than the empty promises of a fallen world. If you are seeking to be loved, seek the One true lover of your soul.

Listen To ...

We cannot help conforming ourselves to what we love.

—*Francis de Sales*

The Proof of Love

Recently, the discovery of considerable offshore oil reserves has caused a dispute over the unpopulated islands between China and Japan. Because the Senkaku Islands and the Diaoyu Islands in the East China Sea were historically claimed as part of the Ryukyu Kingdom, which had ties with the Ming Dynasty of China, China made claim to these islands. Japan occupied the islands in the late nineteenth century and had interests in the islands through World War II, when it was occupied by the United States. In 1972 the United States returned the islands to Japan, leading to Japan's claim with the full backing of the United States.[4]

Proof of ownership can quickly end any dispute, whether over a property, a vehicle, or even a pet. The same goes for proof of love. We can say we love someone; we can even write it down and send it in a letter or text message. But what is the proof of that love? Is it expensive gifts or acts of kindness that go above and beyond the norm?

God showed the proof of His love by giving His Son to die for our sins. By the active sending of His one and only Son, He forever ended the debate with undisputable proof: the sacrifice of Jesus.

Lift Up ...

Dear Lord, I can never repay You for coming to this earth to pay for my sins. You took my place, You took my judgment, and You paid the price in order to bring me life. May I not waste one precious moment of this abundant life. In Jesus' name. Amen.

Look At ...

Yesterday, we learned that God, who is love, is the true source from which all love comes. Only by grasping His unending supply of love can we truly come to understand love.

2 The Son

Only begotten Son is used four times in the New Testament. This title means the only one of its kind. John used it to emphasize the uniqueness of Jesus.[6]

3 The Life

Some people believe they must wait for heaven in order to experience eternal, abundant life. But that isn't God's intention. He wants us to live a full and fruitful life today, in the midst of our present circumstances and difficulties. The only way to live such a life is through a personal relationship with the Lifegiver: Jesus Christ.

5 The Love

God didn't ask for our love before He sent Jesus to cover our sins. He has loved us from the beginning of time. "Yes, I have loved you with an everlasting love; therefore with lovingkindness I have drawn you" (Jer. 31:3). Even without our love, God draws us near to Him through Jesus.

Today, John continues by showing us how God proved His active love for us. He didn't just speak the words and leave it at that. The *IVP Bible Background Commentary* says, "God's supreme character is His love which was revealed on the Cross with Christ."[5] God revealed His love by sending His Son. It was an act of will and choice, not just words on a page.

Read 1 John 4:9–10.

In this the love of God was manifested toward us, that God has sent His only begotten Son into the world, that we might live through Him. In this is love, not that we loved God, but that He loved us and sent His Son to be the propitiation for our sins. 1 John 4:9–10

1. In this verse, *manifest* means to reveal openly. What has been openly revealed to us?

2. How did God manifest His love toward us?

3. Where did God send His Son, and what was His purpose in choosing this particular way to reveal His love?

4. To whose love does John refer? Why is this important?

5. What has been done completely separate from us?

6. What action did God take as a result of His love, and why?

Live Out ...

7. Jesus Christ became the propitiation (appeasement or satisfaction) for our sins when He died on the cross. He paid the price a holy God demands for the sins of the world.

Read Hebrews 7:24–27:

7 The Sacrifice

No one forced the Son of God to lay down His life. Jesus chose to hang on the cross, knowing He could call down legions of angels to save Him. Michael Card's popular Christian song "Why?" sums up the decision Jesus made to be our sacrifice: if there had been no nails at Calvary, "His love would have held Him there."[8]

> But He, <u>because He continues forever</u>, has an unchangeable priesthood. Therefore He is also able to save to the uttermost those who come to God through Him, since He always lives to make intercession for them. For such a High Priest was fitting for us, who is <u>holy, harmless, undefiled, separate from sinners</u>, and has become higher than the heavens; who does not need daily, as those high priests, to offer up sacrifices, first for His own sins and then for the people's, for this <u>He did once for all when He offered up Himself.</u>

Underline or highlight each attribute of Jesus that makes Him worthy to be our propitiation. As you consider His worthiness, do you see yourself as the beneficiary of His sacrifice?

8. It's not surprising that we love God; He is lovable. But how lovable are you? The following statements paraphrase truths about love found in the Scriptures. Read each statement, then rate yourself by circling the word that best reflects how often you obey the command to love.

    a. I love my enemies and pray for them (see Luke 6:27).

      Usually   Sometimes   Rarely

10 The Knowledge

The Lamb of God knows everything about us and still loves us; isn't that shocking? "O LORD, You have searched me and known me. You know my sitting down and my rising up; You understand my thought afar off. You comprehend my path and my lying down, and are acquainted with all my ways" (Ps. 139:1–3).

b. I love others sincerely, without hypocrisy (see Rom. 12:9).

      Usually   Sometimes   Rarely

c. I show love by serving others (see Gal. 5:13).

      Usually   Sometimes   Rarely

d. I love others with genuine affection (see Rom. 12:10).

      Usually   Sometimes   Rarely

e. I show love by being kind and patient (see 1 Cor. 13:4).

      Usually   Sometimes   Rarely

9. Review your answers above. Choose one command where you checked "Sometimes" or "Rarely," and write in your journal about a specific way you will improve your love in this area. Think of someone in particular to whom you have not shown true, sacrificial love, and pray about how you can show them love this week.

10. Jesus Christ knows you intimately. He knows every sin you have ever committed and every sin you've yet to commit. Willingly, He died in your place so that you could spend eternity with Him. What else does Jesus know about you? What else has He done for you? Draw lines to match each scripture reference with its personal application.

Matthew 8:3   He knows my thoughts.

Matthew 11:28   He gives me rest.

Matthew 12:25   He calms my storms.

Matthew 14:30–31   He has compassion for me.

Mark 4:39   He cleanses me.

Luke 7:13   He saves me from sinking.

If you've ever been pulled over for a traffic violation, you know the officer typically asks for three things: proof of a driver's license, proof of registration, and proof of insurance. He is trying to verify that (1) you have the legal right to drive, (2) the vehicle you are operating is yours and is legally registered with the state, and (3) you are insured according to the state law requirements. Some people are reluctant to reach for those items, especially if they are missing one. Simply *telling* the officer you have those things will not suffice; he wants visible proof.

God willingly shows us the proof of His love without us having to ask. Without hesitancy He knows He can provide hard, factual proof to show us the extent of His love. Have you accepted the proof of His love? Do you live each day knowing He loved you before you were made and sent His Son for you?

Listen To ...

Whom should we love, if not Him who loved us, and gave himself for us?
—*Augustus Toplady*

The Pattern of Love

Meteorology is the scientific study of the atmosphere. It comes from the Greek word *metéōros,* meaning lofty, high (in the sky); from *meta,* which means above; and from *aeírō,* meaning to lift up. Part of a meteorologist's field of study is learning to understand weather patterns. In global-scale meteorology, the weather patterns related to the transport of heat from the tropics to the poles are studied.[7]

When there are several consecutive days of dry and hot weather, that is a weather pattern. When it's cold and rainy for several days in a row and then one day it changes to a warm and sunny day, that is a weather pattern change. By studying and identifying seasonal patterns in the temperature and precipitation, meteorologists can predict coming weather.

Just as a skilled meteorologist can identify weather patterns, we can see a clear pattern of God's love throughout the pages of Scripture. From John 3:16, "For God so loved the world," to Romans 5:8, "But God demonstrates His own love toward us, in that while we were still sinners, Christ died for us," we see the everlasting love of God for His children. By understanding this pattern, we should, in turn, imitate the pattern and love those whom God loves.

Lift Up ...

Dear Lord, Your Word is full of examples of the power of Your love. From healing lepers, to freeing slaves, Your love is the ultimate model for my life. You love me sacrificially and selflessly, completely and without reservation. Help me follow Your perfect pattern with people in my life. In Jesus' name. Amen.

Look At ...

Yesterday, we saw that God willingly gave us proof of His love by the sacrifice of His only begotten Son.

In today's lesson, John shows us that God sets a pattern for us to emulate His actions. In John 13:15, Jesus gave us an example of how to serve others by washing the disciples' feet: "For I have given you an example, that you should do as I have done to you." We reveal God's love to others by how we live our lives. John reminds us to love in a continual imitation of His love for us. God set a pattern for believers: He asks us to love as He loved, with devotion and sacrifice.

Read 1 John 4:11–12.

Beloved, if God so loved us, we also ought to love one another. No one has seen God at any time. If we love one another, God abides in us, and His love has been perfected in us. 1 John 4:11–12

1. What name does John use once again for the reader? How does it make you feel to be called such an intimate name?

2. What action does John refer to when he says, "If God so loved us"?

3. What should we do as a result of God's sacrificial, selfless love?

4. Who has seen God? For what time period does your answer apply?

5. If we love one another, what does John say will happen in us?

6. What else will happen?

3 Serving Others

One of the ways we show love to others is by serving them. In serving, we follow the example of our Lord Jesus Christ. He taught His followers that the one who was greatest among them was the one who was a slave to all (see Matt. 20:28).

4 Seeing God

Although we have not literally seen God, we see evidence of His existence all around us. Scripture tells us there is no excuse for denying the existence of God, as He is evident in all creation, from people to the earth, sky, and seas—all that He has made. There is no excuse (see Rom. 1:20).

6 Sanctifying Ourselves

Perfected means accomplished or completed. As we follow God's pattern of love, we see a perfect circle forming: God loves us, so we love others, then God abides in us and His love is completed in us. This circle of love is being completed in us a little more each day (see 2 Cor. 3:18 NLT).

Live Out ...

7. God demonstrated His love for us by sending Jesus to die for our sins. Look up the following scriptures, and describe other ways God has demonstrated that He loves us.

8 Sheltering Believers

While we might not always get along with other believers, we are never to be unloving. First Peter 4:8 says, "And above all things have fervent love for one another, for 'love will cover a multitude of sins.'" If Jesus' blood can cover all of our sins, our love for Him should cover the offenses of others.

Scripture	Ways God Shows His Love for Me
Psalm 3:3	
Psalm 4:7	
Psalm 13:6	
Psalm 23:3	
Psalm 27:1	

8. Love cost God what He held most near and dear. What does your love for others cost you?

a. Check each box that shows what you will invest in or spend on love this week.

❏ Invest some of my time by telephoning a friend in need

❏ Invest some of my money by giving to a homeless shelter or a missionary

❏ Spend some of my energy by helping an elderly neighbor with housework

❏ Spend some of my prayer time by praying for those persecuted for their faith

❏ Spend/invest other: _____

b. Pick one of the boxes you checked, and write a prayer asking God to bless your desire and to help you achieve your plan. Praise Him for being the supreme example of love for you to follow.

9. Verse 12 says no one has ever seen God face to face. Will God always remain such a mystery? Read the following Scriptures, and answer each question.

a. In Exodus 33:20, what did God tell Moses about seeing His face?

b. According to Matthew 18:10, who already sees God's face?

c. From Revelation 22:3–4, who can look forward to seeing His face one day?

9 Waiting Patiently

Do you long to see God in all His glory, to understand His nature, and to be in His presence? One day, He will be very real to you. Job had the assurance that His Redeemer lives and would one day rule the earth. He waited in anticipation for that glorious day (see Job 19:25–26).

10. In today's passage, we see a condition and a promise. Read the following verses, and list the condition and the promise contained in each one.

The Condition	**The Promise**
a. 1 John 4:12b	*We love one another God abides in us*
b. Exodus 19:5	
c. Deuteronomy 8:19	
d. 1 John 1:9	

11. What a wonderful promise God has given! As we love others, He will abide in us. In 1847 Henry F. Lyte wrote the song "Abide with Me."

> *Abide with me: fast falls the eventide;*
> *The darkness deepens; Lord with me abide:*
> *When other helpers fail, and comforts flee,*
> *Help of the helpless, O abide with me!*[8]

Are there times when you feel alone and occasions when it seems no one is there to help you or comfort you? The Lord your God is the Helper of the helpless. In your journal write a prayer to the One who is always there. Pour out your heart to Him. Ask Him to come to you and abide with you. He loves you very much.

In the world of beginner's sewing, it's imperative to follow patterns. The pattern teaches you how to cut the fabric, where the stitching needs to be, and how to pull it all together to accomplish the garment you are looking for. Some experts who have sewn for years can eyeball a pattern and measure it on the fly. But if you aren't one of those practiced seamstresses, you can find yourself with a hem too short, an armhole out of place, or a dress that's two sizes too small.

God gave us the perfect pattern, filled with promise. If we follow it and give the same love He gives us, it will come out perfect every time: He will abide in us and we will be perfected. Often in the church, we can get caught up in being perfect on the outside but not the inside, where God sees. We want to be right in our arguments but not in our hearts. Sometimes, it's hard for us to get along with some fellow brothers and sisters, but according to God's pattern of love, we will be known not for being perfect but for how we have loved. Not by being right, but by being loving, just as He loved us.

Listen To ...

I picked up a man from the street, and he was eaten up alive from worms. Nobody could stand him, and he was smelling so badly. I went to him to clean him, and he asked, "Why do you do this?" I said, "Because I love you."

—*Mother Teresa*

DAY 4

The Proclamation of Love

Presidential proclamations are statements issued by a president on a matter of public policy. Unless authorized by Congress, they do not have the force of law. A president can define a situation or conditions of a situation that *become* legal or economic truths.

Some proclamations are ceremonial, relating to special observances or holidays, like Thanksgiving, Veterans Day, and Father's Day. Others are substantive. These relate to foreign affairs and other sworn executive duties, like international trade, export controls, and tariffs.[9]

President Lincoln issued some of the most well-known proclamations, including the Thanksgiving proclamation and, of course, the Emancipation Proclamation, issued on January 1, 1863. This proclamation declared the freedom of slaves in ten states that were still in rebellion during the Civil War and applied to 3.1 million slaves in the United States.

Just as Lincoln proclaimed the freedom of slaves, Christ came to this world to set us free and to testify, "Therefore if the Son makes you free, you shall be free indeed" (John 8:36). While we don't need an act of Congress to make it a law, we can boldly proclaim our freedom in Christ and testify to the power of the cross.

Lift Up ...

Dear Lord, thank You for freeing me from my sin. Because of Your sacrifice, I can proclaim that I am a free Christian. I pray for the continued strength and boldness to make my confession of faith to everyone I meet, believer and unbeliever alike. Strengthen my witness, I pray. In Jesus' name. Amen.

2 The Spirit of Power

The Holy Spirit is our guarantee that we abide in God and He in us. By His power we can love others; by His strength we can love our enemies; by His might we can walk in obedience.

3 The Savior of the World

The name *Jesus* means Jehovah saves. The Father sent His Son to save us from death, judgment, and eternal separation from God. We must trust in the provision God makes through Jesus, "for there is no other name under heaven given among men by which we must be saved" (Acts 4:12).

5 The God of Change

Not all of John's fellow believers had seen Jesus in the flesh. However, they saw evidence of God's work in their midst when they observed the changed lives and the love of those who testified (reported, bore witness) and followed Jesus.[10]

Look At ...

Yesterday we learned that God has set forth a pattern of His example of substantial love. For the time being, we will not see God, but if we love one another, He abides in us and is seen in our actions. Because He loved us, He has asked us to love others in return.

Today, John guides us in understanding that through God's Spirit, we can testify that God sent Jesus Christ as a sacrifice for our sins. In today's verses, we will see the beautiful work of the Trinity in the lives of believers. It is what gives us the boldness to proclaim the good news of the gospel of Christ to all who do not yet know Him.

Read 1 John 4:13–15.

By this we know that we abide in Him, and He in us, because He has given us of His Spirit. And we have seen and testify that the Father has sent the Son as Savior of the world. Whoever confesses that Jesus is the Son of God, God abides in him, and he in God. 1 John 4:13–15

1. What can we know for certain?

2. How do we know this?

3. What can we see and testify to? What is His purpose for our testimony?

4. What must a true believer confess about Jesus?

5. What phrase is repeated from yesterday's lesson, regarding what will happen in us?

6. Read Romans 10:9–10, and answer the following questions.

    a. List the two conditions for being saved.

    b. Describe the part your heart plays in this confession of faith.

    c. Describe the part your mouth plays.

Live Out ...

7. This week we saw that <u>love for others</u> and <u>belief in Christ</u> are necessary for God to abide in us. Look again at John 14:23. What other tangible action does Christ say is necessary for the Father and the Son to take up residence in your heart?

8. Take a few moments to review some of the truths you have learned in 1 John about abiding in God. Look up the following Scriptures, and record the results of abiding.

    a. 1 John 2:6. If I abide in Him, I will …

    b. 1 John 2:28. If I abide in Him, I will …

    c. 1 John 3:6. If I abide in Him, I will …

    d. 1 John 3:24. If I abide in Him, I will …

9. Today we saw that believers in the early church knew Jesus was the Son of God because of what they *saw*, and they *testified* about what they had witnessed. Now imagine you are explaining the gospel to someone who has never heard of Jesus Christ.

    a. In your journal write about what you have *seen* as a result of your belief in Christ.

    b. *Testify* of what you have witnessed in the lives of fellow believers.

7 The Love of Obedience

Jesus often equates love with obedience in the Scriptures. If you love someone, you will be obedient to what that person says, not just in word, but in deed. "This is love, that we walk according to His commandments. This is the commandment, that as you have heard from the beginning, you should walk in it" (2 John 1:6).

9 The Testimony of Belief

The early disciples should inspire us to testify of what we have seen and heard since becoming Christ's followers. These faithful men and women were threatened and admonished to keep silent. In spite of persecution, they boldly declared that Jesus was the Holy and Anointed One.

10. Using the first line of a famous poem by Elizabeth Barrett Browning, make your own confession of love to the Lord.

How do I love Thee? Let me count the ways …

I love Thee so much that …

I will love Thee even if …

I will love Thee whether or not …

The Emancipation Proclamation did not immediately free slaves, nor did it outlaw slavery altogether, but it was the first step in the abolition of slavery in the United States. It wasn't until the December 1865 ratification of the Thirteenth Amendment that the abolition of slavery would come. But seventy-four years prior to that, the First Amendment of the Constitution of the United States was adopted, establishing the freedom of speech as a constitutional right. It states, "Congress shall make no law respecting an establishment of religion, or prohibiting the free exercise thereof; or abridging the freedom of speech, or of the press; or the right of the people peaceably to assemble, and to petition the Government for a redress of grievances."[11]

While this amendment is often misused in society, it resonates with what today's verse tells us: we have the freedom of speech through God to testify of the power of Christ Jesus in our lives. It is our right to proclaim what He has done in our lives and the many promises He has given us through His Word. If we are abiding in Him, He will abide in us. Through the Holy Spirit, we are free. Is there someone to whom you have not confessed the mighty power of Jesus? Don't wait; the freedom is yours!

Listen To …

God, the Eternal God, is Love. Covet therefore that everlasting gift, that one thing which it is certain is going to stand, that one coinage which will be current in the universe when all other coinages of all the nations of the world shall be useless and unhonored.

—*Henry Drummond*

The Picture of Love

"A picture is worth a thousand words." This phrase was coined around 1911 in a newspaper article about journalism and publicity. It proposed that a complicated situation could best be explained by a single image.

In today's digital age, complete with smartphones, iPads, and other technology, photos are more popular than ever. According to recent data, one site estimated that over the course of photographic history, over 3.8 trillion pictures have been taken. It would take nearly 145 billion iPhones to store that many photos.[12]

This week we have seen that a picture is indeed worth a thousand words. God showed us how much His love spanned time and space in order to reach out and save us through Jesus' death and resurrection.

There are over 780,000 words in the King James Version of the Bible.[13] Yet all that is necessary to sum up the message of the Bible is this: if we abide in God, He will abide in us. Through His everlasting love, He sent His Son to be the Savior of the world.

While the Internet might be inundated daily with pictures of families, food, vacations, and more, God's picture of perfect love is the one we should focus on daily. It's breathtaking—and a solid foundation for us to stand upon.

Lift Up ...

Dear Lord, thank You for loving me intently. You *are* love, and there is no better example than Your gift of salvation through Your Son, Jesus Christ. Help me to be mindful of the depth of Your love. I want to abide in You and serve You each day of my life. In Jesus' name. Amen.

1 God Is Compassionate

The problems and trials of our lives take on less significance when we remember the greatness of the Father's love toward us. His mercies endure forever; His strength is boundless. "His compassions fail not. They are new every morning; great is Your faithfulness" (Lam. 3:22–23).

2 God Is Love

Aren't we thankful that God doesn't love as we love? He loved us when we were dead in our sins, when we were miserable and wretched creatures. Even today, He loves us in spite of, not because of, who we are. Oh, thank You, most merciful God!

Look At ...

Yesterday, we found that through the Spirit, we freely testify that Jesus is the Savior of the world. Through the strength of our testimony, our belief in God, and our obedience that gives substance to our words, we are the lights penetrating a dark world. An abiding relationship with God is one of living in the Word and in prayer, as He resides in us. It's a perfect relationship between the God who loves and the children He saved.

Today, John brings us back again to stand on the powerful love of God, the One who *is* love. He tells us if we abide in love, we abide in God, and God abides in each of us. We have complete assurance of His presence in our lives. Do you want to be an abiding place for God? Then open your heart to His love.

Read 1 John 4:16.

And we have known and believed the love that God has for us. God is love, and he who abides in love abides in God, and God in him. 1 John 4:16

1. What do we know and believe?

2. What distinct phrase is repeated about God?

3. Think about this phrase. What does it mean to you today?

4. Another phrase is also repeated. What is it, and why do you think it's emphasized again?

5. In this week's lesson, count the number of times *love* is used. Now, count the number of times *abide* is used. What do these two words mean to you?

Live Out ...

6. This week we have considered the greatness of God's love. Read Ephesians 2:4–7, and answer the following questions.

    a. How is God's love described? Why do you think you can trust Him with your heart (v. 4)?

    b. Even when we were dead in trespasses, because of God's great love for us, what three things did He do (vv. 5–6)?

    c. Who will we join in the heavenly places (v. 6)?

    d. What do you think God wants to show you (v. 7)?

7. If you abide in love, God has promised that you will abide in Him, and He in you. Read the verse below, and answer the following questions regarding God's promises.

> Behold, this day I am going the way of all the earth. And you know in all your hearts and in all your souls that not one thing has failed of all the good things which the LORD your God spoke concerning you. All have come to pass for you; not one word of them has failed. (Josh. 23:14)

    a. What do you know in your heart?

    b. What have you discovered about the promises of God?

    c. What does this mean for a promise you might be waiting on today?

    d. Write a prayer of praise for what God has done, and if you are waiting on a promise, praise Him for what He is going to do.

5 God Keeps His Promises

God is the great Promise Keeper. His promise to abide in us assures us that He will never leave us alone or defenseless. Throughout His Word, God assures us of His unfailing presence, provided we abide in Him. "For He Himself has said, 'I will never leave you nor forsake you'" (Heb. 13:5).

7 God Is a Rewarder

When we are in trials, God promises not to let them go to waste. "Blessed is the man who endures temptation; for when he has been approved, he will receive the crown of life which the Lord has promised to those who love Him" (James 1:12).

8 Jesus Is the Christ

In the gospel of John, *believe* is used over eighty times. John tells us there is no way to contain all the words and works of Jesus in one book, but we were given the Bible and its contents to increase our faith and strengthen our belief that Jesus is the Christ (see John 20:30–31).

8. We can always believe God and take Him at His Word. Read the following scriptures, and record what we know and believe about God.

Scripture	What We Know and What We Believe
Psalm 32:7	
Psalm 119:64–66	
Psalm 135:5–6	
Psalm 145:8–9	

9. What an assurance that the Lord is with us always and meets our every need! Read Zephaniah 3:17.

    a. Describe a time in your life when you were in turmoil and God quieted you with His love.

    b. Now describe a time when in the midst of your joy, you felt God rejoicing over you with singing.

10. God wants you to *know* how much He loves you and to *believe* that His love will never fail. How does God demonstrate His love to you? (Perhaps He uses other people to minister to you. Perhaps there are particular verses that speak to your heart. Perhaps you feel the loving presence of His Holy Spirit in a powerful way.)

In your journal write about your experience of His love.

———————————

What would you consider the most memorable American photograph of all time? Would it be the 1963 photo of a stunned Jackie Kennedy standing by as Lyndon Johnson was sworn in as president following the assassination of John Fitzgerald Kennedy? Maybe it's the iconic image of the man staring down an approaching army tank in

Tiananmen Square in 1989? Then there's the 1945 photo of the sailor impulsively kissing the nurse in the middle of Times Square after the announcement that Japan had surrendered and the war was over.

Your most memorable photos may be more personal: your wedding or baby's pictures, a graduation, family reunion, or rusty-looking tintypes from generations past. Pictures can bring smiles to our faces, tears to our eyes, joy to our lives, and sadness to our spirits.

This week, we studied the beautiful picture of God's love, which is perfect in form and purity and given totally and without condition. The most powerful picture of God's love is the poignant image of God's only Son hanging on the cross as payment for our sins. No image can compare. His love is ever giving and everlasting, and as we grow in understanding, we stand in awe.

Listen To ...

To love God is the greatest of virtues; to be loved by God is the greatest of blessings.

—*Author Unknown*

Triumphant Living

1 John 4:17–5:5

How would you describe a triumphant life? According to *Webster's Dictionary*, *triumphant* means to delight in success, to be glad in victory, and to be made joyful by something accomplished. Some may argue that a triumphant life means accumulating a lot of money—in other words, the one who has the most toys wins.

But for believers, a triumphant life means experiencing God's perfect love. When we accept Jesus Christ as our Lord and Savior, we receive God's nature and reflect His love to others. Wrapped in God's steadfast love, we can meet the hardships and stresses of life with courage. By obeying the Lord's commands, we can stand strong in the face of worldly opposition.

This deep, triumphant life is ours only because more than two thousand years ago, Jesus paid sin's penalty and broke its power over our lives. We share in His victory over sin through our faith and trust in Him. Keep your eyes fixed on Jesus and experience a truly triumphant life. We are victors, not victims.

Day 1: 1 John 4:17–18   **Perfected in Him**

Day 2: 1 John 4:19–20   **Loved by Him**

Day 3: 1 John 4:21—5:1   **Believe in Him**

Day 4: 1 John 5:2–3   **Unburdened by Him**

Day 5: 1 John 5:4–5   **Victory through Him**

Day 1

———

Perfected in Him

Lift Up ...

Dear Lord, when I am fearful, I am not focused on You. I want to steadily grow in my love for You so that I can better love the people in my everyday life. You alone are perfect, but I strive to be more like You. In Jesus' name. Amen.

Look At ...

In the previous lesson we pondered God's love and power. We considered the abiding life—abiding in God's Word and inviting Him to abide in us through the power of the Holy Spirit. Although such things are hard to grasp, we can be assured of His presence in our lives.

Today, John brings us into the territory of a mature life in Christ Jesus. He tells us that we have reason to be bold and confident, as each of us will one day be held accountable. He goes on to encourage us to strive for a maturity that manifests in dispelling our nagging fears and replacing them with loving trust in the Lord. We are reminded that our fears reveal the imperfections of our faith.

Read 1 John 4:17–18.

Love has been perfected among us in this: that we may have boldness in the day of judgment; because as He is, so are we in this world. There is no fear in love; but perfect love casts out fear, because fear involves torment. But he who fears has not been made perfect in love. 1 John 4:17–18

1. In what way does God want our love for Him to manifest in our life?

2. How can we know our love has been perfected?

3. What day is coming that will require our bold confidence?

4. Who gives us boldness, and how?

5. Perfect love casts out what emotional condition?

6. When fears threaten, what aspect of God's character can we focus on?

7. Persistent fearfulness indicates that something has not yet happened in our lives. Reread verse 18 and write down what it says.

Live Out ...

8. How is love made perfect in us? God's love indwells us in the person of the Holy Spirit. His goal for us is that we pour out His love onto others. In that way, the Lord is manifested to them through us.

 a. What do you think it means to possess God's love in your heart?

 b. Has your recognition of His abiding love increased this past year? In what ways?

 c. Now, think about this past week and describe a moment when you showed His love to someone else.

9. Jesus died so that we would no longer have to fear. The Lord doesn't want us to panic or be immobilized by perceived dangers. Instead, we can challenge our fear with faith and knowledge of His omnipotence.

1 A Mature Love

Perfected love is a mature and productive love, "that state of mind and activity in which the Christian is to find himself when the love of God within him, expressing itself in the believer's own love, has accomplished that which God fully intends it to accomplish."[1]

2 A Confident Life

Believers do not need to fear the future, because Jesus took the punishment for our sins, and so we are beyond the reach of further condemnation. "He who hears My word and believes in Him who sent Me has everlasting life, and shall not come into judgment" (John 5:24).

3 A Bold Future

The day of judgment is an appointed time in the future when God will examine everything. He will judge the wicked and uphold the righteous. As God's children, we need not fear this day, for "we are more than conquerors through Him who loved us" (Rom. 8:37).

We all struggle with fear at various times in our lives. Circle the occurrences listed below that have caused you to feel afraid. Then, describe why you think you are, or were, afraid. Be prepared to briefly share with your group.

9 A Reasonable Fear

Healthy fear is a natural response to a perceived threat. But general fearfulness overwhelms the positive emotions of love and joy. By trusting in Jesus, we can eliminate the strongholds of apprehension and trepidation. In His name the battle is waged; by His power the victory is won.

Your death	Judgment Day
The death of someone you love	Financial reversal
Abuse	Humiliation/bullying
Rejection	Abandonment
Severe illness	Other: _____

I am (or was) afraid of _____ because _____.

10 An Unnecessary Torment

Torment involves feelings of intense fear. We can torment ourselves when we obsess about the future. God wants us to live feeling confident, loved, and secure. We can put aside fear because we are wrapped in the certainty of His love.

10. Match the following references with the message they convey. Think about a persistent fear and replace it with the victory available to you through the Word.

a. Romans 12:2   _c_ I cannot be separated from the love of Christ.

b. Ephesians 6:11–16   _a_ A renewed mind can transform me.

c. Romans 8:35   _b_ God's armor will protect me daily.

_____

Remember studying for spelling tests in elementary school? We started out memorizing short words and worked our way up to the impressive ones like *antidisestablishmentarianism* or *supercalifragilistic-expialidocious*! We were striving for that elusive "A," and step by step, our spelling abilities improved and matured.

When we commit to perfecting God's love in our lives, we undertake another challenge. As new Christians, we learn that God loved us even before we knew Him. Early in our relationship with God, He may have seemed remote and scary, but as we studied His Word, our fears gave way to awe.

Desiring to know and serve Him, we will mature in our faith. It won't happen all at once, but our faith grows stronger as we go through the tests that come in all lives. Warren Wiersbe tells us that "an immature Christian is tossed between fear and love; a mature Christian rests in God's love."[2] Let's strive for love and maturity.

Listen To ...

The knowledge of Christ's love for us should cause us to love Him in such a way that it is demonstrated in our attitude, conduct, and commitment to serve God. Spiritual maturity is marked by spiritual knowledge being put into action.
—*Edward Bedore*

Loved by Him

Human beings require love. We need to know that someone accepts and values us. Without the assurance of love, we are inclined to retreat from life or behave irresponsibly, sometimes thinking that even negative attention is better than none. Until we know someone cares about us, we are stunted in our growth and unsure of our worth.

Our lives are changed when we realize that God not only loves us right now; He loved us before we were born—even before the earth was formed! His love for us will continue throughout eternity. He pays attention; He cares; He accepts us. We are so important to Him that He wants us to know Him and have a real relationship with Him.

Such love can be a difficult concept to grasp. How can we relate to the God who created the universe? How can He care about us personally and individually? And what difference does it make to know that God loves us? The answer may seem almost too simple and too good to be true. Yet once we have sensed our need, confessed our sin, and received Christ as our Savior, the door is thrown open, and we enter into a relationship with Him. As we pray and read the Bible, we begin to understand His absolute love for us.

He cares about us. In every way.

Lift Up ...

Dear Lord, make me aware of Your unfailing love. People can be fickle and hurtful, but I know You are constant and unchanging in Your love for me. Help me love others and, in the process, glorify You. In Jesus' name. Amen.

Look At ...

Last week, we looked at what it means to be a mature believer. John assured us that we need not be focused on fear when we know the One who holds our lives.

Today, John gives us a litmus test to gauge the truth of our love. He told us that we can't profess to love God while hating someone whom God loves. Such an attitude of hatred offends God and reveals the true state of our hearts.

Read 1 John 4:19–20.

We love Him because He first loved us. If someone says, "I love God," and hates his brother, he is a liar; for he who does not love his brother whom he has seen, how can he love God whom he has not seen? 1 John 4:19–20

1. Who do we love?

2. Why do we love Him?

3. If we say we love God but hate other people, what are we?

4. Of our five senses, which sense do we use to get to know other people that we can't use to get to know God?

5. Once we truly see another person, what emotion will we feel?

6. If we do not love other people when we can see them in their humanity, how do you think we will feel about God, whom we cannot see?

3 Perfect Hatred

Hate is a strong negative reaction toward someone perceived as an enemy due to existing conflict. We are encouraged to hate only that which opposes God. "You who love the LORD, hate evil!" (Ps. 97:10).

4 Sight Unseen

Seeing is using the eyes to gain knowledge or awareness of something. It is also grasping by thinking. In other words, seeing encompasses both image and understanding.

5 Brotherly Love

Combining the Greek words *phileo* (to love) and *adelphos* (brother) gives us the word for brotherly love, *philadelphia*. Giving brotherly love means treating others as though they were part of your own family. Jesus' second commandment is "you shall love your neighbor as yourself" (Mark 12:31).

8 First Love

The Lord loved you first. Think about that in the context of the family. Before children have any capacity to love us, we love them. Our love results in nurturing them, guiding them, and providing for their every need. God loves us like that—and more.[3]

7. How would you describe the difference (or the difficulty) between loving someone you can see as compared to loving someone who is invisible?

Live Out ...

8. Hebrews 11:1 tells us that "faith is the substance of things hoped for, the evidence of things not seen." We may not see Him with our eyes, but we see Him with our hearts. Now, read the verses below to discover more about God's unseen love for you.

> Deuteronomy 33:12
>
> Isaiah 38:17
>
> John 14:21
>
> Romans 5:8
>
> Ephesians 2:4–5

9. Sometimes we find ourselves in the company of people for whom we feel no love. We might tell ourselves that this lack of love is okay because, after all, we love God, and that's what really matters. But let's look deeper.

a. Describe a recent encounter you had with someone you do not love.

b. How did you handle that situation?

c. Now, having learned you cannot love God unless you love other people, how will you change your behavior when that situation recurs?

As we study the Bible, we learn to know and love God. Through this process, we are enabled to demonstrate His love to others. Showering love on other people testifies to our love of them and the God who created them in His own image.

10. In a different scenario, we sometimes find ourselves in the company of people who don't love us! The words of Jesus in Matthew 5:44 describe four ways to respond. Please list them.

1.

2.

3.

4.

According to Matthew 5:45, what will your obedience entitle you to be called?

_____

10 Love without Limits

The way we treat other people signifies whether our love for God is real. We are to love others without insisting we receive love in return. We can boldly proclaim the gospel to unbelievers, knowing that the day may come when they receive Christ as their Savior.

Loving God is often easier than loving people. Yet our first love for God enables the second love of others. We are commanded to love other people, and our obedience will be richly rewarded when we come face to face with God. Loving beyond ourselves extracts our fear and confirms our faith.

Humbly, we realize that our love for God originated with His love for us. We are His creation, and just as we love our children, He who created us loves us. "'For all those things My hand has made, and all those things exist,' says the LORD. 'But on this one will I look: On him who is poor and of a contrite spirit, and who trembles at My word'" (Isa. 66:2).

We are given the opportunity to love others as God loves us. Even when we have grieved the Holy Spirit, provoked the Lord, and dishonored the Father, He nevertheless persists in loving us! He will never leave or forsake us, and if we seek Him, He promises to be found. This empowers us to give His love to others.

Listen To ...

*If you are having difficulty loving or relating to an individual,
take him to God. Bother the Lord with this person. Don't
you be bothered with him—leave him at the throne.*

—*Charles Swindoll*

DAY 3

Believe in Him

Question: What is the cornerstone of the Christian life? Answer: Faith.

Hebrews 11:6 explains that "without faith it is impossible to please Him, for he who comes to God must believe that He is, and that He is a rewarder of those who diligently seek Him." Our love for God brings us to belief that creates the desire to both obey and rely on Him. In 1986, Johnny Cash penned the song "Believe in Him."[4] These simple words describe what it means to believe:

> *When your good-luck ship don't come sailin' in,*
> *You must chart another course and try again,*
> *And believe in Him, free yourself from worry,*
> *Go through this life and do your best,*
> *He has promised He will take care of the rest.*[5]

The Lord requires our belief, trust, and obedience. In return, He assures us He will take care of all the rest. Charles Spurgeon summed this up by saying, "Faith and obedience are bound up in the same bundle. He that obeys God, trusts God; and he that trusts God, obeys God."[6]

Lift Up ...

Dear Lord, I know there is a difference between willful unbelief and honest questions. One is an offense to You, and the other is welcomed by You. Help me know my mind and heart and trust supremely in You. In Jesus' name. Amen.

Look At ...

In yesterday's lesson, John confronted the reality of our hard hearts and our reluctance to love others. We learned that we are compelled to generously and genuinely love others; this is the evidence of our faith and gives glory to God.

In today's lesson, John confirms these truths and commands from God. We may try to make loving another a personal ambition, but it is a solemn command and part of the DNA of being a child of God. Our union with God creates a union with our brothers and sisters.

Read 1 John 4:21—5:1.

And this commandment we have from Him: that he who loves God must love his brother also. Whoever believes that Jesus is the Christ is born of God, and everyone who loves Him who begot also loves him who is begotten of Him. 1 John 4:21—5:1

1. How does the Lord emphasize the importance of love?

2. What does He command in this passage of Scripture?

3. If we love God, what *must* we do?

4. How are people born of God?

5. Who is "Him who begot"?

6. Who is "him who is begotten of God"?

1 A Commandment

A *commandment* is an authoritative command. As described in Exodus 20, the Lord gave Moses the Ten Commandments, which are the fundamental principles underlying His covenant relationship with those who believe in Him.

2 A Union

The love of God and the love of our brothers and sisters can never be separated. If one is obeyed, the other must also be obeyed. "Grace be with all those who love our Lord Jesus Christ in sincerity" (Eph. 6:24).

3 A Must

The word *must* does not carry the same meaning as the word *should*. When you must do something, you are required and obligated to do what is asked.

7. What happens to everyone who "loves He who begot"?

Live Out ...

8. Read Leviticus 19:17–18.

    a. Below, copy the five commands believers are given regarding others.

        1.

        2.

        3.

        4.

        5.

    b. Who gave these commands?

    c. Which of these commands are not easy for you to follow? Explain why.

9 An Anointed One

To *anoint* is to rub someone with oil for the purpose of healing, setting apart, or embalming. Priests and kings are ceremonially anointed as a symbol of God's power upon them.[7] Jesus, as the begotten Son of God, was anointed as the Christ. He alone united His godly and human natures.

9. The Hebrew noun *Messiah* and the Greek noun *Christos* are translated as "to anoint." Anointing was used to signify the importance of those commissioned for a special task. Read the verses below, and write the name and title of the person described as an anointed one.

    Leviticus 4:5

    2 Samuel 1:12, 14

    2 Samuel 22:51

    Psalm 105:15

    Luke 4:18–19

10. John explains that if we love the One who begot (God), we will love His begotten (Jesus Christ). This type of love is more than a feeling. We all have to make the choice to love Jesus. With this in

10 A Relationship

To *beget* means to father a child; *begotten* refers to the child of a father. Symbolically, these words describe God's relationship to His Son and His adopted children, who experienced spiritual rebirth "having been born again ... through the word of God which lives and abides forever" (1 Pet. 1:23).

mind, use the word LOVE as an acrostic to write in your journal about how you plan to demonstrate your love of Christ to a brother or sister this week.

L (*e.g., Leave a note of encouragement*)

O

V

E

_____

The Hartford Institute is a research group that has gathered reliable information about religious life in America for the past thirty-five years. It has determined that there are currently about 350,000 religious congregations in the United States. Of these, about 314,000 are Protestant and other Christian churches, and 24,000 are Catholic and Orthodox churches. Approximately 63,000,000 people worship weekly in Protestant and other Christian churches.[8]

Wikipedia defines a megachurch as a Protestant church that has more than 2,000 members. Calvary Albuquerque has a membership of 13,500![9] Any way you look at it, there are a lot of Christians in this country.

The Scripture passage we studied today says, "He who loves God must love his brother also" (1 John 4:21). Does this mean we are to love our family members? Yes, of course. Does this mean we are to love the people who attend our church? Yes, it does.

John gave us further understanding when he wrote, "Whoever believes that Jesus is the Christ is born of God, and everyone who loves Him who begot also loves him who is begotten of Him" (1 John 5:1). In other words, *all* who believe Jesus is the Christ are our brothers and sisters.

Listen To ...

Life becomes harder for us when we live for others,
but it also becomes richer and happier.
—*Albert Schweitzer*

Day 4

Unburdened by Him

We are a much-burdened species.

In the Bible, we read about the scribes and the Pharisees, who bore the weight of hundreds of nitpicky rules on every aspect of their religion and life. Their self-imposed rules were a prideful burden that displeased God.

Today, adults carry psychological and physical burdens that may change in content but are rarely eliminated. Even children are burdened down. *Oregonlive.com* stated that children ages eleven to fourteen commonly complain of back and shoulder pain. One study found that the average weight of a backpack was fifteen or more pounds. For a sixth grader weighing sixty-five pounds, carrying a fifteen-pound backpack is the equivalent of a two-hundred-pound man carrying a forty-five-pound pack. Professionals say that a grade-schooler's backpack should never exceed 15 percent of the child's weight.

While we can fix an overloaded backpack, our internal burdens are more difficult to handle. At times the weight we carry seems too much to bear. So, what can we do?

Jesus changed everything. He eliminated the unattainable rules and declared, "My yoke is easy and My burden is light" (Matt. 11:30). We can become modern-day equivalents of Pharisees when we overload ourselves with too many commitments, self-imposed rules, and meaningless activities. Set down your burdens and ask God to help you prioritize. Number one on your list? Jesus.

Lift Up ...

Dear Lord, I often carry burdens that were never meant for me. Remind me that You are not impressed with my self-imposed worries. You want me to set down my heavy burden at the foot of the cross—Your cross. In Jesus' name. Amen.

Look At ...

Yesterday, John guided us through the undeniable truth that we are compelled to love our brothers and sisters. Our response to this command reveals the condition of our hearts and our personal devotion to the Lord. We considered our joyous opportunity to be in a relationship with Jesus. He is like no other; He alone is the Anointed One.

Today, John concentrates on the family relationship we have with our Father God. Children resemble their father by their behavior, their obedience, and their love. Our love for God should result in obedience, and our obedience then results in loving others. Being rightly related to God makes love possible rather than an impossible burden. Our love for others sets us apart and is an effortless product of our love for God.

Read 1 John 5:2–3.

By this we know that we love the children of God, when we love God and keep His commandments. For this is the love of God, that we keep His commandments. And His commandments are not burdensome. 1 John 5:2–3

1. How can we know that we love the children of God?

2. Who are we to love first and foremost?

3. In what way do we show our obedience?

4. What does it mean to keep God's commands?

2 A Circle of Love

The children of God share a Father and know that whoever loves the Father loves His children and whoever loves His children loves God. Our attitudes toward others originate from our love of God. "For you are all sons of God through faith in Christ Jesus" (Gal. 3:26).

3 Family Obedience

Our active obedience is an example to our biological family and an unbelieving world of how to serve a loving Father and help our brothers and sisters in Christ. We demonstrate this love by keeping God's commandments and willingly doing His work.[10]

4 Keeping Commands

To *keep* can mean to fulfill a promise or other commitment. The Lord loves us enough to give us commands we can keep. When we obey them, we show that we hear Him, love Him, and serve Him.

5. Review the Ten Commandments as found in Exodus 20:2–17. Now look at Matthew 22:37–39, where Jesus names the greatest commandments. Write them in the spaces below.

    a.

    b.

6. What should be our goal when we consider His commandments?

7. Why are His commandments easy for us to keep?

Live Out ...

8. John encouraged us to show how much we love God by showing love to His children. In Philippians 2:1–4, Paul gives a list of ways we can show our love for one another.

    a. Place a check next to the verses that indicate ways you've shown love to a brother or sister in Christ.

        ☑ Being like-minded (v. 2)

        ☑ Not being ambitious at another's expense (v. 3)

        ☑ Esteeming others better than yourself (v. 3)

        ☑ Looking out for another's interests (v. 4)

    b. Think of ways you could better manifest your love for others.

        I will show my love to ...

        by ...

9. Continue thinking about God's commandments in Exodus 20:2–17.

    a. List the Ten Commandments.

    b. Next to each, write down whether this commandment is easy or difficult for you to follow.

        1.

        2.

        3.

4.

5.

6.

7.

8.

9.

10.

c. Some of these commands may seem burdensome to you. Choose one with which you struggle. Explain why this commandment is difficult for you to obey.

d. What commandment is either the easiest or the most difficult for you to obey? Why?

10. The Lord sees us as parts of a unified body of believers.

a. Read 1 Corinthians 12:26 and describe what that means.

b. Examine how you react to the successes of other believers:

When others in my church receive honors and I do not, I feel _____.

When others are praised and I am not, my thought is: _____.

When I am passed over, my usual response is:

_____.

---

9 Pleasing God

We are learning about mature Christian love. Once we are born again as children of God, we can obey His commandments. Our love for God and our brothers and sisters makes obedience desirable. "Do all things without complaining and disputing" (Phil. 2:14).

10 Rejoicing Love

Loving our brothers and sisters allows us to rejoice when others are honored or receive praise and not be offended when we are passed over.

In 1527 at the age of twenty-five, Anthony Zaccaria set up a medical practice in Cremona, Italy. The doctor's work not only included ministering to the sick; he ministered to the dying and bereaved as well. Because he came to believe that many of his patients were spiritually sick as well as physically ill, he began to study theology to learn more about the comfort and ways of God. By 1528 he became an ordained priest as well as a doctor.

Now his work encompassed evaluating a person's spiritual and physical health. For some doctors, that would present too great a burden, but Dr. Zaccaria did not see it that way. Instead, he felt, "That which God commands seems difficult and a burden … the way is rough, you draw back; you have no desire to follow it. Yet do so and you will attain glory."[11]

When we allow ourselves to be instruments in God's hands, He is able to carry our burdens, and we will naturally glorify Him in our accomplishments.

Listen To ...

The first degree of humility is prompt obedience.
—*Saint Benedict*

DAY 5

Victory through Him

The University of Southern California is known as a leading private research university, but it is also known for its dynamic football program. Interest in the football program and its history is so lively, it prompted the writing of a 224-page book about various players' memories and stories.

As with all college teams, victory matters at USC. When a touchdown is scored, a costumed warrior rides onto the field astride a majestic white stallion while the band plays "Conquest." The crowd goes wild. Victory is sweet, but one victory is not enough. Another victory will be required at the next game and the next and the next.

As Christians we find our victory in a different arena—Satan's ongoing battle for our souls and his attempts to draw us away from God. Our triumph is found in our belief that Jesus Christ died on the cross, shedding His blood to pay the price for our sin.

Scripture confirms this: "'O Hades, where is your victory?' The sting of death is sin, and the strength of sin is the law. But thanks be to God, who gives us the victory through our Lord Jesus Christ" (1 Cor. 15:55–57).

Once we have received Jesus as our Savior, the victory is forever won.

Lift Up ...

Dear Lord, although I've experienced many losses in the course of life, I rejoice in the knowledge that I have eternal victory in You. Thank You, Lord. You paid the price for me—a price I could never pay. In Jesus' name. Amen.

Look At ...

Yesterday, John focused on the family—the family of God. As in all functional families, in the family of God, obedience born both of respect and of love is required. When these elements are

1 Born of God

Being born of God comes from belief in Jesus as our personal Savior. A new, powerful, divine nature enters us that draws us to obey the Lord more than to follow the world. Faith begins to manifest as love, and love, in turn, increases our faith.

3 Victory over Sin

Victory over our sin nature arises solely from the strength of God within us. We are unable to resist Satan-inspired temptation in our own strength, but we don't have to: "You are of God, little children, and have overcome them, because He who is in you is greater than he who is in the world" (1 John 4:4).

4 Faith in Christ

Faith leads the Christian to victory when it is grounded in the belief that Jesus is the Christ. The Lord awaits the overcomers and will graciously share His throne with them: "I also overcame and sat down with My Father on His throne" (Rev. 3:21).

in place, we are able to love beyond our natural abilities and to have a powerful impact on the world around us.

Today John brings us to the wonderful results of being born of God through belief in Jesus Christ. We are not only bound for heaven; we are able to function fully in faith while we reside in the world. No longer slaves to sin, we can be victorious in our walk with the Lord and in our witness to others. We are overcomers.

Read 1 John 5:4–5.

For whatever is born of God overcomes the world. And this is the victory that has overcome the world—our faith. Who is he who overcomes the world, but he who believes that Jesus is the Son of God? 1 John 5:4–5

1. What allows us as individuals to overcome the world?

2. When we are born of God, what can we do?

3. What is it called when we overcome the world?

4. How does victory happen?

5. As Christians, what is our goal?

6. How can we achieve that goal?

7. What is a Christian required to believe?

Live Out ...

8. We choose to sin by satisfying the desires of our flesh, hungering for more pleasures of the senses, and focusing on carrying out our own ambitions. Galatians 6:8 tells us that "he who sows to his flesh

will of the flesh reap corruption, but he who sows to the Spirit will of the Spirit reap everlasting life."

Look at the list below and circle any sins you are struggling with at this time in your life. Add any additional sins that are challenging you.

a. Pride in my achievements

b. A never-ending desire for more

c. Envy

d. Addiction

e. Other: _____

Describe how your increasing faith will help you overcome these sins and, in so doing, overcome the world. See Proverbs 17:3; 21:3; and John 1:9 for inspiration.

9. Write about anything that causes you to doubt that your faith is strong enough to overcome this world and ultimately stand confidently before God.

Faith and knowledge rest on our hope of eternal life, which God, who doesn't lie, promised us before the beginning of time (see Titus 1:2). "For God so loved the world that He gave His only begotten Son, that whoever believes in Him should not perish but have everlasting life" (John 3:16).

What assurance do you have that eternal life is yours?

10. Throughout 1 John, we are reminded that as believers, we will overcome. Consider the verses below, and discover the future recognition that awaits those who overcome.

Scripture	Recognition
Revelation 2:7	
Revelation 2:11	
Revelation 3:12	

8 Results of Testing

A pure heart, right actions, and confession of sins empower us to stand strong in the face of temptation. Remember, God loves you just as you are, but He allows your testing so that you will become strong, sure, and mature.

9 Faith in His Strength

Faith means relying on Christ alone for salvation and taking God at His word. In so doing, He honors our faith, and we are able to overcome the world in the power of His strength.

We tend to look for easy fixes in life. We want a pill that will help us lose weight, an exercise program that we can follow while we sleep, and a website that will bring us someone to love or fix the relationship we have. Looking for the simple fix rarely has a positive outcome. Instead, we can become addicted to pills, weak from lack of exercise, and frustrated in our relationships.

Thomas à Kempis wrote of four choices we can make that bring great peace and true liberty into our lives.

1. Seek to do the will of others rather than your own.
2. Always choose to have less rather than more.
3. Look always for the last place and seek to be beneath all others.
4. Always wish and pray that the will of God will be fully carried out in you.[12]

Choosing well moves us from defeat to victory. Belief that Jesus Christ is the Son of God is the ultimate *fix* for our lives. The result of plunging into the vastness of faith in Christ is that we live triumphant lives.

Listen To ...

There is a loftier ambition than merely to stand high in the world.
It is to stoop down and lift mankind a little higher.
—*Henry van Dyke*

Jesus on Trial

1 John 5:6–13

The apostle John witnessed Jesus' life, crucifixion, and resurrection. In verse one of his first epistle, John gave a strong eyewitness testimony: "That which was from the beginning, which we have heard, which we have seen with our eyes, which we have looked upon, and our hands have handled, concerning the Word of life—the life was manifested, and we have seen, and bear witness, and declare to you that eternal life which was with the Father and was manifested to us" (1 John 1:1–2).

As believers, we are called to testify on behalf of Jesus before a jury of unbelievers. They will listen to the facts and make a decision about whether Jesus is really everything the witnesses claim Him to be. Yet this is a mock trial because Jesus is the righteous Judge (see John 5:22), not the defendant. The murmuring voices are silenced as the Judge gives His instructions: "Seek the LORD while He may be found, call upon Him while He is near" (Isa. 55:6).

The "jurors" who refuse to believe the truth about Him are the ones who face a sentence of eternal separation from God. Are you a witness for Him, or are you a juror? Will you seek Him and call upon Him, or will you be found in contempt of the Judge: Almighty God?

Day 1: 1 John 5:6	**Witness 1: The Holy Spirit**
Day 2: 1 John 5:7–8	**Witness 2: The Trinity**
Day 3: 1 John 5:9	**Witness 3: God the Father**
Day 4: 1 John 5:10–11	**Witness 4: The Believer**
Day 5: 1 John 5:12–13	**Witness 5: The Believer's Life**

Witness 1: The Holy Spirit

Lift Up ...

Dear Lord, thank You for revealing Your truth through the Holy Spirit. Create in me a witness that testifies of Your mercy, love, and power. In Jesus' name. Amen.

Look At ...

Last week we learned that victory comes from living a life of obedience and love. Our victory is won not by personal righteousness but from our relationship to Christ, the Victor. Our faith in Him is the key that unlocks power in our time here on earth, and it assures us of an eternity with the Lord we love.

This week, John circles back to the purpose of verifying who Jesus is. Jesus' full humanity and full deity are verified as they were called into question. John essentially brings us into the courtroom to hear testimony from key witnesses as he presents the "case for Christ" and thereby refutes the false teachings of his day. The character of God receives an undeniable testimony of truth. His witness: the Holy Spirit.

Read 1 John 5:6.

This is He who came by water and blood—Jesus Christ; not only by water, but by water and blood. And it is the Spirit who bears witness, because the Spirit is truth. 1 John 5:6

1. What two unique terms does John use to describe how Jesus Christ "came"?

2. What phrase does John use to indicate the importance of Jesus' death on the cross in addition to His baptism?

3. Acts 19:4–5 tells us, "John … baptized with a baptism of repentance, saying to the people that they should believe on Him who would come after him, that is, on Christ Jesus." Imagine John the Baptist's surprise when Jesus came to him to be baptized. Read about this event in Matthew 3:13–17, and answer the following questions:

    a. What did John the Baptist say and do when Jesus came to him (v. 14)?

    b. Why did Jesus need to be baptized (v. 15)?

    c. What three things happened after Jesus came out of the water (vv. 16–17)?

4. Who bears witness to Jesus' deity?

5. Why can this witness's testimony be trusted?

6. Read John 15:26–27. What did Jesus predict the Spirit of truth and His disciples would do?

7. How does Acts 5:29–32 confirm that Jesus' own testimony was truthful?

Live Out ...

8. Baptism was an Old Testament cleansing ritual and a requirement for Gentiles who converted to Judaism. Jews who came to John for baptism were repenting of Gentile-like lifestyles and dedicating themselves to heartfelt service of God in preparation for the coming

1 The Revealed Son

The phrase *came by* is better translated as "revealed through." John focuses on two specific events through which Jesus' identity as God's Son was revealed: His baptism by water, and His death on the cross by blood.

2 Fully Divine/Fully Human

False teachers challenged the nature of Jesus Christ, claiming He was only divine from the time of His baptism until He hung on the cross. John refutes their claims and presents evidence to prove Jesus was both fully God and fully man throughout His earthly life.

3 A God Who Saves

Jesus identified with sinners through His baptism, the first public event of His ministry. Jesus' baptism symbolically foreshadowed His death, burial, and resurrection, through which He fulfilled all righteousness by substituting His righteousness for our sin.[1] Our sinless Lord overcame sin for us (see 2 Cor. 5:21).

8 A New Life

As Jesus Christ identified with us through baptism, so we identify with His death, burial, and resurrection through water baptism. Rather than being a ritual that saves us, it's a biblical practice that enables believers to follow Jesus' example and make a public statement that we "have been crucified with Christ" (Gal. 2:20). We now "walk in newness of life" (Rom. 6:4).

10 Washed by the Word

As believers, we are cleansed from sin for salvation only once, but our "feet" get dirty while walking in this world. Jesus "gave Himself [for us] ... that He might sanctify and cleanse [us] with the washing of water by the word" (Eph. 5:25–26). What needs to be washed off your spiritual feet today?

Messiah.[2] Baptism took on new meaning once Jesus ascended into heaven. Explain its significance according to Romans 6:3–4.

9. In today's text, the water points to the witness of the Father and the Spirit at Jesus' baptism. Water is used symbolically throughout Scripture to portray spiritual cleansing and life. Look up the following verses to discover (1) where living water comes from and (2) what it accomplishes in a believer's life.

Scripture	Source	Functions of Living Water
Ezekiel 36:25–26		
John 7:37–39		
Titus 3:4–6		
Hebrews 10:21–22		

What area in your life, if any, needs the cleansing that can only come from the washing of the Holy Spirit?

10. Jesus used literal water to wash His disciples' feet, a task usually reserved for the lowliest of servants. When you examine your heart, are you willing to stoop down to help others? Does pride prevent you from doing the overlooked and unglamorous tasks? In addition to a lesson on humility, the washing of the disciples' feet portrayed the spiritual cleansing that would soon take place at the cross. Read about what happened as Jesus washed His disciples' feet in John 13:5–10.

a. In your own words, summarize Peter's reactions in verses 6, 8, and 9.

b. What reason did Jesus give for needing to wash His disciples?

c. What do you think Jesus meant by his response to Peter's request for a full bath?

Today's lesson looks at the key witness of Jesus' deity, the Holy Spirit. At Jesus' baptism, the Holy Spirit descended upon Him in the form of a dove, signifying and bearing witness that He was the Son of God (see John 1:33). To *bear witness* comes from the Greek word *martureo,* which means to testify about the truth of what one has seen, heard, or knows.[3] As a member of the Godhead, the Holy Spirit is thoroughly qualified to testify to Jesus' deity.

The Holy Spirit also testified about Jesus through the inspired writings of the Old and New Testaments. Throughout His life on earth and to this day, the Holy Spirit continues to witness on Jesus' behalf. He confirms that Jesus is "the express image of His person, and upholding all things by the word of His power, when He had by Himself purged our sins, sat down at the right hand of the Majesty on high" (Heb. 1:3).

Listen To ...

"Spirit of Jesus, glorify the Master's Name in me; whether I live, or if I die, let Christ exalted be."
—J. Oswald Sanders

DAY 2

Witness 2: The Trinity

When the space shuttle *Atlantis* lifted off from Cape Canaveral on July 8, 2011, Lisa Green was there. If you talked with her today, she could tell you every detail of her experience, describing the sound of the rockets, the smell of the fumes, the colors in the sky, and the emotion of the crowd. An eyewitness can take us to a moment in time and bring life to an experience that we did not see for ourselves.

When the apostle John was old, he gave his eyewitness account of what he had seen, heard, and touched while he was with Jesus. From the beginning of Christ's earthly ministry, John witnessed His miracles, His grace, and His love. He was present at the cross, witnessed the empty tomb, and touched the risen Savior. His eyes beheld the King of Kings in the revelation of Jesus Christ. "The life was manifested, and we have seen, and bear witness, and declare to you that eternal life which was with the Father and was manifested to us" (1 John 1:2). John's goal in writing was that we would *know* Jesus and *continue* steadfast in faith until the end.

Lift Up ...

Dear Lord, although I will never be an eyewitness to Your life, death, or resurrection, make my life a witness of a life of faith in You and Your Word. The world may change, times may pass, but Your Word is established forever. Thank You. In Jesus' name. Amen.

Look At ...

Yesterday we heard the Spirit confirm John's eyewitness testimony that Jesus is an eternal member of the Godhead. We pondered the mysterious fact that Jesus was fully God and fully man. The evidence was clear and the Witness beyond reproach: the Holy Spirit.

Next we zoom in on the testimony of the Trinity throughout Jesus' ministry. The apostle John was an eyewitness of the deity of Christ, but he deferred to the testimony of the Father, the Son, and the Holy Spirit. We hear the Judge's gavel fall as God the Father, God the Son, and God the Holy Spirit establish the truth. Once again, these witnesses defy defamation and are in perfect accord—they are the Godhead.

1 The One

In John's gospel, Jesus is called "the Word [who] became flesh and dwelt among us." John said, "We beheld His glory, the glory as of the only begotten of the Father, full of grace and truth" (John 1:14).

Read 1 John 5:7–8.

For there are three that bear witness in heaven: the Father, the Word, and the Holy Spirit; and these three are one. And there are three that bear witness on earth: the Spirit, the water, and the blood; and these three agree as one. 1 John 5:7–8

1. List the three that bear witness in heaven and describe their relationship.

2. What three names are given to the rider of the white horse in Revelation 19:11–13? Who do you think this passage describes?

3. The evidence is clear: "In Him dwells all the fullness of the Godhead bodily" (Col. 2:9). The following verses testify that Jesus has the same attributes as God, a teaching denied by false prophets.

    a. *Circle* the phrases that testify of his *eternal nature.*

    b. *Underline* the phrases that reveal Him as *Creator.*

    c. *Box* the phrases that demonstrate His *majesty, power, and deity.*

"In the beginning was the Word, and the Word was with God, and the Word was God. He was in the

3 The Three

Most scholars agree that 1 John 5:7 was found in only a few Greek manuscripts. However, its presence or absence doesn't change the teaching of the text, nor does it depart in any way from the overall teachings in the Word. Many verses attest to the doctrine of the Trinity.

6 The Blood

God testified to the accomplishment of His Son's death by ripping the temple veil—a thick curtain separating the Holy Place from the Most Holy Place—from top to bottom. Jesus bridged the gap between God and man "with His own blood [and] entered the Most Holy Place once for all, having obtained eternal redemption" (Heb. 9:12).

beginning with God. All things were made through Him, and without Him nothing was made that was made" (John 1:1–3).

"But to the Son He says: 'Your throne, O God, is forever and ever; a scepter of righteousness is the scepter of Your Kingdom'" (Heb. 1:8).

"He is the image of the invisible God, the firstborn over all creation.… And He is before all things, and in Him all things consist" (Col. 1:15, 17).

4. What three witnesses testify about Jesus on earth, and how do you know their testimonies are consistent?

5. The Holy Spirit testified to Jesus' deity at His baptism, represented by the water in verse 8. Similarly, the Bible reveals the Spirit's active involvement throughout Jesus' life on earth. Match the following scriptures with the evidence described.

a. Created Jesus' physical body   *b* Acts 10:38

b. Anointed Jesus' ministry   *c* Mark 1:12

c. Led Jesus to confront Satan   *a* Luke 1:35

6. The testimony of the blood occurred at the six-hour crucifixion, when God darkened the sky during three midafternoon hours, demonstrating that His Son—not a mere man—had been sacrificed for the sins of the world.

    a. List the other supernatural events that took place according to Matthew 27:51–53.

b. Continue reading through verse 54. Who witnessed these events, and what was their response?

Live Out ...

7. The false teachers of John's day concocted a theory that the Spirit left Jesus at the cross, and He ceased to be the Christ. The witness of "the blood," and what happened on the cross, is the cornerstone of Christianity. Think about your relationship to the Father. Are you at peace with God? Read Colossians 1:19–22.

a. What two things pleased the Father (v. 19–20)?

b. *Reconciliation* means there has been a change in our status before God. What was our status with God prior to reconciliation (v. 21)?

c. For what purpose has He reconciled us to Himself (v. 22)?

d. What is your status before God?

❏ Alienated because of sin ❏ Holy and blameless because of Christ's blood

7 The Redeemed

We have been redeemed with the precious blood of Christ. On the cross, Jesus fulfilled the entire sacrificial system and put an end to it forever. He accomplished with one offering what millions of animals on Jewish altars could never accomplish.[4] Christ alone paid the price for your sin. Have you personally acknowledged His sacrifice? Pray a prayer of thanksgiving for giving His perfect life for yours.

8. Paul continues this discussion on reconciliation with this qualifying statement: "If indeed you continue in the faith, grounded and steadfast ... not moved away from the hope of the gospel" (Col. 1:23).

a. How will you commit to continue in the faith, grounded and steadfast?

☑ Stay in God's Word   ☑ Renounce a particular sin

☑ Share my faith with   ☑ Spend time with other
   others   believers

☑ Pray more often   ❏ Other: _____

9 The Bold

Come to His throne! Hebrews 4:16 says that because of our perfect Savior, we may come boldly to the throne of grace any time of any day, that we may obtain mercy and find grace to help in times of need.

b. What types of things move you away from the hope of the gospel?

❑ Political correctness   ❑ Peer pressure   ❑ Financial frustrations

❑ Health difficulties   ❑ Relationship trouble   ❑ Other: _____

_____

c. Below, write a prayer based on Hebrews 12:1–2: "Let [me] lay aside every weight, and the sin which so easily ensnares [me], and let [me] run with endurance the race that is set before [me], looking unto Jesus, the author and finisher of [my] faith, who for the joy that was set before Him endured the cross."

9. Today we learned that the temple veil was split from top to bottom when Jesus died. For thousands of years, this veil symbolized the separation that existed between Holy God and sinful man. Thank the Lord that you now have the privilege "to enter the Holiest by the blood of Jesus, by a new and living way which He consecrated for us, through the veil, that is, His flesh" (Heb. 10:19–20).

Write in your journal about what it means to you personally to have an open invitation to God's chambers any time of the day or night. How often do you take advantage of this privilege?

_____

Over 80 percent of babies are born with birthmarks.[5] Some of these marks are scarcely visible and some are profound. Many babies acquire these marks as a result of the transformational process of birth, and they are visible their whole lives.

We have been redeemed by the precious blood of Christ and have been made new. As such, born-again believers should bear visible birthmarks! As the Holy Spirit indwells us, we should bear the marks of love and righteousness. Because we have been set free from sin and death, we should be identified with the marks of an overcomer.

Birthmarks of light, grace, and life should be apparent in and through our lives. These marks and witnesses are internal and external signs that we are His children, children of the all-loving, true, and living God!

Listen To ...

Blessed are those who have not seen and yet have believed.

—Jesus

DAY 3

Witness 3: God the Father

Our world continues to put Jesus on trial by challenging the truth about Him as revealed in the Bible. Many people say they are seeking the truth, yet they hear and believe false testimonies from people who are hostile to the gospel.

God the Father's testimony is the most powerful statement of truth and knowledge that could ever be required. Any testimony is only as reliable as the witness. Peter, James, and John were eyewitnesses of the transfiguration of Jesus. Peter was overwhelmed with awe, wanting to memorialize the moment by building a tabernacle for Jesus and one each for Moses and Elijah. At this point, Peter was interrupted with the testimony of God the Father for His Son:

> While he was still speaking, behold, a bright cloud overshadowed them; and suddenly a voice came out of the cloud, saying, "This is My beloved Son, in whom I am well pleased. Hear Him!" And when the disciples heard it, they fell on their faces and were greatly afraid. But Jesus came and touched them and said, "Arise, and do not be afraid." When they had lifted up their eyes, they saw no one but Jesus only. (Matt. 17:5–8)

The presence of Moses on the mount represented the law; Isaiah represented the validity of the prophets, but at that moment, the Father strongly affirmed His witness of the deity of His Son.

The message of the Father is just as valid now as it was then: "Hear Him!"

Lift Up ...

Dear Lord, just like a parent guides a child, I know that sometimes You must get my attention in order to show me what's important. You have given Your Son and You want Him to be my focus. I pray that I will be a reliable witness of love for Your Son. In Jesus' name. Amen.

Look At ...

So far we've heard the testimony of the Spirit at Jesus' baptism followed by the testimony of the triune God throughout the earthly ministry of Christ. John spoke knowingly of Jesus, as he was on the scene and saw, heard, and experienced Jesus up close. As powerful as John's personal account was, it pales in comparison to those of the Father, Son, and Holy Spirit.

Next we turn to the testimony of God the Father. No one can testify on the character and content of a man in quite the way as a father for his son. Today we step into the realm of the Father of all and His testimony for His Son, Jesus Christ. We find that we have a part in the matter of belief—our focus and our heart. There is no peace in our hearts absent the Son of Man.

3 Tried and True

Receiving the witness of men and women means accepting, embracing, or following their instructions. If we readily trust people, how much more should we trust what God says about His Son? Jesus said of Himself: "My judgment is true; for I am not alone, but I am with the Father who sent Me" (John 8:16).

4 A Prophetic Word

The Jews were familiar with Messianic prophecy and should have instantly recognized Jesus as Christ based on God's testimony. Peter wrote, "And so we have the prophetic word confirmed, which you do well to heed as a light that shines in a dark place" (2 Pet. 1:19).

Read 1 John 5:9.

If we receive the witness of men, the witness of God is greater; for this is the witness of God which He has testified of His Son. 1 John 5:9

1. Whose witness does John remind us we readily receive?

2. How does he compare this witness to the witness of God?

3. The witness of God is His testimony about whom?

4. In addition to Jesus' baptism, Scripture records two other times when God the Father testified about His Son in an audible

5 Religious Rejection

Jesus presented this evidence to religious leaders who refused to receive the One who came in the Father's name. He confronted them by saying they would quickly accept and honor someone who came in his own name, although the acceptance of one man by another was meaningless when they rejected the One honored by God (see John 5:43–45).

7 A Godward Gaze

Isaiah the prophet said, "You will keep him in perfect peace, whose mind is stayed on You" (Isa. 26:3). In Hebrews, the term *perfect peace* is actually *shalom shalom*. In the Hebrew, repetition communicates intensity. When we keep our minds settled upon the Lord Himself, then we can be kept in perfect peace.[6]

voice before men. Look up the following scriptures and describe these testimonies, including (1) who was present, (2) what was said, and (3) when or where it took place.

Matthew 17:1–5	John 12:28–29

Who:

What:

When/Where:

5. Jewish law required a testimony to be confirmed by two or three witnesses. Jesus claimed equality with God many times in the Gospels. John the Baptist supported the testimonies of Jesus: "And I have seen and testified that this is the Son of God" (John 1:34). Who or what else testified to Jesus' true identity according to John 5:36–39?

1.

2.

3.

6. Read John 14:8–12. What do you learn about the relationship between the Father and the Son?

Live Out ...

7. John reminds us that we often pay more attention to what *people* say than what *God* says. Examine your thoughts, motives, and actions during the past twenty-four hours. Estimate the time spent on the following:

Witness of People	Witness of God
___ Worrying what others think	___ Asking God His opinion
___ Evaluating how I look to others	___ Looking in the mirror of God's Word
___ Seeking the approval of others	___ Performing acts as unto the Lord
___ Seeking opinions from others	___ Sitting and listening for God's voice
___ Reading self-help books	___ Reading the Bible and applying it
___ Looking for someone to fulfill me	___ Letting God witness through me
___ **Total Hours**	___ **Total Hours**

9 The Heart of the Matter

Reading the Bible every day allows God to transform our hearts by the discerning sword of His Word. "All Scripture is given by inspiration of God, and is profitable for doctrine, for reproof, for correction, for instruction in righteousness" (2 Tim. 3:16).

8. If you weren't able to account for all your waking hours in the question above, you're probably thinking, *My time is spent changing diapers, doing housework, driving the car, or concentrating on work.* Even so, there is an underlying theme to every second of our day. How will you choose to make God's testimony part of everything you do?

- ☑ Listen to Christian teaching/music while I drive, clean, exercise, and so on
- ❑ Talk to my children about Jesus while we eat, play, dress, and so on
- ☑ Keep a scripture by my desk while I'm working or studying
- ☑ Pray in the middle of the night when I can't get back to sleep
- ☑ Invest time in a relationship for God's glory
- ❑ Other: _____

9. Although God testified of Jesus through Old Testament prophets or at times in an audible voice, some people were still unwilling to

recognize Him. Jesus told these religious leaders, "You search the Scriptures, for in them you think you have eternal life …. But you are not willing to come to Me that you may have life" (John 5:39–40).

a. Searching the Scriptures or gaining biblical knowledge is good, but it should always lead us into a deeper relationship with Jesus Christ. Head knowledge *about Him* without heart knowledge *of Him* doesn't bring life. Has your *head knowledge* been transformed into *heart knowledge* during this Bible study? Explain.

b. What change have you noticed in your willingness to come to Jesus on a daily basis (e.g., "I usually go to the mall when I'm feeling low, but now I'm more likely to listen to praise music and read my Bible")?

"Like father, like son" is a saying that was never more true than when it came to Jesus resembling His Father. Hebrews 1:3 states that Jesus is the express image of the Father. Jesus Himself said, "He who has seen Me has seen the Father" (John 14:9). As we might say today of a child, *He's the spitting image of his old man.*

When we consider what this means to us, the significance is clear. When we have the Son in our lives, we also have the Father. If we reject the Son, we also reject the Father. It is simply not possible to love God and hate His Son. The Father and Son are one; to have one is to have the other.[7]

Listen To …

To gather with God's people in united admiration of the Father
is as necessary to the Christian life as prayer.
—*Martin Luther*

Witness 4: The Believer

Paul Revere's famous midnight ride to warn the patriots that "the British are coming" is legendary. As an eyewitness to the approach of the British to Lexington, Revere set out on horseback with a warning and a message. By the time his ride was over, his witness had inspired forty additional riders to branch out to spread Revere's lifesaving message.

As believers, we are called to carry an important message every day and be a witness of what Jesus has done in our lives. God wants us to share what we have experienced through the transforming work of the cross and the resurrection of Jesus.

How wonderful that we don't have to rely on ourselves alone to do this. Jesus said, "You shall receive power when the Holy Spirit has come upon you; and you shall be witnesses to Me in Jerusalem, and in all Judea and Samaria, and to the end of the earth" (Acts 1:8).

When we rely on the leading of the Holy Spirit, we can reliably point the hurting world to the redeeming Christ and the life-changing power of His presence in our lives.

Lift Up ...

Dear Lord, I don't want knowledge to be confined to my intellect. Let my belief in You radiate from the inside out. Though my words may not always be clever or smart, I pray that my love for You will ring out and be a witness to others. In Jesus' name. Amen.

Look At ...

Last week we had the privilege of hearing the voices of both a human witness, John, and a divine witness, God the Father. How generous God is to deal with doubt and skepticism on the part of His own creation. Nothing tops the words of the Father about His Son.

2 Inward Belief

Belief comes from the word *pisteuo* and means more than simply agreeing with the facts. It involves entrusting one's spiritual well-being to Jesus Christ.[8] Someone who believes in the Son of God testifies to the truth about Him.

3 Firsthand Knowledge

Believers need not rely on hearsay; as God's children, they possess firsthand knowledge. They trust Jesus, who promised that the Spirit of truth "will not speak on His own authority, but whatever He hears He will speak; and He will tell you things to come" (John 16:13).

5 Unspoken Lies

John isn't saying that an unbeliever actually makes God a liar because "God is not a man, that He should lie, nor a son of man, that He should repent" (Num. 23:19). Instead, he stresses that disbelieving God's testimony about His Son is like calling God a liar.

Today John encourages believers to do a little self-confrontation. We may try to fool others about our beliefs, but God knows that what is true in our hearts eventually becomes true in our lives. If we fail to possess true faith, our words essentially make God a liar. Can you imagine sitting on the witness stand and calling God the Father a liar? Today it's time to examine our own testimony.

Read 1 John 5:10–11.

He who believes in the Son of God has the witness in himself; he who does not believe God has made Him a liar, because he has not believed the testimony that God has given of His Son. And this is the testimony: that God has given us eternal life, and this life is in His Son. 1 John 5:10–11

1. John introduces the next witness in his case. Who is it?

2. What does this person have in himself?

3. Read Galatians 4:6–7, and answer the following questions.
   a. How is someone who believes in the Son related to God?
   b. Who speaks to the heart of this person, and what does He say?

4. With whom does John contrast the believer?

5. What does this person make God and why?

6. What two specific details does God give in His testimony about Jesus Christ?

7. Read John 3:16. What motivated God to give us eternal life?

Live Out ...

8. We've learned a lot about witnesses this week. The Holy Spirit bears witness to believers that we belong to God and confirms the truth about Jesus Christ found in God's Word. Jesus said, "You shall receive power when the Holy Spirit has come upon you; and you shall be witnesses to Me in Jerusalem, and in all Judea and Samaria, and to the end of the earth" (Acts 1:8).

Honestly evaluate what kind of witness you are for Jesus Christ.

- ☒ Silent
- ☐ Reluctant
- ☒ Holy Spirit-empowered
- ☐ Inconsistent
- ☒ Timid
- ☐ Other: _____

In your journal write a prayer asking God to give you (1) the power to be His witness, (2) the desire to testify about what He's done in your life, and (3) the discernment to know when and where He wants you to speak.

9. In today's text, we are reminded that God has given the gift of eternal life through the death of His Son. Read what Paul says about life in Colossians 3:1–4.

a. What two truths do these verses reveal about your life (vv. 3–4)?

b. In light of these truths, what instructions does Paul give (vv. 1–2)?

10. Since our lives are hidden in Jesus Christ, and He *is* our lives, we are "eternally secure, protected from all spiritual enemies, with full access to all His blessings."[10] Sometimes, however, we lose sight of the security we have in Him.

a. Which of the following earthly concerns threaten to shake your security in Christ?

8 Overflowing Life

Of the many depictions of God's ideal life for the believer, our Lord Himself describes the most alluring. He portrayed a life of perpetual fullness and of torrential, overflowing life.[9] "If anyone thirsts, let him come to Me and drink [and] ... out of his heart will flow rivers of living water" (John 7:37–38).

9 Ongoing Life

Eternal life begins when we first believe and adds joy and satisfaction to our days on earth. Although the gift of eternal life is free, it isn't everywhere or in everyone. God wrapped eternal life in the most costly, sacrificial package He could find—His only begotten Son, Jesus Christ.

☒ Finances   ☒ Fear of failure   ☒ Stressful situations

☒ Fear of evildoers   ❏ Difficult people   ❏ Other: _____

b. If you are a believer, your future couldn't be more secure—it's hidden in Christ with God! Write a statement below committing every possession and concern—including your own life and the lives of your loved ones—into God's able hands.

Heavenly Father, I commit these things to You for safekeeping to do with as You please …

_____

It might be the fragrance of balsam pine, peppermint kisses, or warm, homemade bread that prompt us to recall a long-ago Christmas morning in the company of family and friends. A distinct fragrance has the ability to transport us through time and fill us with wonderful memories. We all know the way it smells after a spring rain or the pure sweetness of a freshly bathed baby—such fragrances are packed with meanings that require no words.

Isn't it wonderful to think that when we enter a room, God's divine love and grace permeate the atmosphere? There is no counterfeit for the real thing here. Nothing can mimic the aroma of a life genuinely lived with Christ.

On the other hand, sometimes our mere presence is a reminder of the sobering consequences of living in rebellion to the Son of God. "For we are to God the fragrance of Christ among those who are being saved and among those who are perishing. To the one we are the aroma of death leading to death, and to the other the aroma of life leading to life" (2 Cor. 2:15–16).

When we are willing to walk by the Spirit's leading, He will pour out the fragrance of Christ through our lives to either minister to or convict those around us.

Listen To …

"Let God be true but every man a liar" is the language of true faith.

—*A. W. Tozer*

DAY 5

Witness 5: The Believer's Life

Last words are often a person's most important and memorable words. They express what the individual wants others to know before he or she parts. In 1 John, it was as if the apostle were saying, "There is something that I want you to *know*." He had seen, heard, and touched the living Christ, and now he wanted to encourage all believers to fully experience the love and eternal life that Christ offers all who will believe.

Near the end of his life, pastor Chuck Smith was asked, "What would an older Chuck Smith tell a younger Chuck Smith?" His reply was simple and much like the apostle John's. "Stay the course," he replied.

As we finish this portion of 1 John today, be encouraged. Keep your eyes fixed on our Savior. Stay the course!

Lift Up ...

Dear Lord, we have so few assurances in this earthly life, but I thank You for the assurance of eternal life through Your Son. Help me confidently live and speak of my love and my belief in You. Your Word is life, and Your Son is the Word. In Jesus' name. Amen.

Look At ...

At this point, John has presented a rock-solid case for Christ. Although an eyewitness himself, he backs up his own testimony with the testimonies of the Trinity and other believers. Believers speak volumes simply by their lives. Belief is a decision that verifies the ultimate truth of God. Our lives overflow with purpose and joy during our time as witnesses here on earth. We then have the promise of eternity.

Today John reminds us that true believers demonstrate their faith through their lives. Being faithful in our devotion verifies the presence of Christ to others and to ourselves. Belief inspires belief. There can be no vague association with Jesus—we who believe continue in this life and the life to come.

1 Holding Fast

Has is translated from the word *echo*, which means to hold fast with love and devotion. Whoever has this type of relationship with the Son has life. "In Him was life, and the life was the light of men" (John 1:4).

4 Knowing God

Know comes from the word *eido* and describes the perception, awareness, or intuitive knowledge that can only come from a relationship with God." John wants us to *know* we have eternal life and a relationship with God through Jesus Christ, His Son. "This is eternal life, that they may know You, the only true God, and Jesus Christ whom You have sent" (John 17:3).

5 Continuing On

If salvation depends on our own righteousness, we will never have peace about the future. But we can be certain we have eternal life if our hope rests in Jesus and His redeeming work on the cross. Based on what Jesus has done for me, I know I'm saved!

Read 1 John 5:12–13.

He who has the Son has life; he who does not have the Son of God does not have life. These things I have written to you who believe in the name of the Son of God, that you may know that you have eternal life, and that you may continue to believe in the name of the Son of God.
1 John 5:12–13

1. What two types of people does John contrast in this verse, and what is the main difference between them?

2. What did Peter—another eyewitness of the Son's majesty—confirm in Acts 4:12?

3. To whom is John writing these words?

4. What two reasons does he give for writing?

5. The apostle John not only wanted believers to know Christ; he also wanted them to continue in their belief. Write about practical measures you can take to ensure continued growth in your faith.

6. Third John 1:4 reflects John's heart in writing his epistles for the believer. Read this verse and personalize it in your own life.

Live Out ...

7. Today we learned that true believers have the assurance of eternal life because of their relationship with Jesus Christ.

> a. Think about someone with whom you have a close, loving relationship. List some characteristics of your relationship (*e.g., spend time together, talk daily, and so on*).
>
> b. Now circle the characteristics listed above that also describe your relationship with Jesus Christ. What is revealed about the depth of your relationship with Him?

7 Assuring Words

God wants His children to know they belong to Him. The Spirit inspired John to write his gospel to assure us that "Jesus is the Christ, the Son of God" (John 20:31). He wrote this epistle so that we may be sure that we are the children of God (see 1 John 5:2, 19).[12]

8. In today's text, John stresses the need to continue to believe. Peter gave similar instructions. Read his specific instructions in 2 Peter 1:5–8, then answer the following questions.

> a. What should we add to our faith in Christ?
>
> b. Which of the above abound in your life? Underline them. Now evaluate which are lacking and circle them.
>
> c. What happens when we make every effort to add these things to our lives? (v. 8)
>
> d. Write a prayer asking God to help you be fruitful. Ask in confidence, knowing that "His divine power has given to us all things that pertain to life and godliness, through the knowledge of Him who called us by glory and virtue" (2 Pet. 1:3).

8 Growing Roots

We need God's resources to bear fruit, but we determine where we place our roots. Only as we grow them deeply into the spiritual resources of God's grace will we produce fruit. Make the Bible your spiritual resource. Delight in it and feed your soul with its truth.[13]

9. As believers who bear witness to the truth about Jesus Christ, we have the assurance of eternal life. The hymn "Blessed Assurance"

beautifully reflects the security found in an intimate relationship with Jesus Christ. The first verse and the refrain to the hymn are written below:

Blessed assurance, Jesus is mine!
O what a foretaste of glory divine!
Heir of salvation, purchase of God,
Born of His Spirit, washed in His blood.

This is my story, this is my song,
Praising my Savior, all the day long;
This is my story, this is my song,
Praising my Savior, all the day long[14]

a. Focus on the words in the refrain. Every life tells a story and has a theme song. What was *your* song before you knew Jesus personally?
- ☑ "(I Can't Get No) Satisfaction"
- ❏ "Girls Just Wanna Have Fun"
- ❏ "Looking for Love in All the Wrong Places"
- ❏ Other: _____

b. What is your song now? If it hasn't changed, what do you think God wants it to be?

———————————

Imagine once again a courtroom trial. A critical witness is called to the stand to testify to the character and integrity of the defendant. She is sworn in, sits down, and listens to the questions. And then, she responds with—silence.

She would certainly be found in contempt, but more important, the jury would assume that if she would not testify *for* the defendant, she was in essence, testifying *against* the defendant.

Now imagine that the one in question had given his life to save the life of that witness. He was innocent, but he loved her so much that he took her penalty—the penalty of death she deserved.

Our words, our lives, our beliefs, and our boldness are the witness of our Savior, Jesus Christ. We can't say we love Him and then deny Him when we are in crucial situations. What is deeply ingrained in our hearts must be evident in every aspect of our lives.

If you have not yet given your life to Christ, He is calling you. Now. You have been presented with the case for Christ; you have heard the witnesses—both divine and common. You are not just the jury; you are on the stand. Your answer will determine your fate. If you haven't already, call upon the name of the Lord, and you shall be saved.

The question is not original, but it is penetrating: If you were arrested for being a Christian, would there be enough evidence to convict you?

Listen To ...

His voice leads us not into timid discipleship but into bold witness.
—Charles Stanley

Lesson Twelve

Without a Doubt

1 John 5:14–21

Muhammad Ali, born Cassius Clay Jr., is one of the greatest heavyweight boxers in the history of the sport. He was just a teenager when he became a gold medal winner in the 1960 Summer Olympics and all of twenty-two years old when he upset Sonny Liston to win the world heavyweight title. He is credited with having the fastest hands and feet ever seen in a heavyweight fighter.[1]

Muhammad Ali changed the look of boxing forever. His skill was unprecedented, but so was his outspoken personality. He thrived in the media spotlight, entertaining the public by antagonizing his opponents and boasting about himself. Ali was completely confident in himself and his abilities, and he reveled in expressing this confidence to the world. He is famous for such statements as "I am the greatest," "I believed in myself," and "It's hard to be humble when you're as great as I am."[2]

Muhammad Ali placed his confidence in himself. He decided he was "the greatest," and that was all he needed to know. Although his attitude was entertaining, it was also misdirected. Confidence placed in human power and ability will always fall short of expectation and potential. Today, John tells us where our confidence should be placed and shows us that true victors don't believe in themselves but come boldly before One who is far *greater*!

       Day 1: 1 John 5:14–15   **Praying His Will**
       Day 2: 1 John 5:16a–b   **Pardoned from Sin**
       Day 3: 1 John 5:16c–17   **Penalty of Death**
       Day 4: 1 John 5:18–19   **Protected from Evil**
       Day 5: 1 John 5:20–21   **Perceiving the Truth**

Praying His Will

Lift Up ...

Dear Father, thank You for teaching me to pray, "Thy will be done." Your answers to my prayers are always perfect because You know exactly what is best for me. Help me to be confident in that knowledge and to boast only about You. In Jesus' name. Amen.

Look At ...

Last week John made it clear that life, eternal life, is found in the Son of God. It is a black or white situation: if we have the Son, we have life; if we don't have the Son, we don't have life. John stated that we are to hold fast in our beliefs and be confident in our knowledge of God. Our confidence rests in our certainty of what Jesus has done for us.

In today's lesson, John instructs and encourages about the effectiveness of prayer. He tells us who to pray for and instills confidence that our prayers are heard. A confident prayer life comes from learning to pray in God's will, not in our own will. This is not always easy, because the world encourages and rewards self-confidence. Nothing is more powerful than a prayer prayed in accordance with God's will.

Read 1 John 5:14–15.

Now this is the confidence that we have in Him, that if we ask anything according to His will, He hears us. And if we know that He hears us, whatever we ask, we know that we have the petitions that we have asked of Him. 1 John 5:14–15

1. According to John, what do we have in God?

2. Explain what action we can take as a result of our confidence in God.

3. What word delineates the parameters of what we are allowed to ask? Define this word in your own words.

4. Which word in this verse indicates that our asking is a choice?

1 In Confidence

Confidence in this verse literally means boldness. As believers we can come confidently before Jesus and speak to Him without fear or reservation. He will hear us if what we are asking pleases Him and is in accordance with His will.

5. Describe the condition that must be present for God to hear our prayers.

6. Take a moment to consider the words of verse 15: "And if we know that He hears us, whatever we ask." Do you know and believe that He hears whatever you ask in His will? Pray about this, and then write a short statement of belief.

5 In Accordance

God hears us and honors our prayers when they line up with His will. The question is, how do we know what His will is? First, pray in accordance with what we know from His Word. Next, abide closely with Him every hour of every day (see John 15:7).

7. Once we believe that God *hears* us, then we trust that we can know what?

Live Out ...

7 In Response

A *petition* is simply a request. We are directed to be anxious about absolutely nothing but rather take our concerns to God. The result of our request comes straight from the Father: "The peace of God, which surpasses all understanding, will guard your hearts and minds through Christ Jesus" (Phil. 4:7).

8. Today we read about the confidence we can have in God. Have you placed your confidence in your heavenly Father and in Him alone? Do you trust Him with everything? What is your current level of confidence in these areas of your life?

I trust Him ...

~~with my money~~
with my health
with my heart
with my loved ones
with my future

9 In Him

"In most people's minds prayer is a means to which God's will is changed to include the concern of the one praying. But prayer is not so much getting God to pay attention to our requests as it is getting our requests in line with His perfect and desirable will for us. It is learning to think God's thoughts after Him and to desire His desires."[3]

10 In Private

In Matthew 6, Jesus instructs His disciples with a model for prayer. He encourages them to pray privately and sincerely, knowing God is aware of their needs before they ask. Therefore, our prayers should be coherent and trusting—a private conversation between Father and child (see Matt. 6:6).

9. God hears us when we prayerfully ask anything in His will. Read the following verses, and list the aspects of praying God's will that are revealed in each verse.

Scripture	Aspects of God's Will
Matthew 7:7–8	
Matthew 21:22	
John 14:13–14	
1 John 3:22	

10. In Matthew 6:10, Jesus taught us to pray, saying, "Your will be done on earth as it is in heaven." Do you need to lay down your will and pray that your Father's will be done? Is there something or someone you need to surrender to the Lord? Spend some quiet time in prayer today, asking God for *His will* to reign in your life. Write a few words to help solidify this conversation with God in your heart.

———————————

Scripture is full of unexpected answers to prayer. Moses called out to God when the children of Israel were trapped between the Red Sea and the advancing Egyptian army. How could he have known that God would answer his dilemma by parting the waters and allowing His people to walk across on dry land?

Consider Daniel's defiance of the king's decree to pray only to him by continuing in his custom to pray to God before an open window. Do you think Daniel could imagine surviving the night after he was thrown into a den of ravenous lions as punishment?

And then, on the day of Pentecost, Peter must have been stunned as the power of the Holy Spirit used his prayerful words to reach three thousand people who professed their newfound faith in Christ.

As we place our trust and confidence in the Lord's plans for us, we, too, need to expect the unexpected. God is still a God of protection, power, and immense creativity. When we insist on placing confidence in our own abilities, we limit God's will and plan. Let's humble ourselves before our great and mighty God and watch Him work!

Listen To ...

Prayer is not conquering God's reluctance, but taking hold of God's willingness.
—*Phillip Brooks*

DAY 2

Pardoned from Sin

The phrase "I beg your pardon" is often used when we offend someone or accidentally intrude in some way. We hope that others will overlook our shortcomings and pardon our mistakes.

A public example of a *pardon* is found in a presidential pardon. American presidents have the ability and power to issue an official pardon to anyone of their choosing. This pardon forgives its recipients of their offenses and restores their lost civil liberties, such as the right to vote, to serve on a jury, and to own a firearm. Unlike most presidential powers, the president's authority to grant a pardon cannot be reviewed or overturned by Congress.

Some of the most well-known pardon recipients are Brigham Young, Jimmy Hoffa, and Patty Hearst. Perhaps the most famous was President Richard Nixon. Nixon had resigned from office amid accusations of participation in the infamous Watergate scandal. President Gerald Ford offered complete clemency to Nixon before he had been officially charged, thereby covering all federal crimes that the former president had "committed or may have committed or taken part in" during his term of office.[4]

The presidential pardon offers a legal avenue to forgiveness and redemption. As Christians, we are the recipients of a much greater pardon. If we ask God and believe, we receive forgiveness for our sins, resulting in the restoration of our relationship with God and the promise of eternal life.

Lift Up ...

Dear Lord, I continually fall short and sin. Yet You have granted me a pardon based on Jesus' full payment for my sin. How can I even understand the enormity of that act? Help me understand, and help me be forever grateful. In Jesus' name. Amen.

Look At ...

Yesterday we received a wonderful promise. John told us that if we pray confidently in God's will, He will hear and answer. We are to go to Him in private and pray. It is amazing that the God of the universe hears and answers our prayers and petitions.

Today, John gives us an example of how to pray in God's will. If we are aware that any fellow believer is committing sin, we are instructed to pray for that person. John continually tells us to love one another, and there is no greater act of love than to ask the Lord Almighty to intervene in the life of a friend. When a fellow believer is suffering or is out of harmony with God's will, we suffer along with that person and pray for his or her restoration (see 1 Cor. 12:26).

Read 1 John 5:16.

If anyone sees his brother sinning a sin which does not lead to death, he will ask, and He will give him life for those who commit sin not leading to death. 1 John 5:16

1. To what general group is John speaking in this verse?

2. Based on what you have learned in this study, define the word *brother*.

3. State what we are to watch for concerning our fellow believers.

4. To whom is John referring when he says, "He will ask"? What does the phrase mean?

2 Do God's Will

You were born into an earthly family, hopefully consisting of a mother, father, and siblings. When you were born again, you became part of an eternal, spiritual family with God as your Father and fellow believers as your brothers and sisters. The DNA proof of our relationship with God is doing His will.

3 See the Sin

The word *sees* is translated from a Greek word that encompasses the idea of physical sight as well as the concept of perception, awareness, knowing, and understanding.[5] Sin in ourselves, as well as in others, may be *seen* without actually being observed (see Acts 28:27).

4 Side by Side

As believers, we can be part of a personal restoration process. When we pray for our erring brothers and sisters, we intentionally come alongside Jesus as He intercedes on behalf of His people. "He always lives to make intercession for them" (Heb. 7:25).

7 Examine Yourself

Anytime we pray for a fellow believer, we must be careful to examine our own lives. Jesus told His followers not to look for small sins in their brothers while overlooking huge sins of their own. First, we are to correct ourselves before presuming to correct others (see Matt. 7:3, 5).

5. When we see a fellow believer committing sin, our responsibility is to pray for that person. What is God's response to that type of prayer?

6. Name the particular type of sin for which John is instructing us to pray.

Live Out ...

7. All sin is serious to God; He never downplays or ignores it. What is your reaction when a fellow believer sins? Check the box or boxes below that describe your recent reaction(s) to the sin of another.

❏ I ignore the sin and don't think or say anything about it.

❏ I minimize the sin and say, "Oh, it's no big deal."

❏ I don't say anything, but I form an opinion about the sinner.

❏ I gossip about the sin to others.

❏ I pray for the person who is sinning.

❏ I reach out in love to a fellow sinner.

Is your response different from what God tells you to do? If so, align your will with God's will.

8. Today's text tells us to pray for those who sin. This is a privilege and a responsibility. Ask the Lord to reveal the person He is asking you to pray for. Write a prayer for that person in your journal. Include the following steps in your prayer.

a. Thank the Lord for trusting you with those whom He loves.

b. Ask the Lord to give you His heart for the sinner— a broken heart—and not a critical heart.

c. As you develop a burden for the sinner, ask the Lord to restore him or her in grace and love.

9. God knows we are not perfect and will sin from time to time. Read Psalm 130:1–5, the prayer of a repentant sinner, and answer the following questions.

a. From the depths of his despair, to whom did the psalmist cry out?

b. What did he want from the Lord?

c. In your own words, describe why he is thankful God keeps no record of sins.

d. In what does the psalmist put his hope?

10 Enjoy Freedom

Jesus warned us that when we sin, we become slaves of that sin. Being a slave may initially come with a false sense of security, but it is temporary and will strip us of freedom. When we are free in the Son of God, we are absolutely free (see John 8:35–36).

10. Perhaps you are currently involved in sin unknown to anyone— except God. Are you guilty of committing a secret sin? Do you long to be set free from this sin so you can resume sweet fellowship with your Savior?

a. Confess your sin to your loving Lord and ask Him for pardon.

b. Write a prayer of confession and repentance. Your heavenly Father desires to restore you to fellowship, and He longs to give you His peace and joy.

c. Confess to a trusted sister in Christ and ask her to come alongside of you for prayer and accountability.

———————————

A pardon is not effective unless the person to whom the pardon is granted chooses to accept it. A 1915 Supreme Court case decided that it must be left up to the recipient of the pardon to decide whether the person wants to receive the pardon. No one can be forced to embrace clemency or forgiveness.[6]

It seems crazy to have freedom and forgiveness handed to us and then refuse that offer, but that is exactly what many people do with Jesus. He paid our debt. He bore our penalty. He freely offers us a full and complete pardon, but each person has to accept or reject this offer of forgiveness. Pardon from sin is a priceless gift! Refuse the offer and spend eternity paying for your sin. Accept and live an everlasting, abundant life!

Listen To ...

The voice of sin may be loud, but the voice of forgiveness is louder.

—*D. L. Moody*

DAY 3

Penalty of Death

Life is full of decisions. Each day we contemplate which road to take and whose lead to follow. All roads lead somewhere, and the leader we choose to follow will determine where we end up.

Perhaps there is no better example of following the leader than that of the Flying Thunderbirds, the highly trained, premier maneuver-flying team of the United States Air Force. This team flies their fighter jets in formation, sometimes performing maneuvers at five hundred miles per hour while flying only eighteen inches from one another. During maneuvers, the pilots follow the signals of Thunderbird Number One, the lead plane.

In January 1982, during a regularly scheduled practice session, tragedy struck. While flying a famous Diamond Loop maneuver, all four planes impacted the ground at a high rate of speed. It was determined that the lead plane suffered a malfunction, which prevented the pilot from pulling out of the loop. The other three pilots were trained to cue visually to the Number One plane, not on their proximity to the ground, and all three planes followed Thunderbird Number One to death.[7] The pilots did nothing wrong. They were performing exactly as they had been trained, but one malfunction—one failure—led to catastrophe.

Today, John reminds us that sin can take us where we do not want to go. If we are not careful, we might follow the lead of sin directly to death.

Lift Up ...

Lord, thank You for the leading of the Holy Spirit in my life. When I follow Him closely, He will spare me from the pain of being led astray. Lord, help me keep my eyes on You. In Jesus' name. Amen.

Look At ...

Yesterday, John instructed us to pray for those in the household of faith who are caught up in sin. We all experience times of weakness when we are tempted by sin, and during these times it reassures us to know that other believers are praying for us.

In today's lesson, John differentiates between two types of sin. The first is "sin leading to death," for which we are not commanded to pray. The second is "sin not leading to death," for which he instructed us to pray. John does not elaborate on the specifics of this sin, but notice that his emphasis is on the prayer, not on the sin. God's heart is always for repentance, and our prayer should be for the same.

1 Mercy for the God-Fearing

God hates all sin, yet in His great mercy He forgives us through the atoning sacrifice of His Son. How grateful we are that "He has not dealt with us according to our sins, nor punished us according to our iniquities. For as the heavens are high above the earth, so great is His mercy toward those who fear Him" (Ps. 103:10–11).

2 Death for the Godless

Sin leading to death is often referred to as sin leading *unto* death or *toward* death or as sin *punished* by death. "Such a sin could be any unconfessed sin that causes the Lord to determine to end a believer's life. It is not one particular type of sin, but the sin that is the final one in the tolerance of God."[8]

3 Prayer for One Another

John is *not* telling his fellow believers to cease praying for each other. Scripture tells us to confess our sins and pray for one another. He is simply telling the church that they are not *commanded* to pray for the unrepentant one whom God chooses to punish with death.

Read 1 John 5:16–17.

There is sin leading to death. I do not say that he should pray about that. All unrighteousness is sin, and there is sin not leading to death. 1 John 5:16c–17

1. Based on yesterday's lesson, how are we to react to sin *not* leading to death? How will God respond to this action?

2. What other type of sin does John refer to in this passage?

3. Restate what John does *not* command the brethren to do.

4. John's emphasis in this week's text is prayer. We are to pray in God's will and intercede in prayer for believers caught in the snare of sin. Look at these verses, and note the different aspects of intercessory prayer that are highlighted.

Scripture	Aspects of Intercessory Prayer
Philippians 4:6–7	
James 5:16	
Hebrews 4:16	

5. According to 1 John 5:17, what is sin?

6. John equates sin to unrighteousness. In 1 John 3:4, what words does John use to describe sin? Explain how these two words both exemplify sin.

Live Out ...

7. In our text, John is writing to *believers,* telling them to pray for fellow believers who find themselves in sin. The phrase "sin leading to death" is part of this discussion. The most widely accepted interpretation of this text is that sometimes God punishes sin with physical death. Read the following biblical examples, and briefly restate what sin was committed.

    Leviticus 10:1–3

    2 Samuel 6:5–8

    Acts 5:1–10

8. Read 1 John 5:16–17 below, and

    a. Underline every instance where you find "sin not leading to death."

    b. Circle each instance where you read "sin leading to death."

If anyone sees his brother sinning a <u>sin which does not lead to death</u>, he will ask, and He will give him

5 Wrong with God

Unrighteousness or iniquity is a condition of not being right with God according to the standard of His holiness and righteousness.[9] We are not victims of unrighteousness; we are responsible for the condition of our relationship with God (see Ezek. 18:20).

7 Death Leading to Life

God chose to deal with these individuals by taking their physical lives. They were members of the church body, so we cannot assume anything about their hearts, whether of belief or unbelief. God chastens us as He sees fit. "But when we are judged, we are chastened by the Lord, that we may not be condemned with the world" (1 Cor. 11:32).

9 A Hardened Heart

If a person continues in unbelief and chooses to reject Jesus Christ even when the Holy Spirit tells him or her otherwise, that person eventually hardens his or her heart against Jesus Christ. This choice is irrevocable, and the individual will die in sin, leading to spiritual death.

life for those who commit sin not leading to death. There is sin leading to death. I do not say that he should pray about that. All unrighteousness is sin, and there is sin not leading to death.

John's focus is clearly on sin "not leading to death." He wants his readers to love each other enough to pray for each other during periods of weakness and sin. For whom is God prompting you to pray? Ask the Lord to give life to those believers struggling with sin. Write out your thoughts and prayer.

9. According to Scripture, there is only one unforgivable sin. Participating in this sin can lead to *spiritual death*. Look at the following verses and note what sin was committed.

     Matthew 12:31–32

     Mark 3:28–29

     Luke 12:10

Add to your prayer list those you fear are in danger of rejecting the truth of Jesus Christ as witnessed by the Holy Spirit. Commit to pray for them!

———————————

In the Southwest United States, the onset of winter is loudly proclaimed by the migration of the graceful sandhill cranes. They fly across the sky from north to south in a perfect V formation behind the lead crane.

How they know when to travel, where to go, and who to follow is privileged information shared only between the cranes and their Creator. But their behavior holds lessons for us. The cranes know who to follow, and they instinctively trust their journey to that leader. We can, and must, have the same confidence to follow our Creator, our Guide, Our Lord, as He leads us through the seasons of our lives.

Alexander MacLaren says it this way: "Our hearts will turn to Christ as naturally as … the migrating birds seek the sunny south, turning by instinct that they do not themselves understand."[10] Don't follow anyone or anything to death when the road and Giver of life is beckoning.

Listen To ...

A great leader never sets himself above his followers except in carrying responsibilities.

—*Jules Ormont*

Protected from Evil

"Raise shields" is a familiar phrase to avid *Star Trek* fans. Whenever the starship *U.S.S. Enterprise* was under attack, Captain Kirk would order the invisible force field, generally referred to as "the shields," to be engaged for protection from the evil attacking forces. The deflector shields operated by creating and wrapping layers of energy around the ship. Neither physical matter nor highly concentrated energy could penetrate a shield when it was engaged at full power. Deflector shields were essential equipment on any starship.[11]

The shields on the *Enterprise* served to deflect any incoming fire and render the enemy powerless. As believers, we have a protection system, too. The Holy Spirit shields us and enables us to withstand any attack initiated by the wicked one of this world. His weaponry cannot touch us when we are protected by the one true and Almighty God. He alone is our protector and our shield.

Lift Up ...

Dear Lord, thank You for keeping me safe from the Evil One. I am so thankful that You are greater than the ruler of this world. You, Lord, are my shield. In Jesus' name. Amen.

Look At ...

Yesterday we observed that God is serious about sin and that we should not judge one another. Instead, we are to humbly and avidly pray for one another. None of us are immune from sinfulness. "All have sinned and fall short of the glory of God" (Rom. 3:23). We are to tend our own hearts and see that we do not become hardened to unrighteousness.

Today, John reassures us that when we are members of God's family, we are off limits for Satan. What good news! When we belong to God, He is always near to us and protects us from evil. Satan is real and at work in this world, but he is not able to touch those who belong to God.

Read 1 John 5:18–19.

We know that whoever is born of God does not sin; but he who has been born of God keeps himself, and the wicked one does not touch him. We know that we are of God, and the whole world lies under the sway of the wicked one. 1 John 5:18–19.

1. According to 1 John 5:18, what do we know?

2. Based on all we have learned in this study, what does the phrase "does not sin" mean?

3. John says that one born of God does what? (v. 18)

4. Throughout the book of 1 John, we see evidence that we are born of God. What evidence is revealed in each of these verses?

   1 John 2:29

   1 John 3:9

   1 John 4:7

   1 John 5:1

   1 John 5:4

   1 John 5:18

5. What is the desired result of keeping himself?

6. In verse 19, John again tells us what we know. What two points does he make?

   1.

   2.

2 Refrain from Sin

John is not saying that once we come to faith in Jesus Christ, we will never sin again, because we will. But the believer who abides in God makes a conscious effort to refrain from indulging in repetitive, habitual sin. As children of God, we desire to live in obedience to the will of the Father.

3 He Keeps Us

Keeps himself is more clearly translated as "keep him," implying that God participates with us in this process. Keeping ourselves from sin is an effort too great to accomplish alone. Only by the power of the Holy Spirit within us are we able to avoid the lure and snare of sin.

5 Divine Boundaries

The word *touch* means to lay hold of or to grasp in order to harm. Although Satan attempts to gain control, believers belong to God, and Satan is required to follow His rules.

7 The Tempter's Attempts

As long as we are in the world, Satan will try to tempt us away from obedience to God. But Jesus prayed to the Father on our behalf. He asked God to protect and *keep* us while we are living in the world (see John 17:15).

9 The Believer's Sword

The Holy Spirit empowers us to resist temptation, and the Word of God equips us. We, in essence, are armed for warfare by carrying God's Word in our hearts and minds. God's "divine power has given to us all things that pertain to life and godliness, through the knowledge of Him who called us by glory and virtue" (2 Pet. 1:3).

Live Out ...

7. God will prevent Satan from destroying His children, but He expects us to take an active role in holding evil at bay. Complete the chart below by describing how God's Word instructs believers to respond to evil.

Scripture	What We Should Do about Evil
Psalm 34:14	
Proverbs 4:27	
Zechariah 8:17	
1 Peter 3:10	
3 John 1:11	

8. There are essentially two camps of people: those who belong to Jesus and those who belong to the wicked one.

    a. Who lies under the sway of the wicked one?

    b. Read Matthew 12:30. What relationship does this verse have with 1 John 5:19?

    c. How does 1 John 4:4 address the reality of being in the sway of the wicked one?

9. In the Gospels we read that Satan tried to tempt Jesus in the wilderness. Jesus overcame each temptation by quoting Scripture. We must also rely on the Word of God as our defense. Answer the following questions about the power of God's Word within us.

    a. Read Joshua 1:8. Why are we to meditate day and night on the Word of God?

    b. According to Psalm 119:11, what is the benefit of hiding God's Word in our hearts?

c. What does Isaiah 40:8 tell us about the longevity of the Word?

d. According to John 17:17, what is God's Word?

As we learned today, being born of God comes complete with a built-in protection system. The Holy Spirit living in us enables us to deflect the schemes and temptations of Satan while protecting our hearts and lives. God is our invisible "force field," our shield. While He offers us protection and direction in the middle of the battle, He doesn't always remove us from the fight.

We live in a world ruled by the wicked one. Every day offers new opportunities and temptations to be swayed away from right living and abiding in Christ. Yet if we place our trust and hope in the power of the Lord, we will be victorious. Remember, the power does not come from ourselves. Our strength and power are the vicarious results of another's: God. He is not only greater than we are; He's greater than "he who is in the world" (1 John 4:4).

Listen To …

God's Word is pure and sure, in spite of the devil, in spite of your fear, in spite of everything.

—R. A. Torrey

Perceiving the Truth

To Tell the Truth is an American television game show that originated in 1956 and aired intermittently for forty-five years. The show challenged a celebrity panel to correctly identify which of three contestants was actually the person that all three claimed to be.

The host of the show would relate an unusual story about one contestant, and the panel would question all three challengers to determine which one belonged to the story. The catch was that the imposters were allowed and encouraged to lie, but the legitimate contestant was sworn to tell the truth.[12]

Although it was just a game show, in some ways it mirrored real life. One team was based on lies and deceit, and the other was based on the truth. There is still a battle for control in our lives, and one will win and the other will lose.

In this final day of our study, John reassures us in the knowledge that we can recognize and choose truth. Truth is right in front of us, but we must listen, believe, and act accordingly. There is no gray area here. If we pray for the truth, we will recognize the author of truth.

Lift Up ...

Dear Lord, I don't need to look any further than Your only begotten Son to find truth. Yet sometimes the lie is so appealing. Give me strength and discernment to see You and cleave to Your side. In Jesus' name. Amen.

Look At ...

In yesterday's lesson, John made it clear that although the world is under the influence of the wicked one, believers have safety and security in their relationship to God. We are not exempt from sin, but neither do we engage in repetitive disobedience. God has set boundaries to restrict Satan's access in our lives.

Today, as John closes his letter to the church, he skillfully summarizes the heart and soul of the message. Throughout this letter, he presents the facts and emphasizes the tangible truths that we recognize and believe: Jesus, the ultimate truth, came to earth to live among us, to impart understanding and knowledge, and to give us the gift of eternal life. Jesus Christ is the true, genuine, and everlasting God.

1 One and the Same

The expression "Son of God" reminds us that Jesus is of the same nature as God. Jesus and God are separate yet One—Jesus *is* God! The Lord explained this relationship when He said, "He who has seen Me has seen the Father" (John 14:9).

Read 1 John 5:20–21.

And we know that the Son of God has come and has given us an understanding, that we may know Him who is true; and we are in Him who is true, in His Son Jesus Christ. This is the true God and eternal life. Little children, keep yourselves from idols. Amen. 1 John 5:20–21

5 The True

Truth means that which is real or genuine. Jesus Christ is real—He is truth! Jesus is God in human form. He laid aside His heavenly glory and put on the humble robes of humanity. He died and rose and lives again to give us eternal life.

1. a. In the first ten words of this text, what do we know?

    b. What does it mean that "the Son of God has come"?

2. What is the first thing John suggests that the Son of God has given us?

3. Through this God-given understanding, what can we know?

4. Who is included in "Him who is true"?

5. What two remarkable things does this text reveal to us about Jesus Christ?

    1.

    2.

7 The False

"Anything that comes in-between your soul and the path of obedience to God is an idol. Listening to the world's philosophies and priorities can lead us into idolatry."[13] Paul told us not to tolerate idolatry but to flee from it (see 1 Cor. 10:14).

8 The Gift

Romans 6:23 states two absolute truths: Eternal life is a free gift for those who believe in the Son, and death is the paycheck received for those who remain in sin. We are saved by grace through faith. It is a gift of God (see Eph. 2:8).

10 The Counterfeit

According to 1 John, "Anything that detracts from God is idolatrous, for He is the true God, the true revelation of the Father, the true atone-ment for sin, the true bread, and the true vine. He is the beginning and the end of all true religion. Consequently, to know Him is to know the true God and eternal life."[14]

6. According to John 17:3, what is eternal life?

7. What is John's final instruction to his little children?

Live Out ...

8. Many people are deceived into thinking they must earn eternal life. Read Romans 6:23, and answer the following questions.

    a. What will sin earn you?

    b. Can you earn eternal life? Why or why not?

    c. In whom is eternal life found?

9. In this week's text, 1 John 5, there are several "we know" statements. Carefully review them and then complete the statements below:

    a. (v. 15a) And we know that _____

    b. (v. 15b) We know that we have the _____

    c. (v. 18a) We know that whoever is _____

    d. (v. 19) We know that we are _____

    e. (v. 20a) And we know that _____

    f. (v. 20b) That we may know _____

Thank God for these truths in your life. Now, summarize them into a personal statement of faith.

10. In our culture, we don't necessarily worship carved images, but we can still be guilty of serving something other than God. Whatever we serve, whatever we place above God, becomes our idol.

a. Review this list and mark anything that you might hold as an idol.

___ Home   ___ Job   ___ TV

___ Spouse   ___ Church   ___ Food

___ Children   ___ Health   ___ Friends

___ Money   ___ Telephone   ___ Possessions

b. Write a prayer asking the Lord to reveal and replace the idols in your life.

"I promise to tell the truth, the whole truth, and nothing but the truth." This oath is administered to every witness preparing to testify in any United States courtroom. We may have heard it so many times that we take it for granted—but we shouldn't. This statement indicates that truth is the goal of the judicial system. As we have studied 1 John, we have been presented with a pure and honest truth. In the face of truth, we are left with a decision.

First John is all about reaffirming the fundamental truths of our faith. And while 1 John oozes with love, it is not without this sobering reality: "He who has the Son has life; he who does not have the Son of God does not have life" (1 John 5:12). In this letter, inspired by His passion for God and love for his readers, John stated and restated these truths. His goal was that "we know that we know Him"—the true and Holy God—and that Jesus Christ reigns in each of our hearts and lives.

Did John succeed? Does Jesus reign as truth in your life? If not, this is a critical moment. No Bible study, no matter how diligently followed, can replace a true relationship with God. Knowing facts about God is a sad substitute for actually knowing *Him*.

Living brilliantly starts the instant you receive Jesus Christ as your Lord and Savior. It's a challenging journey, but it is rich with love and rewards and relationship—a relationship with none other than the Creator of the universe. It is a relationship that continues on for eternity. Brilliant!

Listen To ...

*I have been driven many times upon my knees by the overwhelming
conviction that I had nowhere else to go.*

—Abraham Lincoln

With Gratitude

Heartfelt appreciation to my family, who enrich my life: thanks to my husband, Skip, for providing a latte each morning and a kiss each night; to my son, Nathan, for a sense of humor that provokes deep belly laughs; to my daughter-in-love, Janaé, for her throw-down loyalty in the face of opposition; to my grandchildren, Seth and Kaydence, for adding such joy to my life.

Special thanks to Misty Foster, Maria Guy, Vicki Perrigo, Trisha Petero, Laura Sowers, and Christy Willis, whose contribution to writing this book is priceless. I'm grateful for the incredible influence of these sisters.

Notes

Introduction

1. Adapted from "Chapter 3: The Ages," God's Kingdom Ministries, accessed August 13, 2017, https://gods-kingdom-ministries.net/teachings/books/the-restoration-of-all-things/chapter-3-the-ages/.

Lesson 1: Partners in Faith

1. John F. Walvoord and Roy B. Zuck, *The Bible Knowledge Commentary* (Colorado Springs: Cook Communications Ministries, 1985), 883.

2. Adapted from Ronald F. Youngblood , F. F. Bruce, and R. K. Harrison, *Nelson's Illustrated Bible Dictionary*, Biblesoft PC Study Bible, Version 4.2b, 1988–2004.

3. Adapted from Ronald F. Youngblood , F. F. Bruce, and R. K. Harrison, *Nelson's Illustrated Bible Dictionary*, Biblesoft PC Study Bible, Version 4.2b, 1988–2004.

4. Adapted from Wikipedia, "Thomas Edison," accessed August 13, 2013, http://en.wikipedia.org/wiki/Thomas_Edison.

5. Jamie Frater, "Top 10 Fascinating Deathbed Confessions," ListServe, September 29, 2009, http://listverse.com/2009/09/29/top-10-fascinating-deathbed-confessions.

6. Adapted from Wikipedia, "Sinners in the Hands of an Angry God," accessed July 11, 2013, http://en.wikipedia.org/wiki/Sinners_in_the_Hands_of_an_Angry_God.

7. John F. Walvoord and Roy B. Zuck, *The Bible Knowledge Commentary* (Colorado Springs: Cook Communications Ministries, 1985), 886.

8. John F. Walvoord and Roy B. Zuck, *The Bible Knowledge Commentary* (Colorado Springs: Cook Communications Ministries, 1985), 887.

9. Adapted from James Strong, *New Exhaustive Strong's Numbers and Concordance,* Biblesoft PC Study Bible, Version 4.2b, 1988–2004.

Lesson 2: The Genuine Article

1. Wikipedia, "Dietrich Bonhoeffer," accessed August 2013, https://en.wikipedia.org/wiki/Dietrich_Bonhoeffer.

2. John MacArthur, *The Gospel According to the Apostles* (Nashville: W Publishing Group, 1993), 168.

3. C. S Lewis, *Mere Christianity* (New York: Macmillan, 1952), 77.

4. Spiros Zodhiates, *The Complete Word Study Dictionary: New Testament* (Chattanooga, TN: AMG Publishers, 1992), 374.

5. John MacArthur, *The MacArthur Study Bible* (Nashville: Thomas Nelson, 1997), 1405.

6. *Encyclopædia Britannica Online*, s.v. "Apprenticeship," accessed June 9, 2013, www.britannica.com/EBchecked/topic/30748/apprenticeship.

7. John MacArthur, *The MacArthur Study Bible* (Nashville: Thomas Nelson, 1997), 1614.

8. Warren W. Wiersbe, *Be Real: Turning from Hypocrisy to Truth* (Colorado Springs: David C Cook, 2009), 46.

9. James Montgomery Boice, *The Epistles of John* (Grand Rapids, MI: Baker, 2006), 53.

10. Spiros Zodhiates, *The Complete Word Study Dictionary: New Testament* (Chattanooga, TN: AMG Publishers, 1992), 987.

11. Gary M. Burge, *Letters of John*, The NIV Application Commentary (Grand Rapids, MI: Zondervan, 1996), 102.

12. Warren W. Wiersbe, *Be Real: Turning from Hypocrisy to Truth* (Colorado Springs: David C Cook, 2009), 46.

Lesson 3: What in the World

1. *Jon Courson's Application Commentary* (Nashville: Thomas Nelson, 2005), 1620.

2. Adapted from Merrill F. Unger and R. K. Harrison, *The New Unger's Bible Dictionary*, Biblesoft PC Study Bible, Version 4.2b, 1988–2004.

3. Adapted from James Strong, *Strong's Greek/Hebrew Definitions*, Biblesoft PC Study Bible, Version 4.2b, 1988–2004.

4. Wikipedia, "Imprinting (Psychology)," accessed August 2013, https://en.wikipedia.org/wiki/Imprinting_%28psychology%29.

5. Wikipedia, "Bill Lishman," accessed August 2013, http://en.wikipedia.org/wiki/Bill_Lishman.

6. Kevin Quinn, "Woman Runs Over Armed Carjacker Who Threatened Kids in Baytown," ABC News, June 15, 2013, http://abclocal.go.com/ktrk/story?section=news/local&id=9139434.

7. James Montgomery Boice, *The Epistles of John* (Grand Rapids, MI: Baker, 2006), 59.

8. Molly Cochran, "Science and Psychology: Why People Ignore Tornado Warnings," Accuweather.com, May 21, 2013, www.accuweather.com/en/weather-news/despite-advancements-in-tornad/11971708.

9. "Heart Disease Facts," Center for Disease Control and Prevention, August 2013, www.cdc.gov/heartdisease/facts.htm.

10. "Disparities in Adult Awareness of Heart Attack Warning Signs and Symptoms—14 States, 2005," Center for Disease Control and Prevention, August 2013, www.cdc.gov/mmwr/preview/mmwrhtml/mm5707a3.htm.

11. "Statistics by Country for Agoraphobia," Right Diagnosis, August 2013, www.rightdiagnosis.com/a/agoraphobia/stats-country.htm.

12. Craig Mackenzie, "Woman Who Hasn't Left Her Home for Three Years Becomes a Global Superstar Despite Her Fear of the Outdoors," *Daily Mail*, July 22, 2012, www.dailymail.co.uk/news/article-2177200/Jemma-Pixie-Hixon-Teenager-left-home-THREE-YEARS-global-superstar.html.

13. Adapted from James Strong, *Strong's Numbers and Concordance with Expanded Greek-Hebrew Dictionary*, Biblesoft PC Study Bible, Version 4.2b, 1988–2004.

14. Frances Black, "Christopher Knight and the World's Most Famous Hermits," Yuppee, April 29, 2013, www.yuppee.com/2013/04/29/christopher-knight-and-the-worlds-most-famous-hermits/.

15. Dareh Gregorian, "James Gandolfini Will a Tax 'Disaster,' Says Top Estate Lawyer," *NY Daily News*, July 5, 2013, www.nydailynews.com/entertainment/james-gandolfini-tax-disaster-top-estate-lawyer-article -1.1391181.

16. Rob Nelson and Alexis Shaw, "Boy Trapped beneath Sand Dune May Have Been Saved by Air Pocket, Officials Say," ABC News, July 13, 2013, http://abcnews.go.com/US/boy-rescued-indiana-sand-dune -critical-condition/story?id=19657457.

Lesson 4: Nothing but the Truth

1. Warren W. Wiersbe, *Be Real: Turning from Hypocrisy to Truth* (Colorado Springs: David C Cook, 2009), 88.

2. Wikipedia, "David (Michelangelo)," accessed August 2013, https://en.wikipedia.org/wiki/David _(Michelangelo).

3. Warren W. Wiersbe, *Be Real: Turning from Hypocrisy to Truth* (Colorado Springs: David C Cook, 2009), 92.

4. Skip Heitzig, from the sermon "Four Part Harmony," Calvary Alburquerque, November 17, 2001, www.calvaryabq.org/teachings_view.asp?ServiceID=2049&AcceptsCookies=yes.

5. Adapted from "Apologetic Sermon Illustration #23: Why One Way and the Firefighter," Domain for Truth, June 25, 2014, https://veritasdomain.wordpress.com/2014/06/25/apologetic-sermon-illustration-23-why -one-way-and-the-firefighter/.

6. Henry Ketcha, "The Life of Abraham Lincoln," Authorama, accessed July 1, 2013, www.authorama.com/life -of-abraham-lincoln-21.html.

7. Amy Carmichael, *You Are My Hiding Place* (Minneapolis, MN: Bethany House, 1991), 50.

8. Charles Haddon Spurgeon, "The Holy Ghost—the Great Teacher," *Blue Letter Bible*, accessed July 1, 2013, www.blueletterbible.org/Comm/spurgeon_charles/sermons/0050.cfm.

Lesson 5: Anchor of Hope

1. IMDB, "Chariots of Fire," accessed June 2, 2013, www.imdb.com/title/tt0082158/quotes.

2. Wikipedia, "Eric Liddell," accessed August 2013, http://en.wikipedia.org/wiki/Eric_Liddell.

3. J. I. Packer, *Knowing God* (Downers Grove, IL: InterVarsity Press, 1993), Kindle edition, 224.

4. Doug Lemov, "Practice Makes Perfect—and Not Just for Jocks and Musicians," *The Wall Street Journal*, October 26, 2012, http://online.wsj.com/article/SB10001424052970204530504578078602307104168.html.

5. IMDB, "Love Story," accessed June 7, 2013, www.imdb.com/title/tt0066011/synopsis.

6. Robert J. Morgan, *Then Sings My Soul, Book 2* (Nashville: Thomas Nelson, 2004), 162–63.

7. "Karyn Williams Talks about 'Rest in the Hope,'" YouTube, accessed July 3, 2012, www.youtube.com /watch?annotation_id=annotation_121078&feature=iv&index=2&list=UUIIPGSWezt67XnlqMaswAbA& src_vid=hb8o4BMOdkw&v=aJMTwFTCwPU.

8. "Rest in the Hope – Official Lyric Video – Karyn Williams," YouTube, accessed June 8, 2013, www.youtube .com/watch?v=6ea3x3B4HZ4,.

9. Julieanne Smolinski, "Women, How Often Do You Look in the Mirror? Study Says 8 Times a Day," *Today*, May 15, 2012, www.today.com/klgandhoda/women-how-often-do-you-look-mirror-study-says-8-773394.

10. Helen Howarth Lemmel, "Turn Your Eyes upon Jesus," Hymnal.net, accessed August 13, 2017, www.hymnal.net/en/hymn/h/645.

11. Mike Pflanz, "World Water Day: Dirty Water Kills More People Than Violence, Says UN," *Christian Science Monitor*, March 22, 2010, www.csmonitor.com/World/Africa/2010/0322/World-Water-Day-Dirty-water -kills-more-people-than-violence-says-UN.

12. "Rainer Maria Rilke," Goodreads, accessed June 6, 2013, www.goodreads.com/quotes/140193-believe-in-a -love-that-is-being-stored-up-for.

Lesson 6: Family Tree

1. Ross Bonander, "Top 10 American Outlaws," Ask Men, accessed August 8, 2013, www.askmen.com/top_10 /entertainment/206c_top_10_list.html.

2. Adapted from *Vines Complete Expository Dictionary of Old and New Testament Words* (Nashville: Thomas Nelson, 1996).

3. Thomas Percy, *Reliques of Ancient English Poetry* (London: J. Dodsley, 1847), 75.

4. Frank Sinatra, "My Way," Lyricsfreak, accessed August 10, 2013, www.lyricsfreak.com/f/frank+sinatra/my +way20056378.html.

5. Wikiquote, "Sherlock Holmes," accessed August 10, 2013, https://en.wikiquote.org/wiki/Sherlock_Holmes.

6. George Sweeting, *Who Said That?* (Chicago: Moody Press, 1995), 430.

7. John F. Walvoord and Roy B. Zuck, *The Bible Knowledge Commentary* (Colorado Springs: Cook Communications Ministries, 1985), 894.

8. Adapted from Ronald F. Youngblood, F. F. Bruce, and R. K. Harrison, *Nelson's Illustrated Bible Dictionary* (Nashville: Thomas Nelson, 1986), 986.

9. Warren W. Wiersbe, *Be Real: Turning from Hypocrisy to Truth* (Colorado Springs: David C Cook, 2009), 119.

10. Lindor Reynolds, "Bus Driver Walks the (Charity) Walk," *Winnipeg Free Press*, September 20, 2012, www.winnipegfreepress.com/local/bus-driver-walks-the-charity-walk-170464686.html.

11. Warren W. Wiersbe, *Be Real: Turning from Hypocrisy to Truth* (Colorado Springs: David C Cook, 2009), 111.

12. Annie Murphy Paul, "The Myth of 'Practice Makes Perfect,'" *Time*, January 25, 2012, http://ideas.time.com /2012/25/the-myth-of-practice-makes-perfect/#ixzz2c3NILso3.

13. Geoffrey Colvin, "What It Takes to Be Great," *Fortune*, October 19, 2006, http://archive.fortune.com /magazines/fortune/fortune_archive/2006/10/30/8391794/index.htm.

14. John MacArthur, *The MacArthur Study Bible* (Nashville: Thomas Nelson, 1997), 1969.

15. Adapted from *Vine's Complete Expository Dictionary of Old and New Testament Words* (Nashville: Thomas Nelson, 1996).

16. Otis Chandler, "Quotes about Comparisons," Goodreads.com, accessed August 12, 2013, www.goodreads .com/quotes/tag/comparisons.

17. Geoffrey Colvin, "What It Takes to Be Great," *Fortune*, October 19, 2006, http://archive.fortune.com /magazines/fortune/fortune_archive/2006/10/30/8391794/index.htm.

18. "Child's Definition of Love," Roger Knapp, accessed August 2, 2013, http://rogerknapp.com/inspire /childsdeflove.htm.

19. Adapted from *Vine's Complete Expository Dictionary of Old and New Testament Words* (Nashville: Thomas Nelson, 1996).

20. "Child's Definition of Love," Roger Knapp, accessed August 2, 2013, http://rogerknapp.com/inspire /childsdeflove.htm.

Lesson 7: All We Need Is Love

1. Adapted from "Summer of Love and Woodstock," The Cold War Museum, accessed August 2013, www.coldwar.org/articles/60s/summeroflove.asp.

2. Adapted from Wikipedia, "All You Need Is Love," accessed August 2013, http://en.wikipedia.org/wiki/All _You_Need_Is_Love.

3. John MacArthur, *The MacArthur Study Bible* (Nashville: Thomas Nelson, 1997), 1970.

4. Richard Selzer, *Mortal Lessons* (New York: Simon and Schuster, 1976), 45.

5. Adapted from Warren W. Wiersbe, *Be Real: Turning from Hypocrisy to Truth* (Colorado Springs: David C Cook, 2009), 129.

6. Adapted from Wikipedia, "William Hunter (Martyr)," accessed August 13, 2017, https://en.wikipedia.org /wiki/William_Hunter_(martyr).

7. Adapted from Chris V. Thangham, "Dog Faithfully Awaits Return of His Master for Past 11 Years," *Digital Journal*, August 18, 2007, http://digitaljournal.com/article/218509.

Lesson 8: Spirit Savvy

1. Robert Schrader, "Austin's Bizarre—but Ubiquitous—Bats," TripSavvy, updated February 14, 2017, www.tripsavvy.com/austins-bizarre-but-ubiquitous-bats-3499014.

2. Andrea Canning, "Exclusive Club Has One Rule: Just Give," *ABC News*, December 23, 2007, http://abcnews .go.com/WN/story?id=4045409&page=1.

3. *Encyclopedia Britannica Online*, s.v. "Cuckoo," accessed August 20, 2013, www.britannica.com/EBchecked /topic/145811/cuckoo.

4. Spiros Zodhiates, *The Complete Word Study Dictionary: New Testament* (Chattanooga, TN: AMG Publishers, 1992), 1244, 1492.

5. John MacArthur, *The MacArthur Study Bible* (Nashville: Thomas Nelson, 1997), 1405.

6. "Grandma's Cooking Secret," Snopes, accessed August 21, 2013, www.snopes.com/weddings/newlywed/secret .asp.

7. "How to Tell if a Designer Bag Is Fake," WikiHow, accessed August 25, 2013, www.wikihow.com/Tell-if-a -Designer-Bag-Is-Fake.

8. John MacArthur, *The MacArthur Study Bible* (Nashville: Thomas Nelson, 1997), 1971.

9. Spiros Zodhiates, *The Complete Word Study Dictionary: New Testament* (Chattanooga, TN: AMG Publishers, 1992), 882.

10. John MacArthur, *The MacArthur Study Bible* (Nashville: Thomas Nelson, 1997), 1971.

11. Mary Bellis, "Biography of Galileo Galilei," About, accessed September 8, 2013, http://inventors.about.com /od/gstartinventors/a/Galileo_Galilei.htm.

12. "How Do 3D Films Work?," Physics.org, January 7, 2010, www.physics.org/article-questions.asp?id=56.

13. Spiros Zodhiates, *The Complete Word Study Dictionary: New Testament* (Chattanooga, TN: AMG Publishers, 1992), 1166.

14. John MacArthur, *Rediscovering Expository Preaching* (Dallas, TX: Word Publishing, 1992), 105–6.

Lesson 9: Love Defined

1. *Merriam-Webster*, s.v. "Love," accessed December 1, 2013, www.merriam-webster.com/dictionary/love.

2. John F. Walvoord and Roy B. Zuck, *The Bible Knowledge Commentary* (Colorado Springs: Cook Communications Ministries, 1985), 898.

3. Wikipedia, "I Wanna Be Loved by You," accessed December 1, 2013, http://en.wikipedia.org/wiki/I_Wanna _Be_Loved_by_You.

4. Jason Ditz, "US Backs Japan in Senkaku Islands Dispute with China," AntiWar.com, November 27, 2013, http://news.antiwar.com/2013/11/27/us-backs-japan-in-senkaku-islands-dispute-with-china.

5. Adapted from John H. Walton, Victor H. Matthews, and Mark W. Chavalas, *The IVP Bible Background Commentary: New Testament* (Downers Grove, IL: InterVarsity Press, 2000), 743.

6. Adapted from Ronald F. Youngblood , F. F. Bruce, and R. K. Harrison, *Nelson's Illustrated Bible Dictionary*, Biblesoft PC Study Bible, Version 4.2b, 1988–2004.

7. Wikipedia, "Meteorology," accessed December 1, 2013, http://en.wikipedia.org/wiki/Meteorology.

8. "Michael Card—Why," Song Meanings, accessed August 13, 2017, http://songmeanings.com/songs/view /3530822107859134944/.

9. Wikipedia, "Presidential Proclamations," accessed December 1, 2013, http://en.wikipedia.org/wiki /Presidential_proclamation.

10. Adapted from John F. Walvoord and Roy B. Zuck, *The Bible Knowledge Commentary* (Colorado Springs: Cook Communications Ministries, 1985), 899.

11. "U.S. Constitution: First Amendment," Cornell Law School Legal Information Institute, accessed September 8, 2017, www.law.cornell.edu/constitution/first_amendment.

12. Hunter Schwarz, "How Many Photos Have Been Taken Ever?," BuzzFeed, September 24, 2012, www.buzzfeed.com/hunterschwarz/how-many-photos-have-been-taken-ever-6zgv.

13. Nic Kizziah, "King James Bible Statistics, Theological Research," BibleBelievers, accessed December 1, 2013, www.biblebelievers.com/believers-org/kjv-stats.html.

Lesson 10: Triumphant Living

1. James M. Boice, *The Epistles of John* (Grand Rapids, MI: Baker, 1979), 119.

2. Warren W. Wiersbe, *Be Real: Turning from Hypocrisy to Truth* (Colorado Springs: David C Cook, 2009), 157.

3. "Thomas Merton Quotes," Brainy Quote, accessed August 17, 2013, www.brainyquote.com/quotes/authors/t /thomas_merton.html.

4. Wikipedia, "Believe in Him," accessed August 25, 2013, http://en.wikipedia.org/wiki/Believe_in_Him.

5. Adapted from "Lyrics, Believe in Him, Johnny Cash," YouTube, accessed August 25, 2013, www.youtube.com /watch?v=r-jETjc_mlA.

6. Charles H. Spurgeon, *Faith in All Its Splendor* (Lafayette, IN: Sovereign Grace, 2001), 57.

7. Adapted from *Holman's Illustrated Bible Dictionary* (Nashville: Holman, 2004), 70.

8. Adapted from "Fast Facts about American Religion," Hartford Institute, accessed August 30, 2013, http://hirr.hartsem.edu/research/fastfacts/fast_facts.html#numcong.

9. Wikipedia, "List of the Largest Protestant Churches in the United States," accessed August 20, 2013, http://en.wikipedia.org/wiki/List_of_the_largest_Protestant_churches_in_the_United_States.

10. Warren W. Wiersbe, *Be Real: Turning from Hypocrisy to Truth* (Colorado Springs: David C Cook, 2009), 160.

11. James Bentley, *A Calendar of Saints* (London: Orbis, 1986), 128.

12. Thomas à Kempis, *The Imitation of Christ* (Peabody, MA: Hendrickson, 2004), 83.

Lesson 11: Jesus on Trial

1. John MacArthur, *The MacArthur Study Bible* (Nashville: Thomas Nelson, 1997), 1397.

2. John MacArthur, *The MacArthur Study Bible* (Nashville: Thomas Nelson, 1997), 1396.

3. Spiros Zodhiates, *The Complete Word Study Dictionary: New Testament* (Chattanooga, TN: AMG Publishers, 1992), 945.

4. Warren W. Wiersbe, *Be Quoted* (Grand Rapids, MI: Baker, 2000), 45.

5. "Birthmarks," Baby Center Medical Advisory Board, February 2012, www.babycenter.com/0_birthmarks_75 .bc.

6. D. Guzik, *Text Commentaries: David Guzik*, Blue Letter Bible: Isaiah, July 7, 2006, www.blueletterbible.org /Comm/guzik_david/StudyGuide2017-Isa/Isa-26.cfm.

7. Adapted from C. Smith, *Text Commentaries: Chuck Smith,* Blue Letter Bible: Hebrews, June 1, 2005, www.blueletterbible.org/Comm/smith_chuck/c2000_Hbr/Hbr_001.cf.

8. Adapted from James Strong, *New Exhaustive Strong's Numbers and Concordance*, Biblesoft PC Study Bible, Version 4.2b, 1988–2004.

9. J. Oswald Sanders, *Christ Indwelling and Enthroned* (Santa Ana, CA: Calvary Chapel, 2002), 99.

10. John MacArthur, *The MacArthur Study Bible* (Nashville: Thomas Nelson, 1997), 1837.

11. Spiros Zodhiates, *The Complete Word Study Dictionary: New Testament* (Chattanooga, TN: AMG Publishers, 1992), 509.

12. Warren W. Wiersbe, *Be Real: Turning from Hypocrisy to Truth* (Colorado Springs: David C Cook, 2009), 174.

13. Warren W. Wiersbe, *Be Quoted* (Grand Rapids, MI: Baker, 2000), 66.

14. Fanny Crosby, "Blessed Assurance," Hymntime.com, accessed August 13, 2017, www.hymntime.com/tch /htm/b/l/e/s/blesseda.htm.

Lesson 12: Without a Doubt

1. "Muhammad Ali," Biography, accessed September 8, 2013, www.biography.com/people/muhammad-ali -9181154.

2. "Muhammad Ali Quotes," Goodreads, accessed September 8, 2013, www.goodreads.com/author/quotes /46261.Muhammad-Ali?page=2.

3. James Montgomery Boice, *The Epistles of John* (Grand Rapids, MI: Baker, 2006), 139.

4. Andrews, Evans, "7 Famous Presidential Pardons," History, July 23, 2013, www.history.com/news/history-lists/7-famous-presidential-pardons.

5. Adapted from James Strong, *Strong's Exhaustive Concordance of The Bible* (Nashville: Thomas Nelson, 1990).

6. Josh Clark, "How Presidential Pardons Work," How Stuff Works, accessed September 9, 2013, http://people.howstuffworks.com/presidential-pardon6.htm.

7. Wikipedia, "United States Air Force Thunderbirds," accessed September 10, 2013, http://en.wikipedia.org/wiki/United_States_Air_Force_Thunderbirds.

8. John MacArthur, *The MacArthur Study Bible* (Nashville: Thomas Nelson, 1997), 1974.

9. Adapted from *Vine's Complete Expository Dictionary of Old and New Testament Words* (Nashville: Thomas Nelson, 1996).

10. George Sweeting, *Who Said That?* (Chicago: Moody Press, 1985), 423.

11. Wikipedia, "Shields (Star Trek)," accessed November 7, 2013, http://en.wikipedia.org/wiki/Shields_(Star_Trek).

12. "Archive of American Television," Emmys, accessed November 8, 2013, http://emmytvlegends.org/interviews/shows/to-tell-the-truth.

13. H. A. Ironside, *The Epistles of John and Jude: An Ironside Expository Commentary* (Grand Rapids, MI: Kregel, 2008), 130.

14. James Montgomery Boice, *The Epistles of John* (Grand Rapids, MI: Baker, 2006), 149.